HARROW

→ DONE COME BACK ←

COUNTY ™

HARROW

◄— DONE COME BACK —►

COUNTY ™

Script
CULLEN BUNN

Art and Lettering
TYLER CROOK

DARK HORSE BOOKS

President and Publisher
MIKE RICHARDSON

Editor
DANIEL CHABON

Assistant Editor
BRETT ISRAEL

Designer
KEITH WOOD

Digital Art Technician
CHRISTIANNE GILLENARDO-GOUDREAU

NEIL HANKERSON Executive Vice President · TOM WEDDLE Chief Financial Officer · RANDY STRADLEY Vice President of Publishing
NICK McWHORTER Chief Business Development Officer · MATT PARKINSON Vice President of Marketing
DALE LaFOUNTAIN Vice President of Information Technology · CARA NIECE Vice President of Production and Scheduling
MARK BERNARDI Vice President of Book Trade and Digital Sales · KEN LIZZI General Counsel · DAVE MARSHALL Editor in Chief
DAVEY ESTRADA Editorial Director · CHRIS WARNER Senior Books Editor · CARY GRAZZINI Director of Specialty Projects
LIA RIBACCHI Art Director · VANESSA TODD-HOLMES Director of Print Purchasing · MATT DRYER Director of Digital Art and Prepress
MICHAEL GOMBOS Director of International Publishing and Licensing · KARI YADRO Director of Custom Programs

Published by Dark Horse Books
A division of Dark Horse Comics, Inc.
10956 SE Main Street
Milwaukie, OR 97222

First edition: October 2018
ISBN 978-1-50670-663-4

Comic Shop Locator Service: comicshoplocator.com

Harrow County Volume 8: Done Come Back

This volume collects Harrow County #29–#32.

10 9 8 7 6 5 4 3 2 1
Printed in China

DarkHorse.com

Library of Congress Cataloging-in-Publication Data

Names: Bunn, Cullen, author. | Crook, Tyler, artist, letterer.

Title: Done come back / script, Cullen Bunn ; art and lettering, Tyler Crook.

Description: First edition. | Milwaukie, OR : Dark Horse Books, October 2018.
  Series: Harrow County ; Volume 8 | "This volume collects Harrow County
  #29-#32"

Identifiers: LCCN 2018017130 | ISBN 9781506706634 (paperback)

Subjects: LCSH: Comic books, strips, etc. | BISAC: COMICS & GRAPHIC NOVELS / Horror.
COMICS & GRAPHIC NOVELS / Fantasy. | COMICS & GRAPHIC NOVELS / General.

Classification: LCC PN6728.H369 B858 2018 | DDC 741.5/973--dc23

LC record available at https://lccn.loc.gov/2018017130

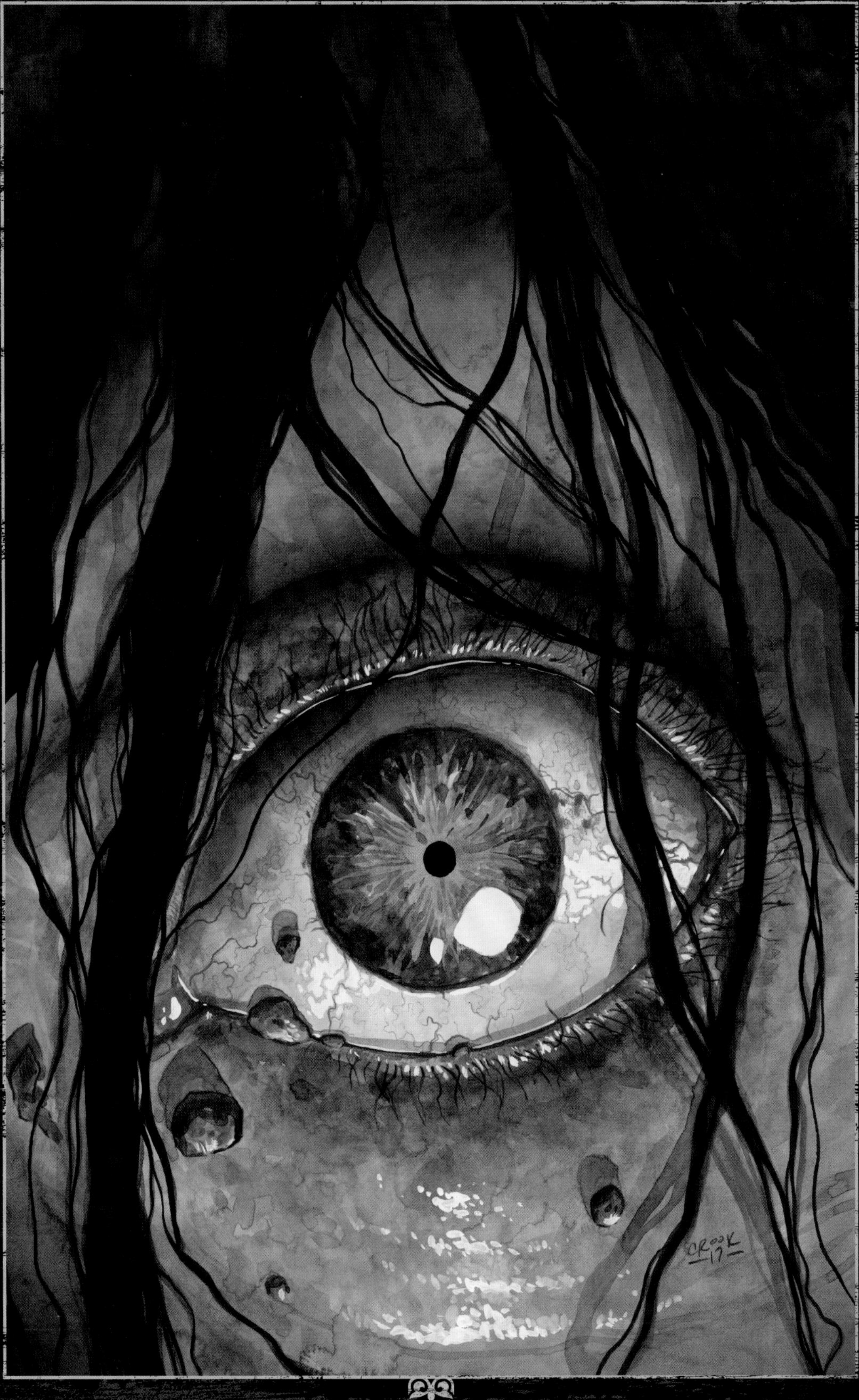
CROOK
17

ONE

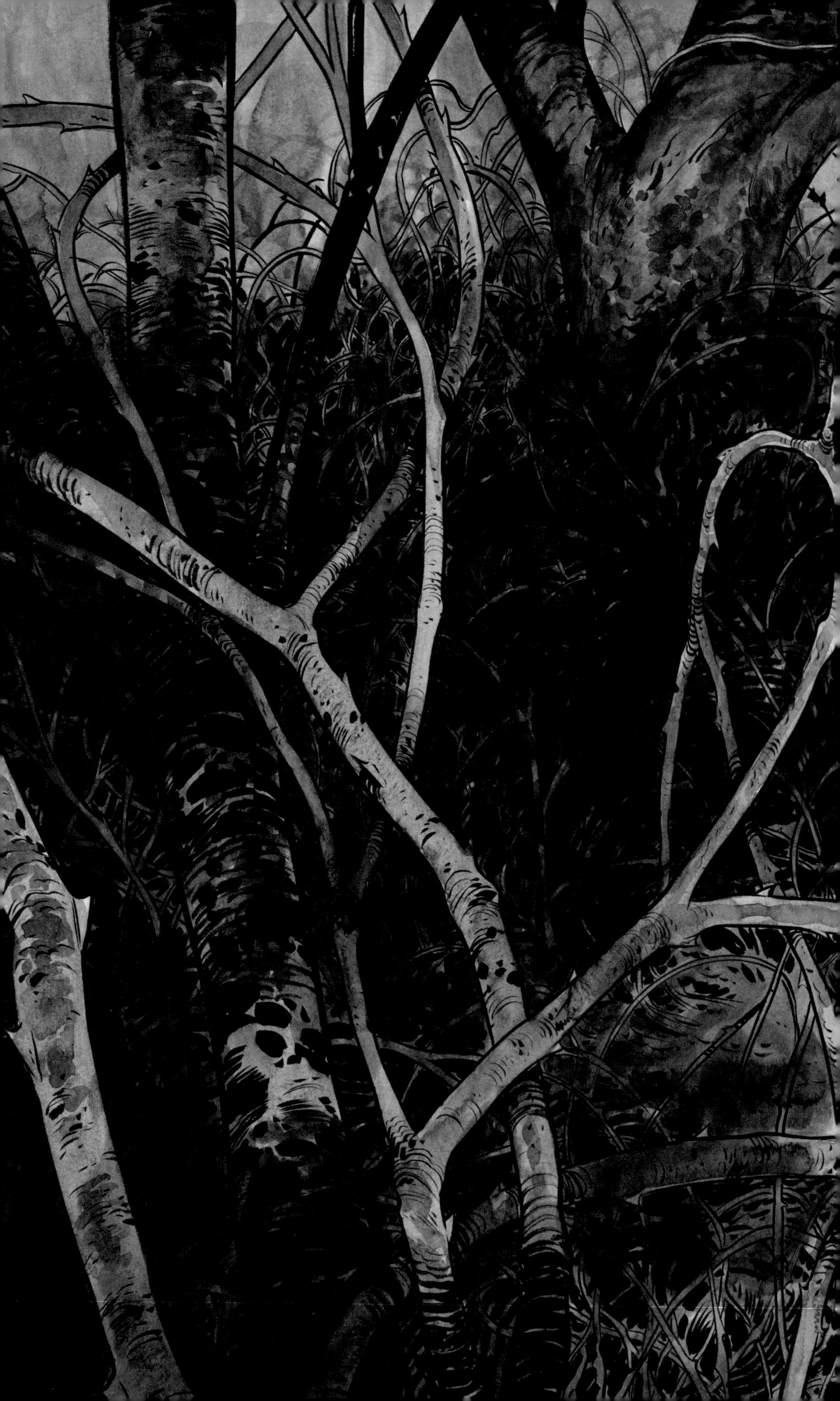

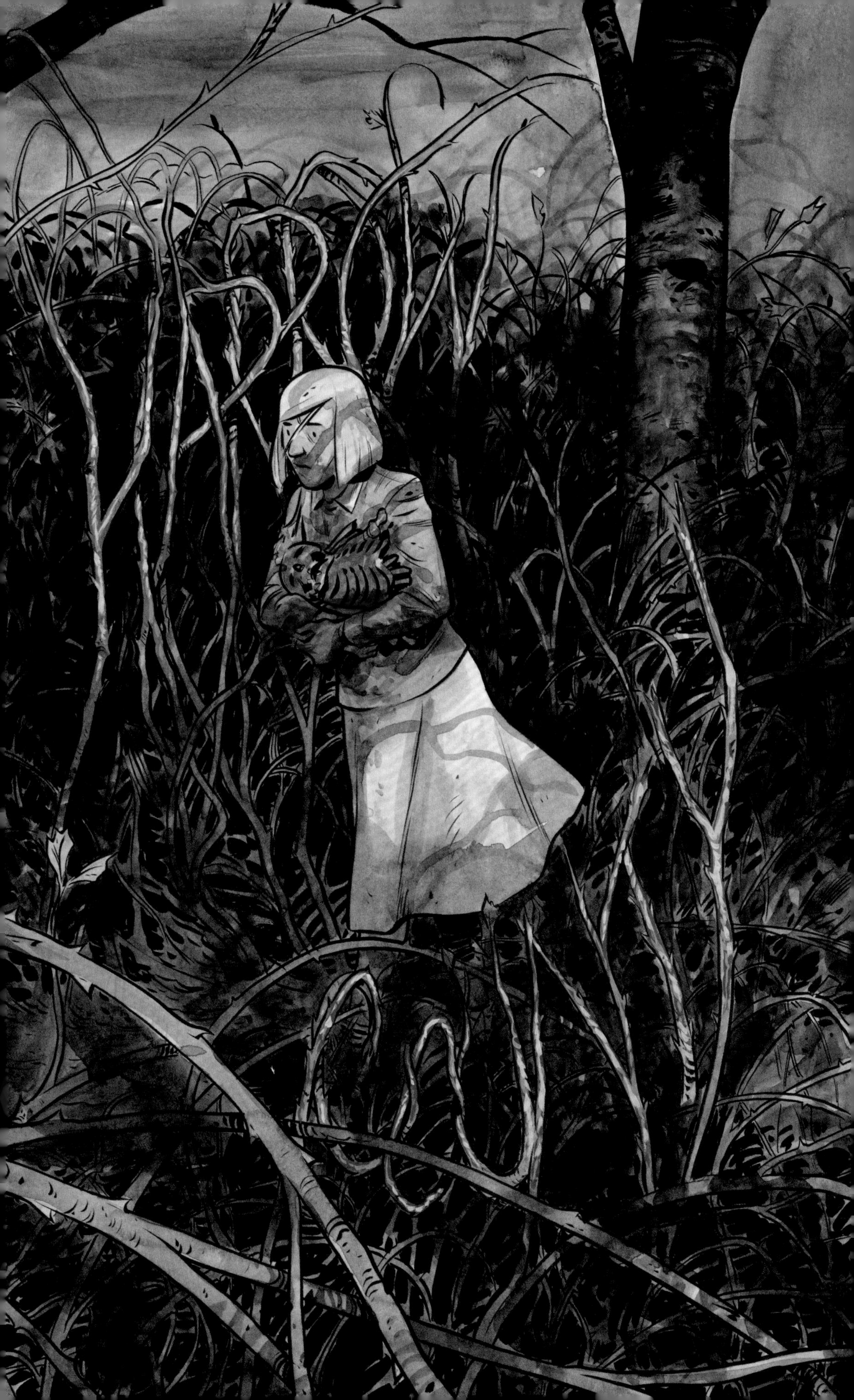

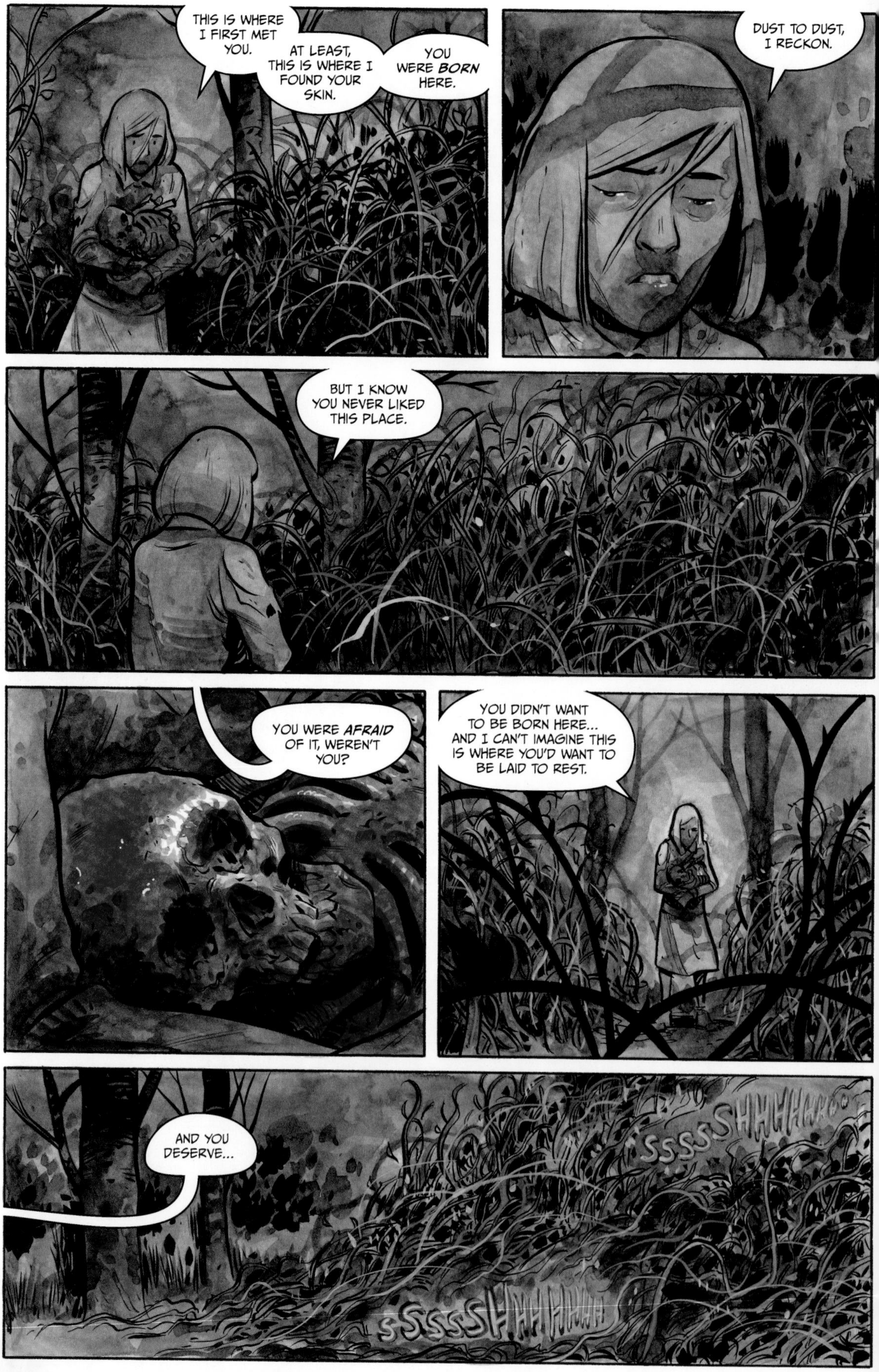
THIS IS WHERE I FIRST MET YOU.
AT LEAST, THIS IS WHERE I FOUND YOUR SKIN.
YOU WERE *BORN* HERE.
DUST TO DUST, I RECKON.
BUT I KNOW YOU NEVER LIKED THIS PLACE.
YOU WERE *AFRAID* OF IT, WEREN'T YOU?
YOU DIDN'T WANT TO BE BORN HERE... AND I CAN'T IMAGINE THIS IS WHERE YOU'D WANT TO BE LAID TO REST.
AND YOU DESERVE...
SSSSSHHHHHH
SSSSSHHHHHHHH

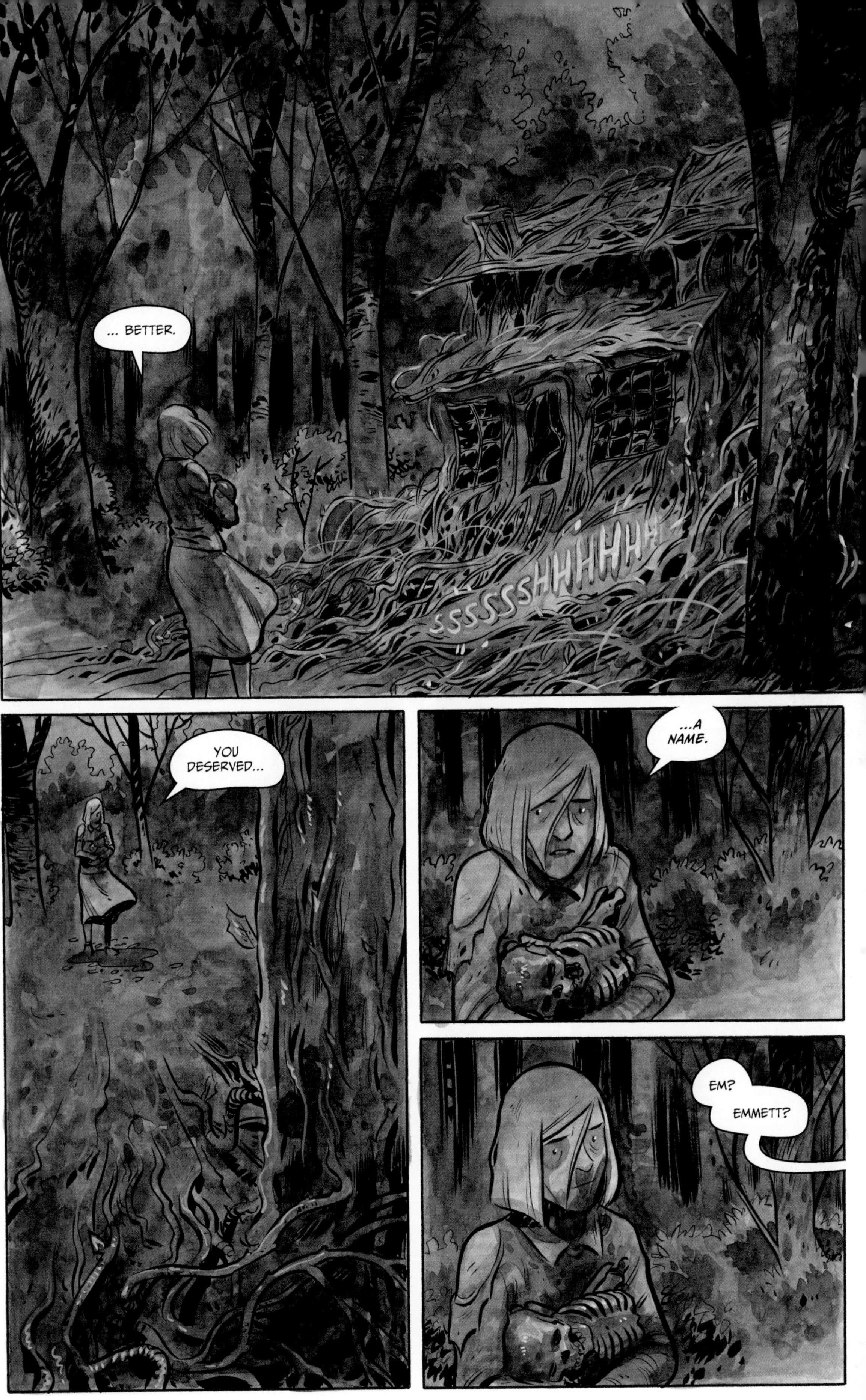
... BETTER.
SSSSSSHHHHHHH
YOU DESERVED...
...A NAME.
EM?
EMMETT?

EMMETT-- YOU COME ON IN NOW!

YOU DON'T WANT TO BE LATE FOR SUPPER!

IT'S TIME TO COME HOME!

YOU HEARD HER.

GO ON.

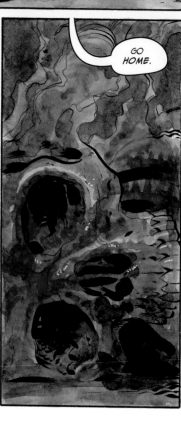

GO HOME.

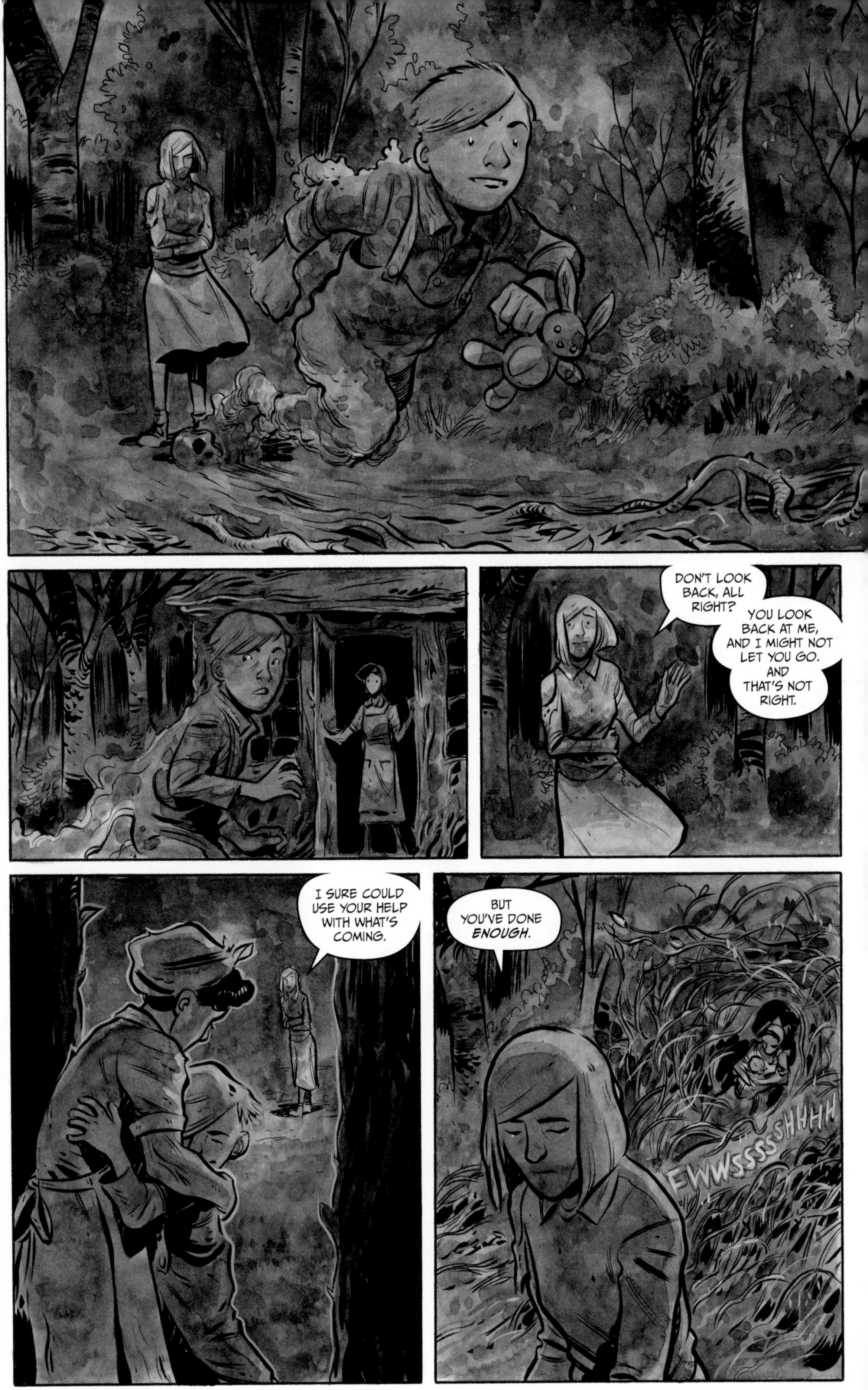

DON'T LOOK BACK, ALL RIGHT?
YOU LOOK BACK AT ME, AND I MIGHT NOT LET YOU GO. AND THAT'S NOT RIGHT.
I SURE COULD USE YOUR HELP WITH WHAT'S COMING.
BUT YOU'VE DONE *ENOUGH.*
EWWSSSSSHHHH

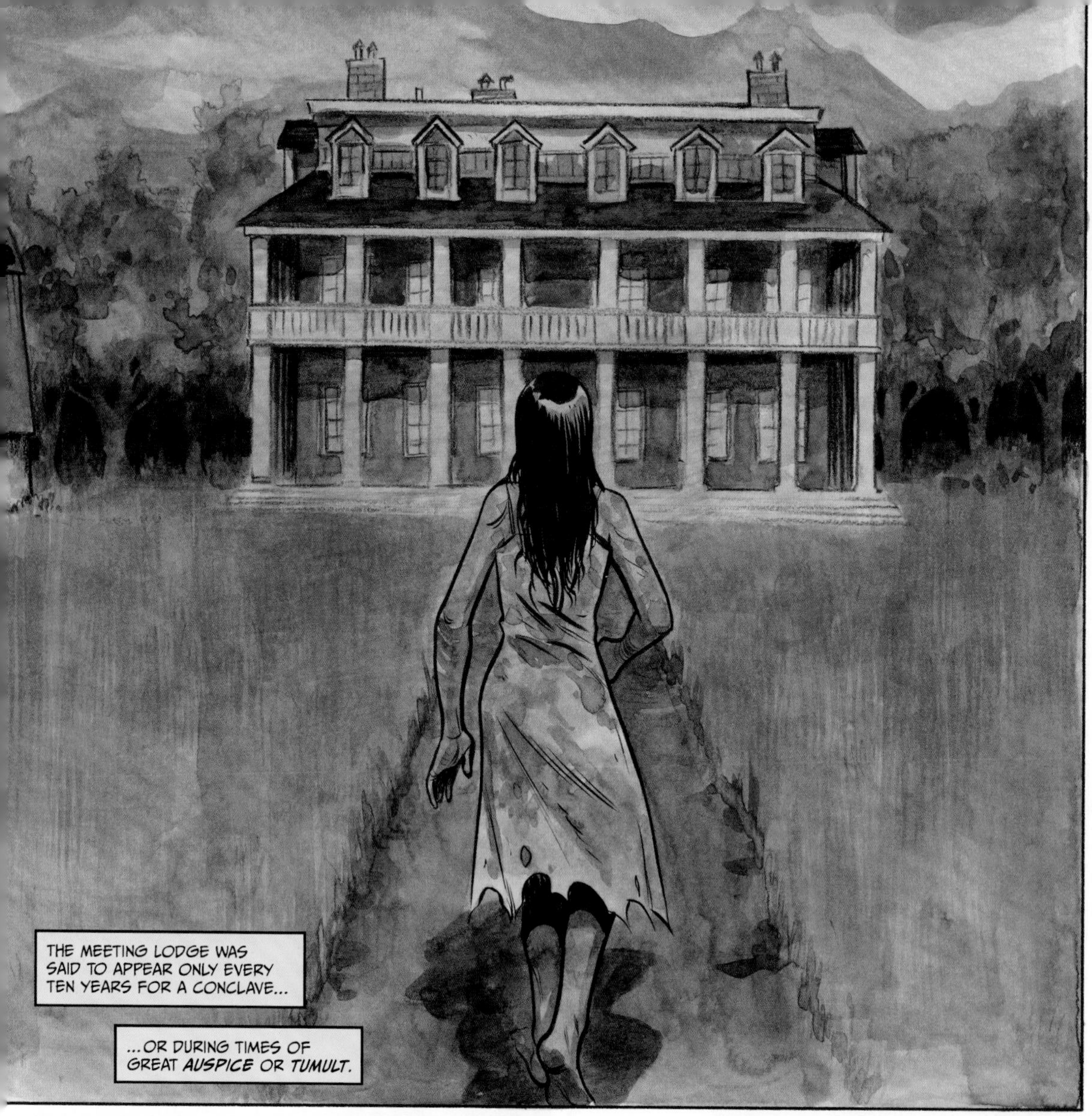
THE MEETING LODGE WAS SAID TO APPEAR ONLY EVERY TEN YEARS FOR A CONCLAVE...
...OR DURING TIMES OF GREAT *AUSPICE* OR *TUMULT*.

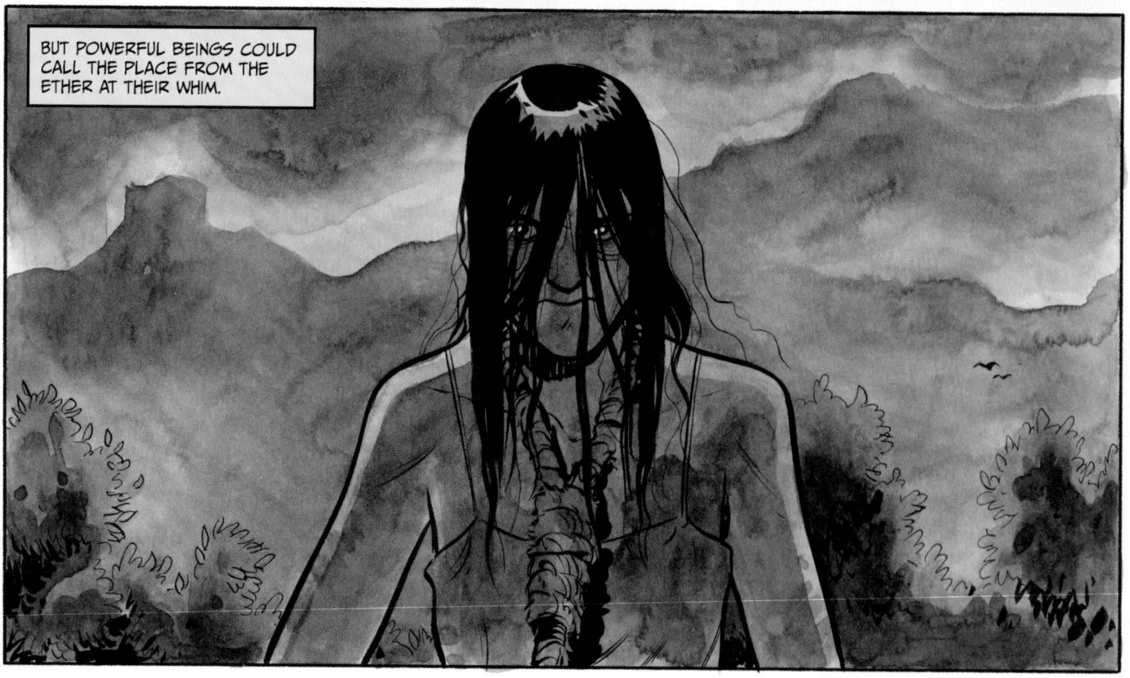
BUT POWERFUL BEINGS COULD CALL THE PLACE FROM THE ETHER AT THEIR WHIM.

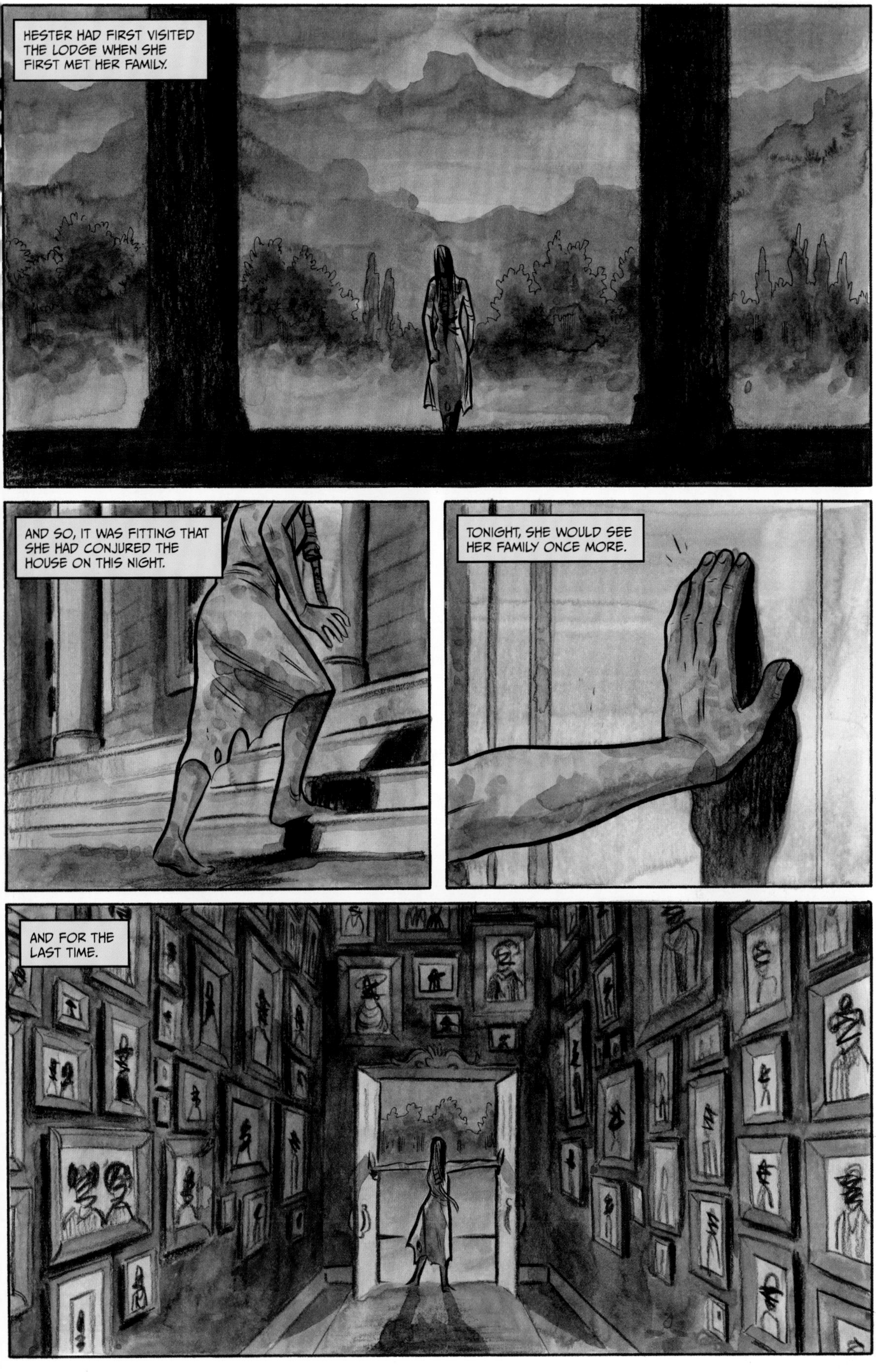
HESTER HAD FIRST VISITED THE LODGE WHEN SHE FIRST MET HER FAMILY.
AND SO, IT WAS FITTING THAT SHE HAD CONJURED THE HOUSE ON THIS NIGHT.
TONIGHT, SHE WOULD SEE HER FAMILY ONCE MORE.
AND FOR THE LAST TIME.

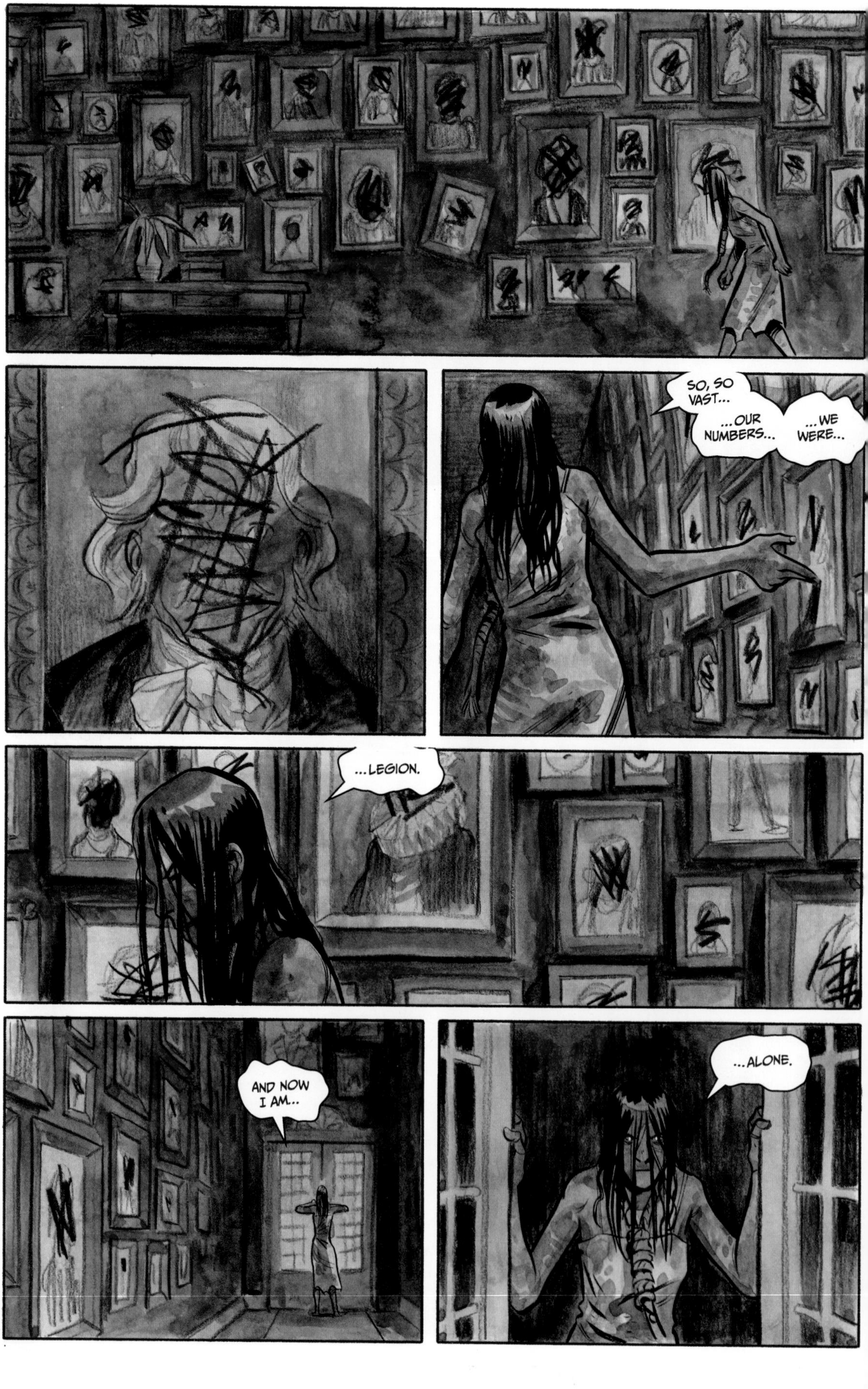

SO, SO VAST...
...OUR NUMBERS...
...WE WERE...
...LEGION.
AND NOW I AM...
...ALONE.

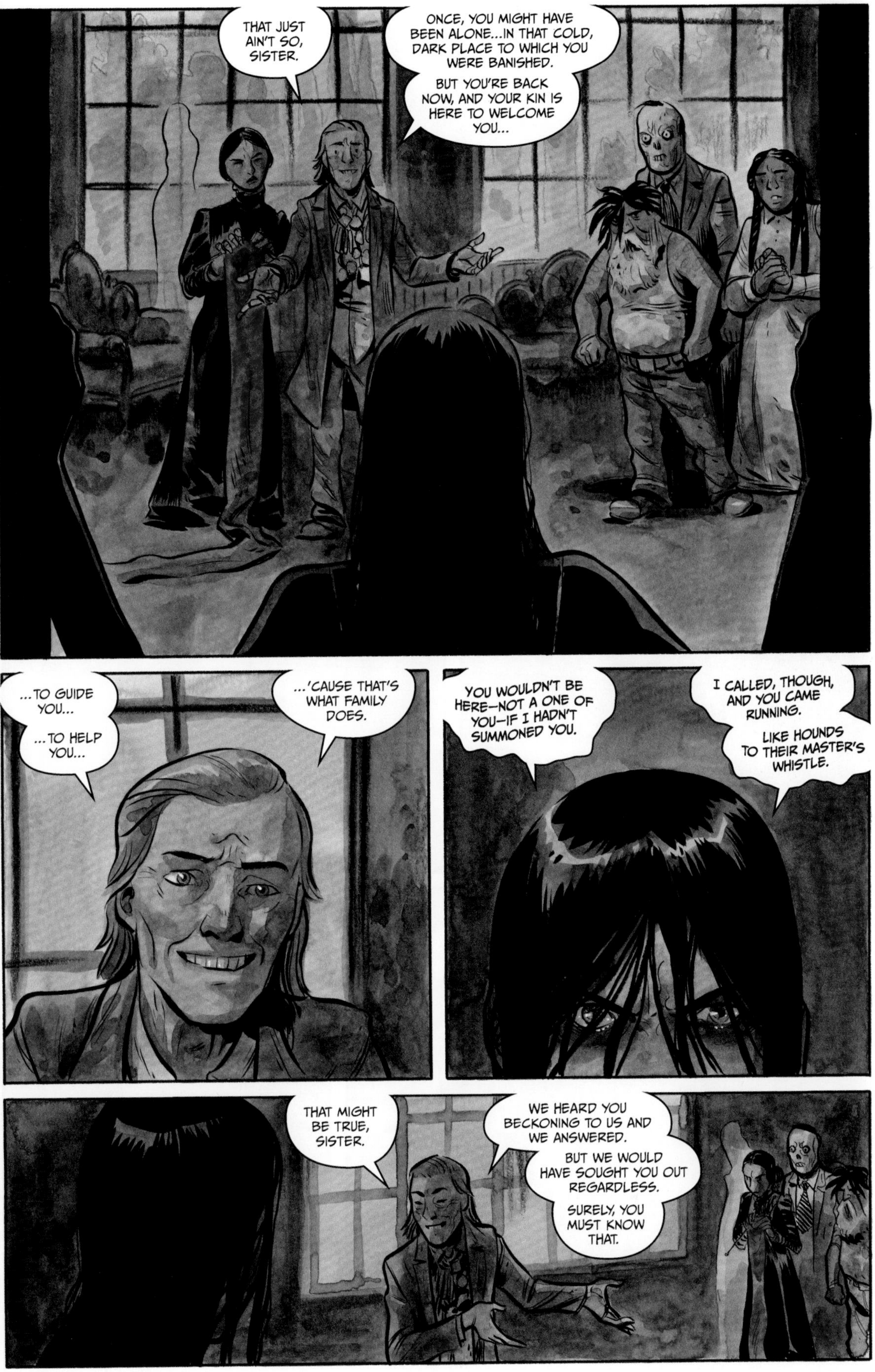
THAT JUST AIN'T SO, SISTER.
ONCE, YOU MIGHT HAVE BEEN ALONE...IN THAT COLD, DARK PLACE TO WHICH YOU WERE BANISHED.
BUT YOU'RE BACK NOW, AND YOUR KIN IS HERE TO WELCOME YOU...
...TO GUIDE YOU...
...TO HELP YOU...
...'CAUSE THAT'S WHAT FAMILY DOES.
YOU WOULDN'T BE HERE—NOT A ONE OF YOU—IF I HADN'T SUMMONED YOU.
I CALLED, THOUGH, AND YOU CAME RUNNING.
LIKE HOUNDS TO THEIR MASTER'S WHISTLE.
THAT MIGHT BE TRUE, SISTER.
WE HEARD YOU BECKONING TO US AND WE ANSWERED.
BUT WE WOULD HAVE SOUGHT YOU OUT REGARDLESS.
SURELY, YOU MUST KNOW THAT.

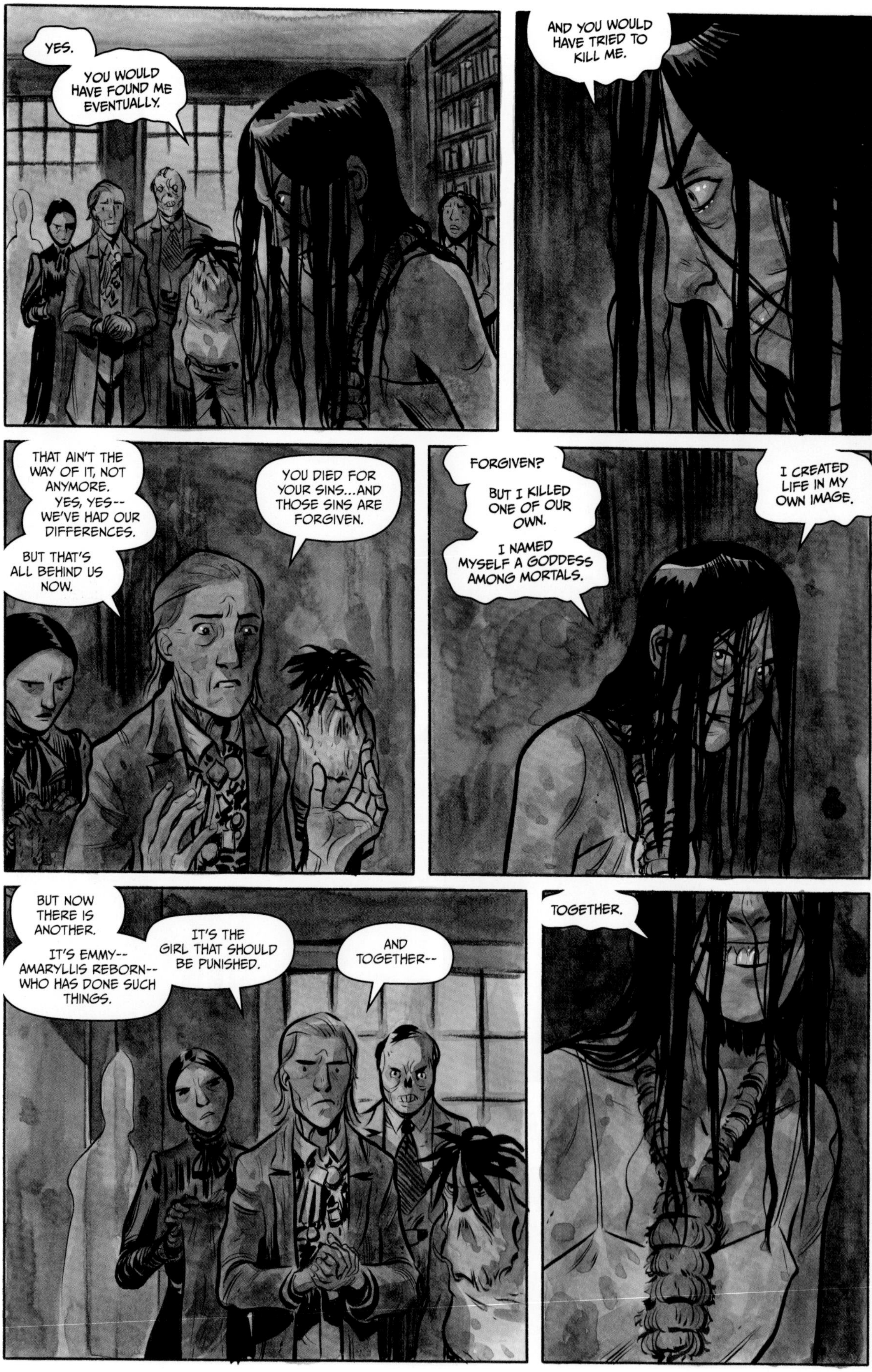
YES.
YOU WOULD HAVE FOUND ME EVENTUALLY.
AND YOU WOULD HAVE TRIED TO KILL ME.
THAT AIN'T THE WAY OF IT, NOT ANYMORE.
YES, YES-- WE'VE HAD OUR DIFFERENCES.
BUT THAT'S ALL BEHIND US NOW.
YOU DIED FOR YOUR SINS...AND THOSE SINS ARE FORGIVEN.
FORGIVEN?
BUT I KILLED ONE OF OUR OWN.
I NAMED MYSELF A GODDESS AMONG MORTALS.
I CREATED LIFE IN MY OWN IMAGE.
BUT NOW THERE IS ANOTHER.
IT'S EMMY-- AMARYLLIS REBORN-- WHO HAS DONE SUCH THINGS.
IT'S THE GIRL THAT SHOULD BE PUNISHED.
AND TOGETHER--
TOGETHER.

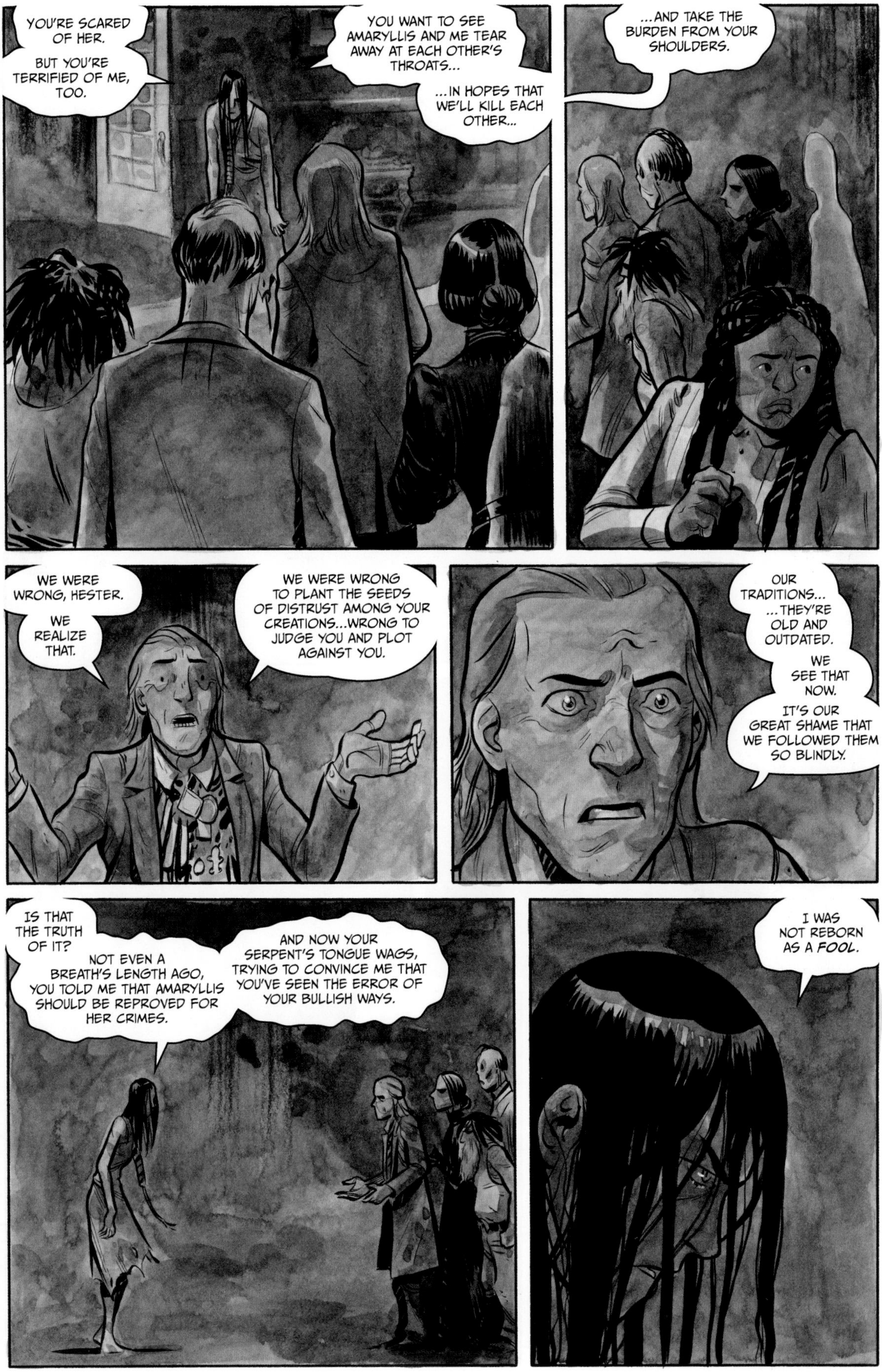
YOU'RE SCARED OF HER.
BUT YOU'RE TERRIFIED OF ME, TOO.
YOU WANT TO SEE AMARYLLIS AND ME TEAR AWAY AT EACH OTHER'S THROATS...
...IN HOPES THAT WE'LL KILL EACH OTHER...
...AND TAKE THE BURDEN FROM YOUR SHOULDERS.
WE WERE WRONG, HESTER.
WE REALIZE THAT.
WE WERE WRONG TO PLANT THE SEEDS OF DISTRUST AMONG YOUR CREATIONS...WRONG TO JUDGE YOU AND PLOT AGAINST YOU.
OUR TRADITIONS... ...THEY'RE OLD AND OUTDATED.
WE SEE THAT NOW.
IT'S OUR GREAT SHAME THAT WE FOLLOWED THEM SO BLINDLY.
IS THAT THE TRUTH OF IT?
NOT EVEN A BREATH'S LENGTH AGO, YOU TOLD ME THAT AMARYLLIS SHOULD BE REPROVED FOR HER CRIMES.
AND NOW YOUR SERPENT'S TONGUE WAGS, TRYING TO CONVINCE ME THAT YOU'VE SEEN THE ERROR OF YOUR BULLISH WAYS.
I WAS NOT REBORN AS A *FOOL*.

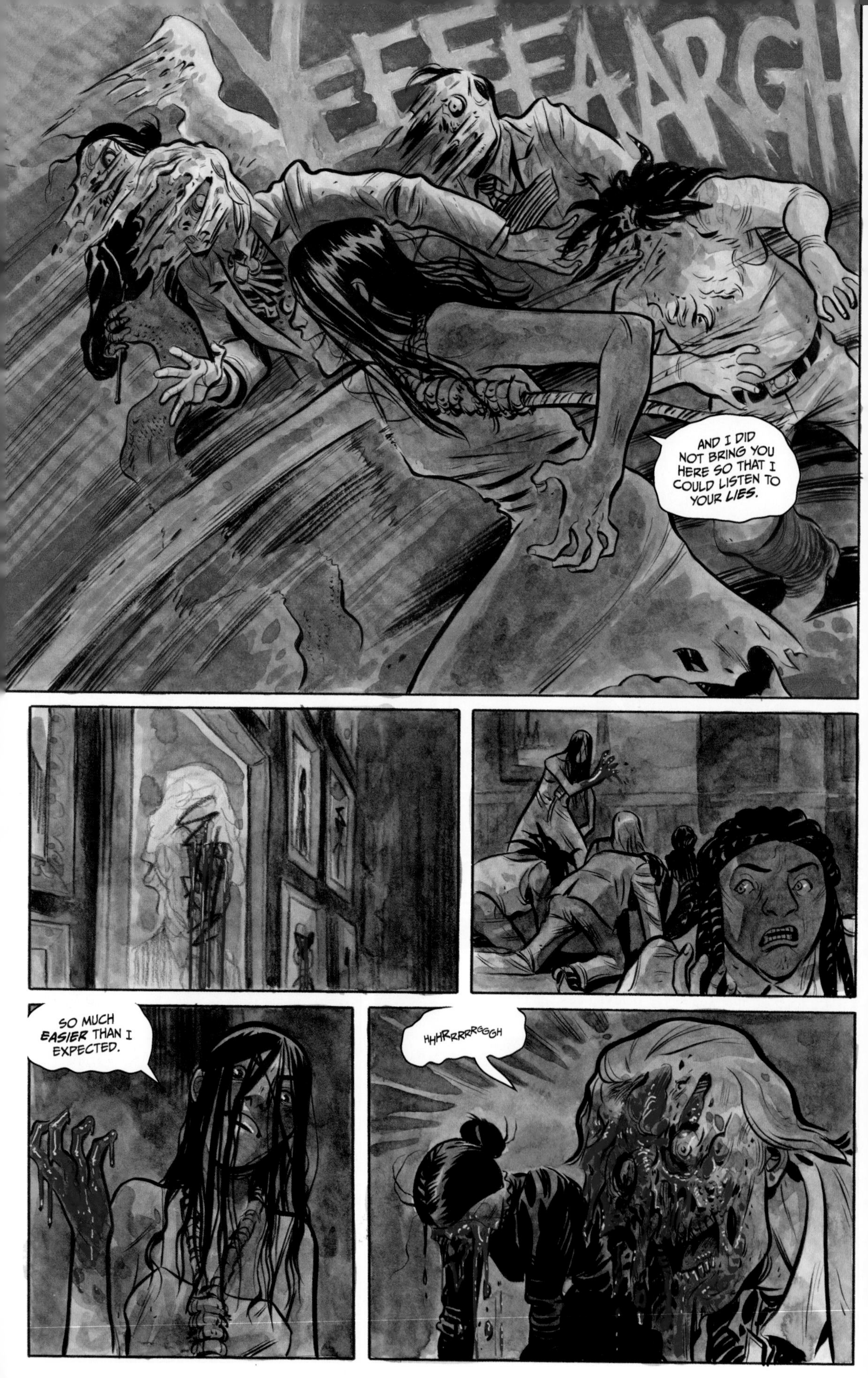
YEEEARGH
AND I DID NOT BRING YOU HERE SO THAT I COULD LISTEN TO YOUR LIES.
SO MUCH EASIER THAN I EXPECTED.
HHHRRRRRGGGH

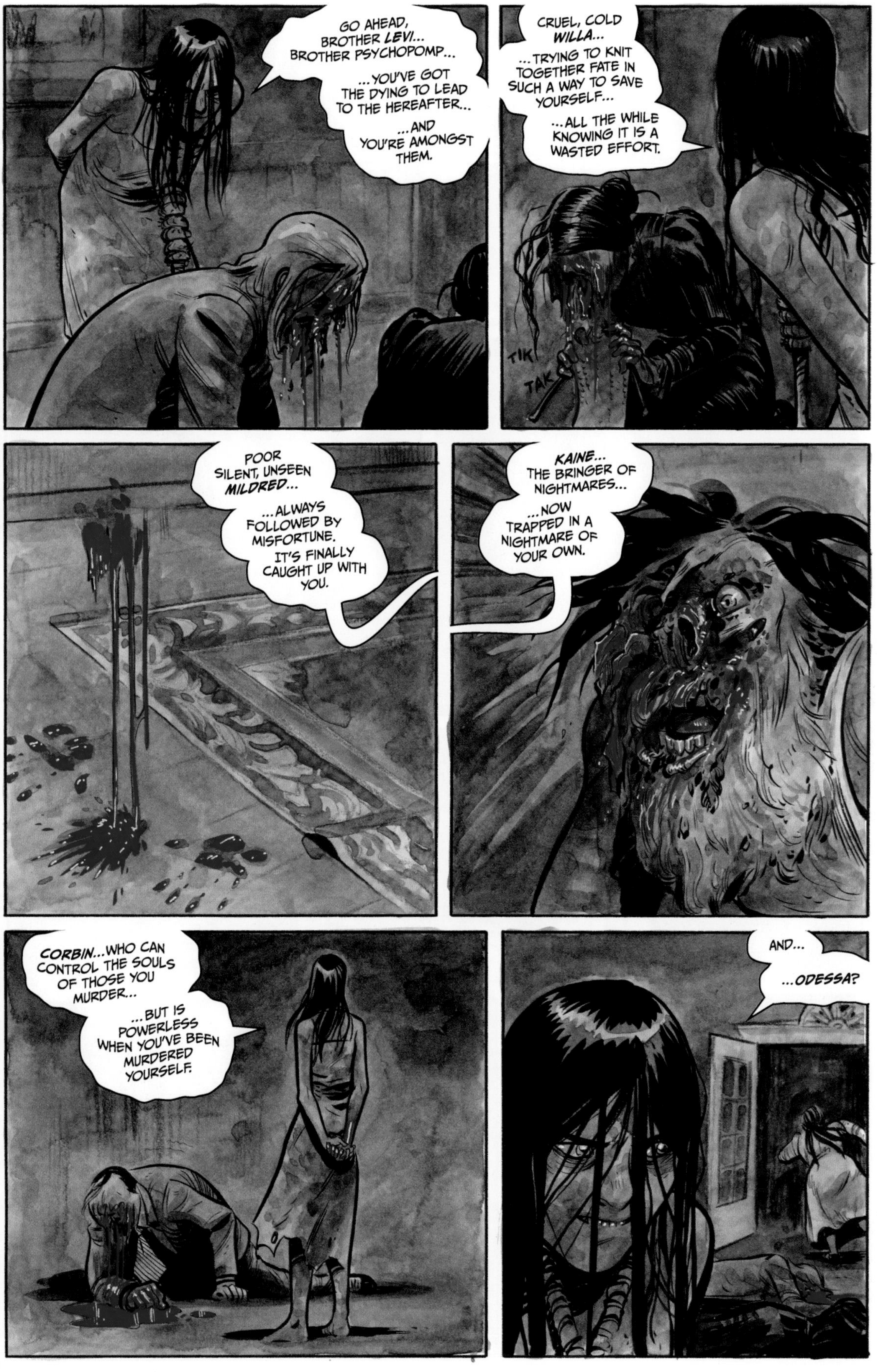
GO AHEAD, BROTHER LEVI... BROTHER PSYCHOPOMP...
...YOU'VE GOT THE DYING TO LEAD TO THE HEREAFTER...
...AND YOU'RE AMONGST THEM.
CRUEL, COLD WILLA...
...TRYING TO KNIT TOGETHER FATE IN SUCH A WAY TO SAVE YOURSELF...
...ALL THE WHILE KNOWING IT IS A WASTED EFFORT.
TIK
TAK
POOR SILENT, UNSEEN MILDRED...
...ALWAYS FOLLOWED BY MISFORTUNE.
IT'S FINALLY CAUGHT UP WITH YOU.
KAINE... THE BRINGER OF NIGHTMARES...
...NOW TRAPPED IN A NIGHTMARE OF YOUR OWN.
CORBIN...WHO CAN CONTROL THE SOULS OF THOSE YOU MURDER...
...BUT IS POWERLESS WHEN YOU'VE BEEN MURDERED YOURSELF.
AND...
...ODESSA?

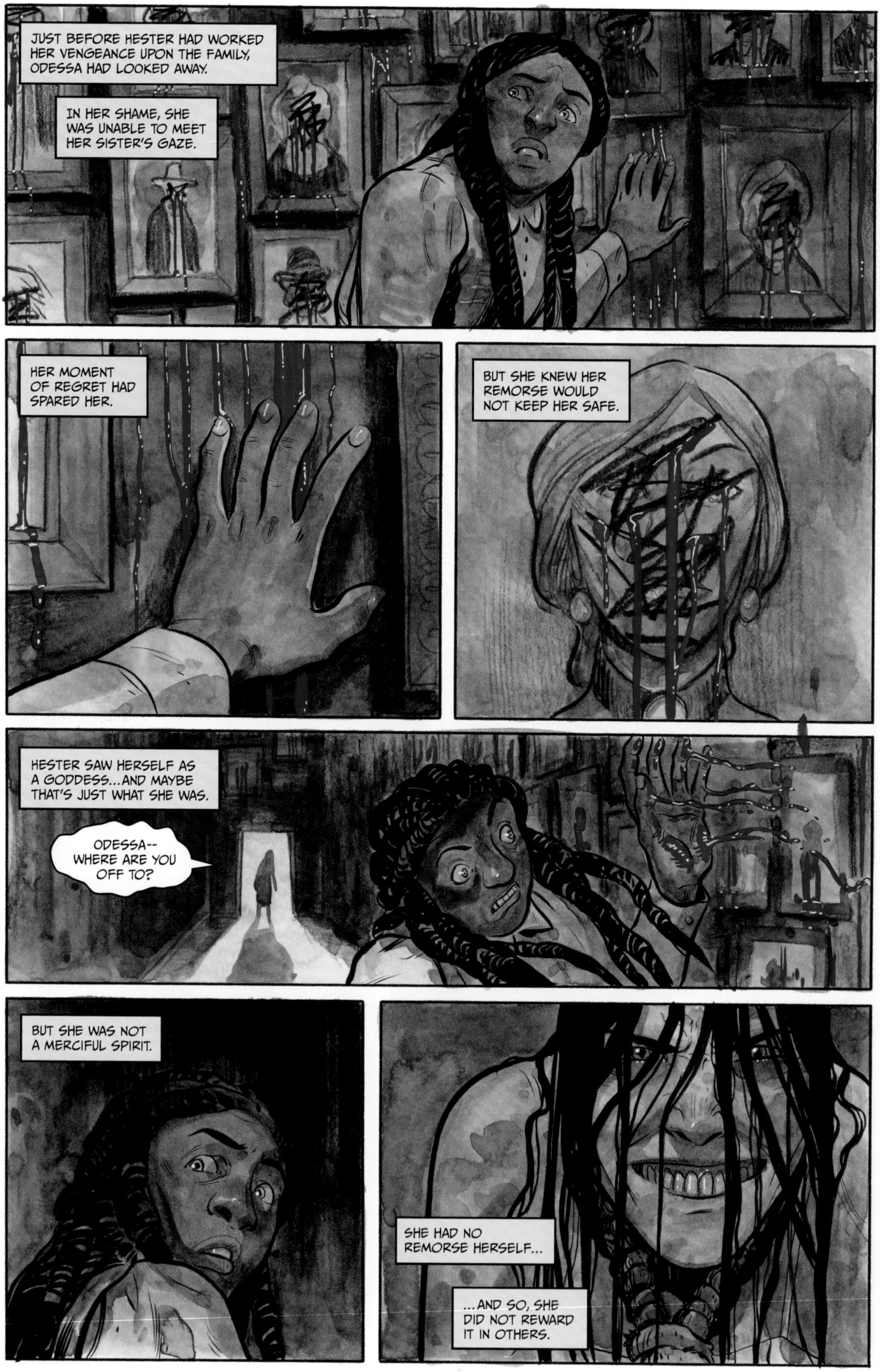
JUST BEFORE HESTER HAD WORKED HER VENGEANCE UPON THE FAMILY, ODESSA HAD LOOKED AWAY.
IN HER SHAME, SHE WAS UNABLE TO MEET HER SISTER'S GAZE.
HER MOMENT OF REGRET HAD SPARED HER.
BUT SHE KNEW HER REMORSE WOULD NOT KEEP HER SAFE.
HESTER SAW HERSELF AS A GODDESS...AND MAYBE THAT'S JUST WHAT SHE WAS.
ODESSA-- WHERE ARE YOU OFF TO?
BUT SHE WAS NOT A MERCIFUL SPIRIT.
SHE HAD NO REMORSE HERSELF...
...AND SO, SHE DID NOT REWARD IT IN OTHERS.

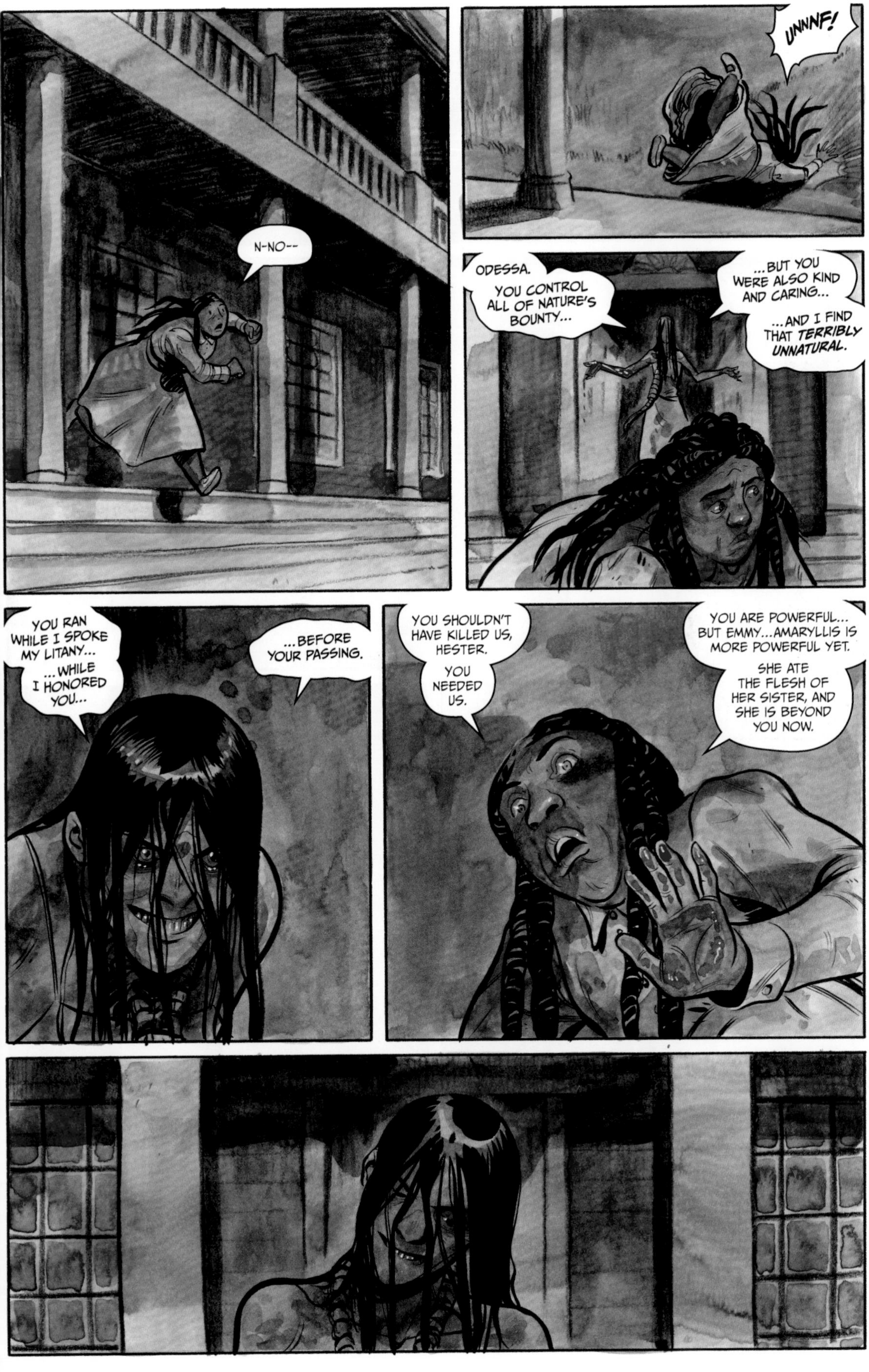
N-NO--
UNNNF!
ODESSA.
YOU CONTROL ALL OF NATURE'S BOUNTY...
...BUT YOU WERE ALSO KIND AND CARING...
...AND I FIND THAT *TERRIBLY UNNATURAL.*
YOU RAN WHILE I SPOKE MY LITANY...
...WHILE I HONORED YOU...
...BEFORE YOUR PASSING.
YOU SHOULDN'T HAVE KILLED US, HESTER.
YOU NEEDED US.
YOU ARE POWERFUL... BUT EMMY...AMARYLLIS IS MORE POWERFUL YET.
SHE ATE THE FLESH OF HER SISTER, AND SHE IS BEYOND YOU NOW.

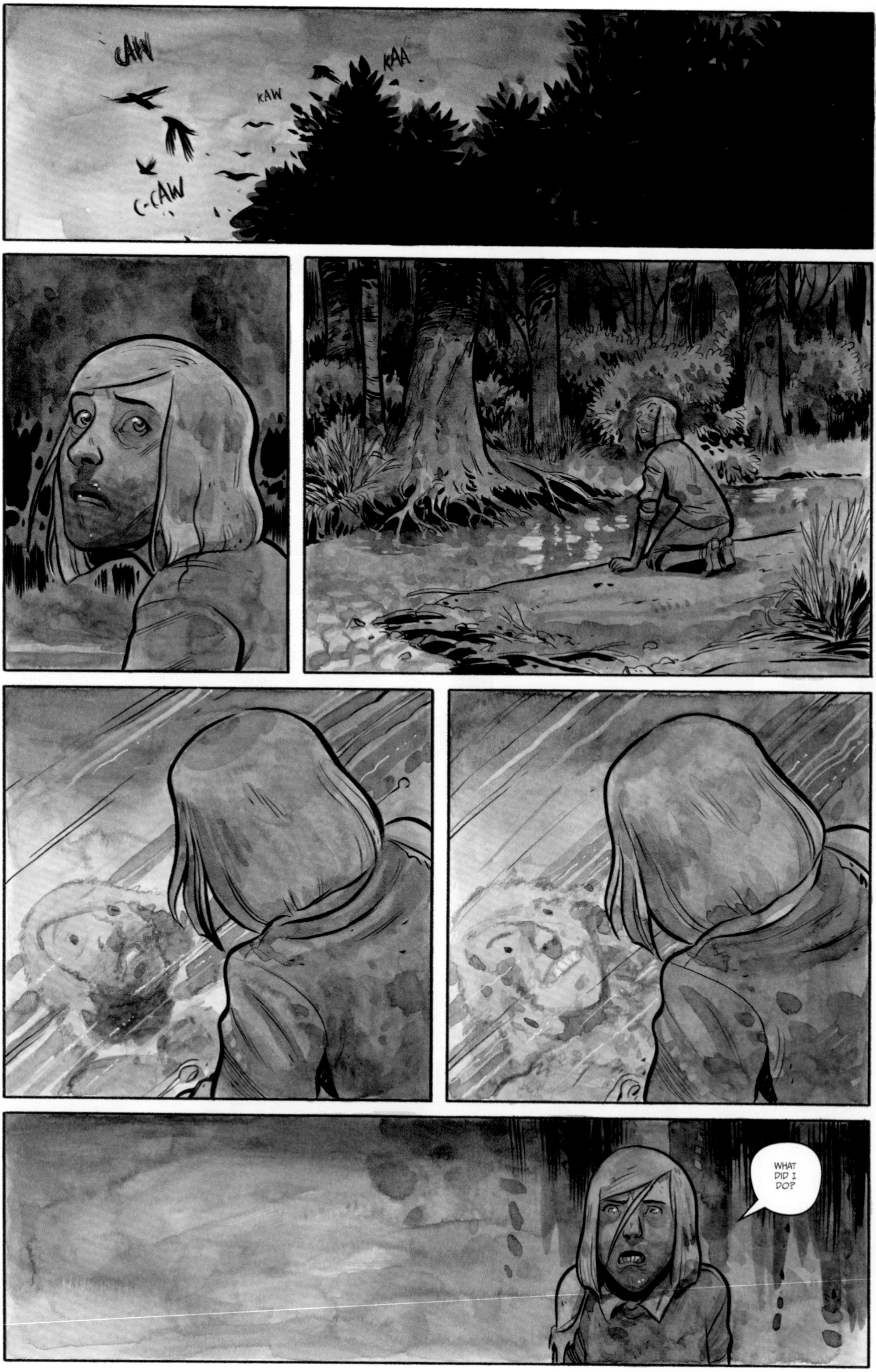
CAW
KAA
KAW
C-CAW
WHAT DID I DO?

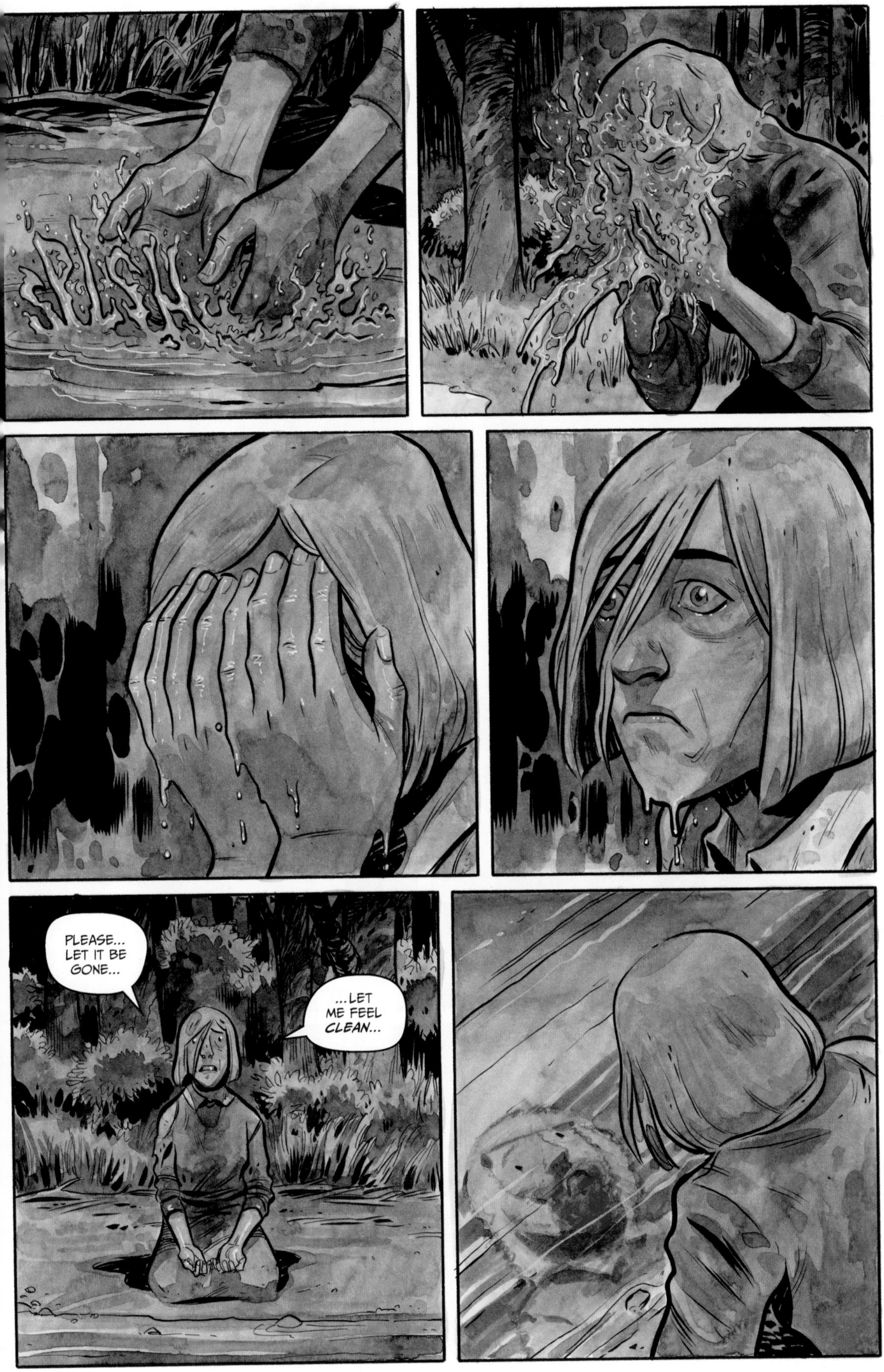
PLEASE... LET IT BE GONE...
...LET ME FEEL *CLEAN*...

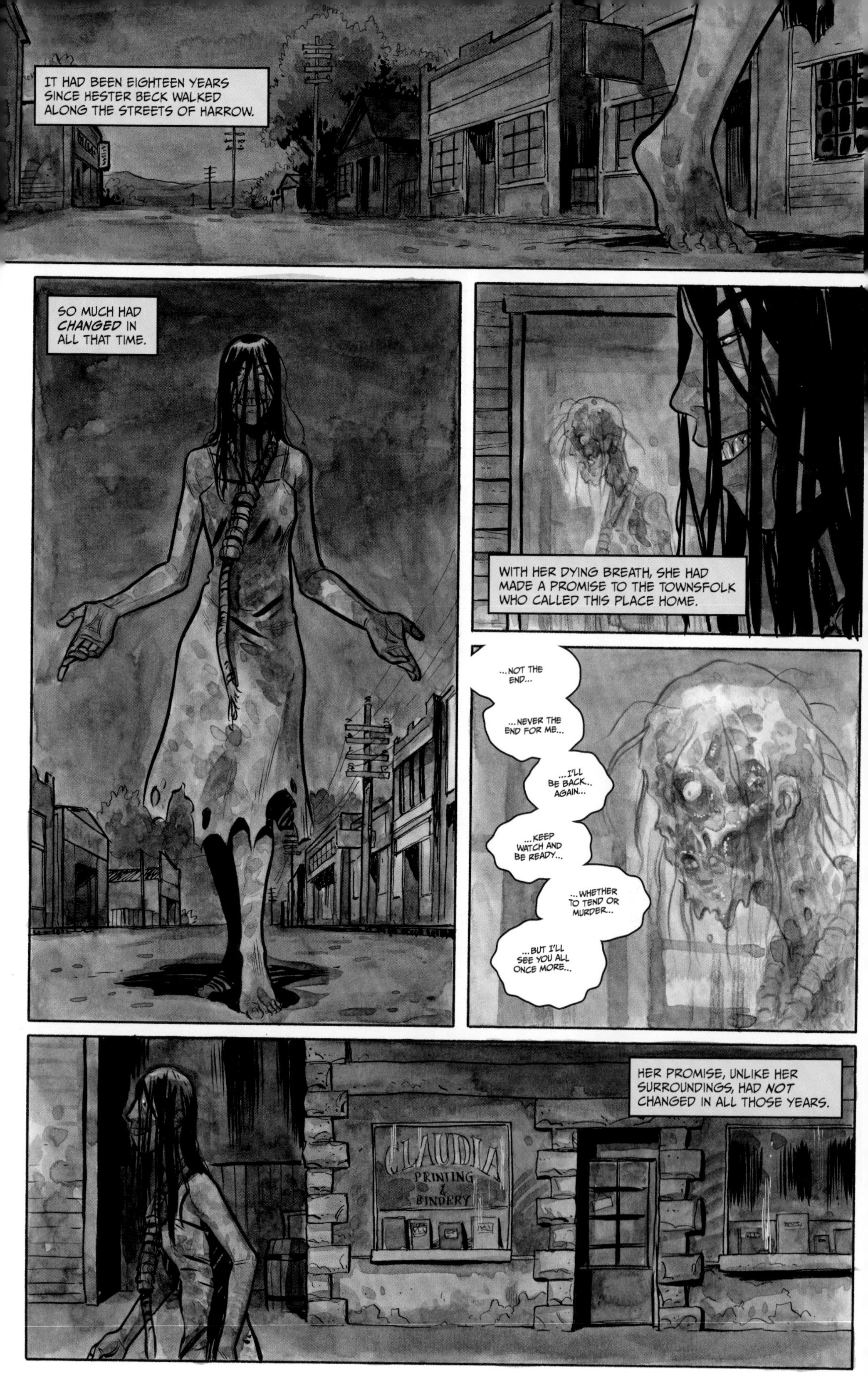
IT HAD BEEN EIGHTEEN YEARS SINCE HESTER BECK WALKED ALONG THE STREETS OF HARROW.
SO MUCH HAD *CHANGED* IN ALL THAT TIME.
WITH HER DYING BREATH, SHE HAD MADE A PROMISE TO THE TOWNSFOLK WHO CALLED THIS PLACE HOME.
...NOT THE END...
...NEVER THE END FOR ME...
...I'LL BE BACK.. AGAIN...
...KEEP WATCH AND BE READY...
...WHETHER TO TEND OR MURDER...
...BUT I'LL SEE YOU ALL ONCE MORE...
HER PROMISE, UNLIKE HER SURROUNDINGS, HAD *NOT* CHANGED IN ALL THOSE YEARS.
CLAUDIA
PRINTING & BINDERY

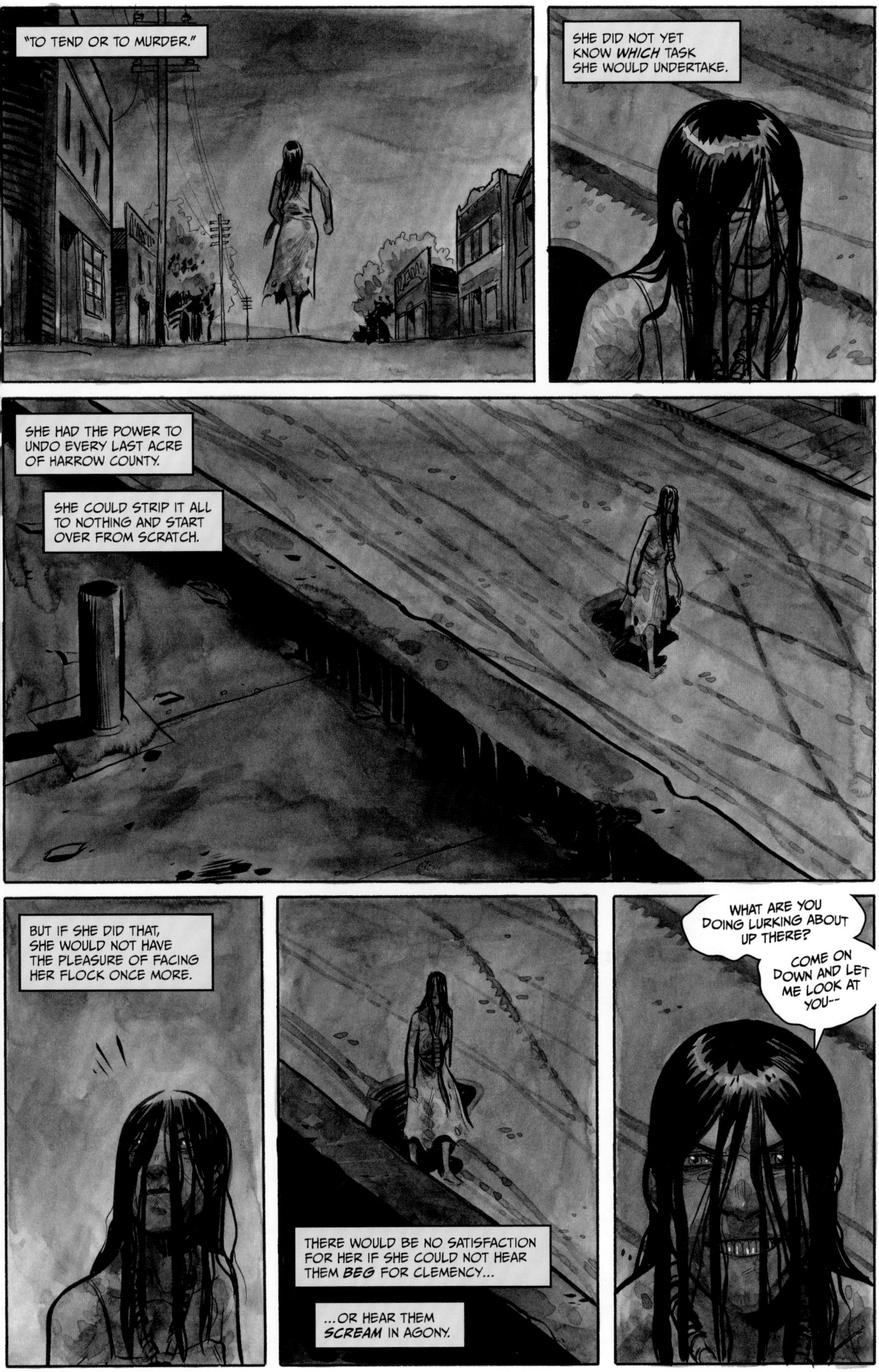
"TO TEND OR TO MURDER."
SHE DID NOT YET KNOW *WHICH* TASK SHE WOULD UNDERTAKE.
SHE HAD THE POWER TO UNDO EVERY LAST ACRE OF HARROW COUNTY.
SHE COULD STRIP IT ALL TO NOTHING AND START OVER FROM SCRATCH.
BUT IF SHE DID THAT, SHE WOULD NOT HAVE THE PLEASURE OF FACING HER FLOCK ONCE MORE.
THERE WOULD BE NO SATISFACTION FOR HER IF SHE COULD NOT HEAR THEM *BEG* FOR CLEMENCY...
...OR HEAR THEM *SCREAM* IN AGONY.
WHAT ARE YOU DOING LURKING ABOUT UP THERE?
COME ON DOWN AND LET ME LOOK AT YOU--

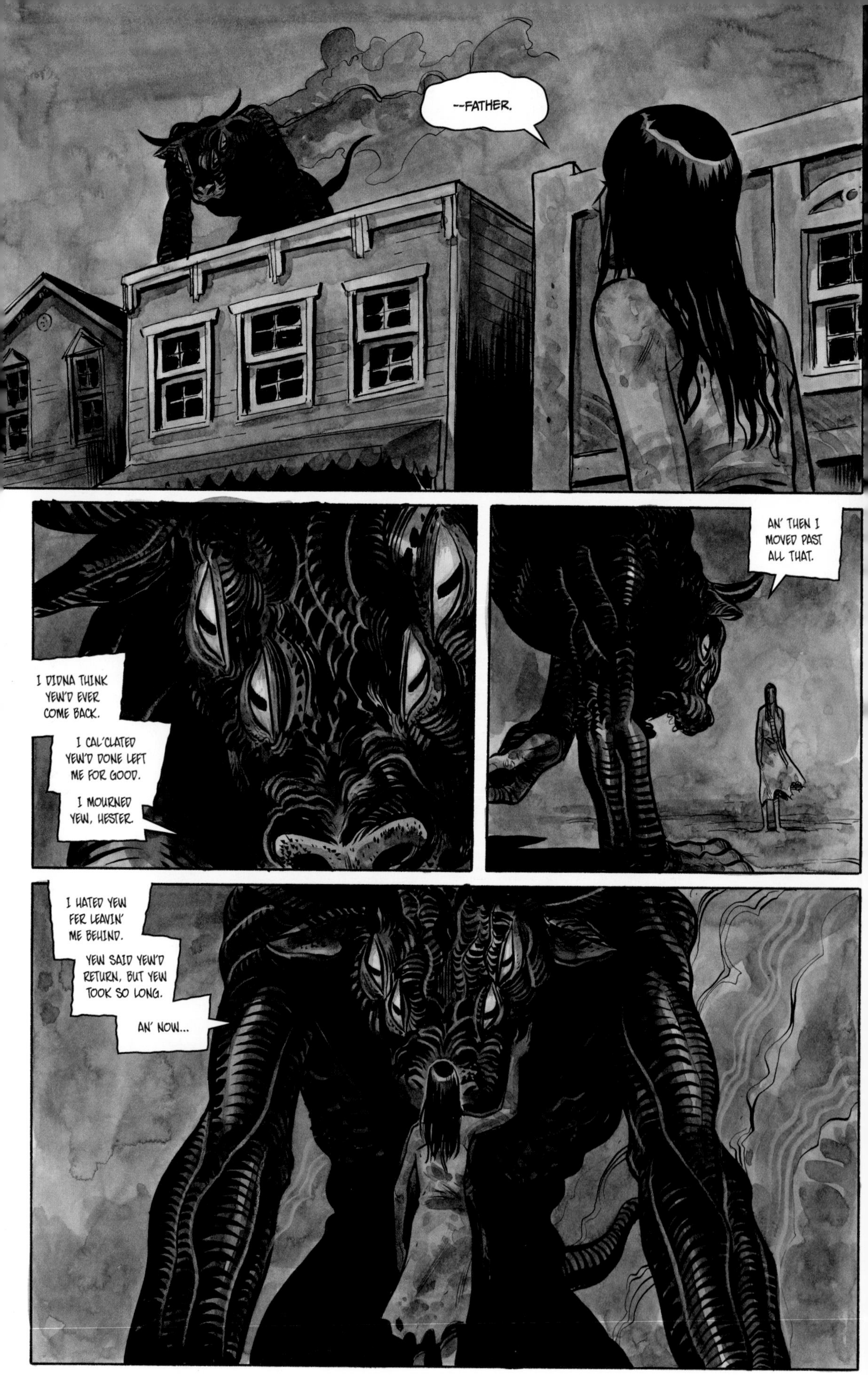
--FATHER.
I DIDNA THINK YEW'D EVER COME BACK.
I CAL'CLATED YEW'D DONE LEFT ME FOR GOOD.
I MOURNED YEW, HESTER.
AN' THEN I MOVED PAST ALL THAT.
I HATED YEW FER LEAVIN' ME BEHIND.
YEW SAID YEW'D RETURN, BUT YEW TOOK SO LONG.
AN' NOW...

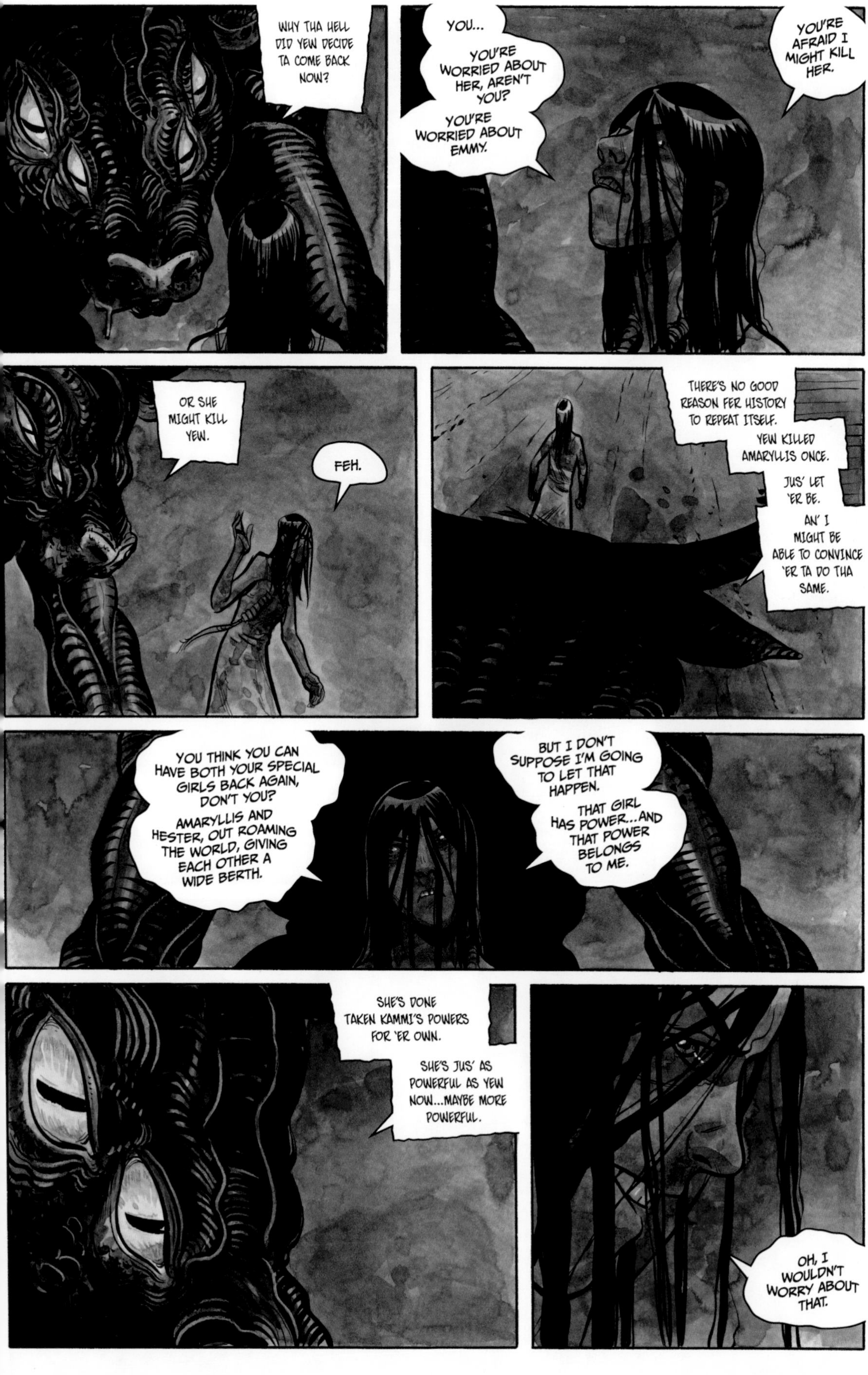
WHY THA HELL DID YEW DECIDE TA COME BACK NOW?
YOU...
YOU'RE WORRIED ABOUT HER, AREN'T YOU?
YOU'RE WORRIED ABOUT EMMY.
YOU'RE AFRAID I MIGHT KILL HER.
OR SHE MIGHT KILL YEW.
FEH.
THERE'S NO GOOD REASON FER HISTORY TO REPEAT ITSELF.
YEW KILLED AMARYLLIS ONCE.
JUS' LET 'ER BE.
AN' I MIGHT BE ABLE TO CONVINCE 'ER TA DO THA SAME.
YOU THINK YOU CAN HAVE BOTH YOUR SPECIAL GIRLS BACK AGAIN, DON'T YOU?
AMARYLLIS AND HESTER, OUT ROAMING THE WORLD, GIVING EACH OTHER A WIDE BERTH.
BUT I DON'T SUPPOSE I'M GOING TO LET THAT HAPPEN.
THAT GIRL HAS POWER...AND THAT POWER BELONGS TO ME.
SHE'S DONE TAKEN KAMMI'S POWERS FOR 'ER OWN.
SHE'S JUS' AS POWERFUL AS YEW NOW...MAYBE MORE POWERFUL.
OH, I WOULDN'T WORRY ABOUT THAT.

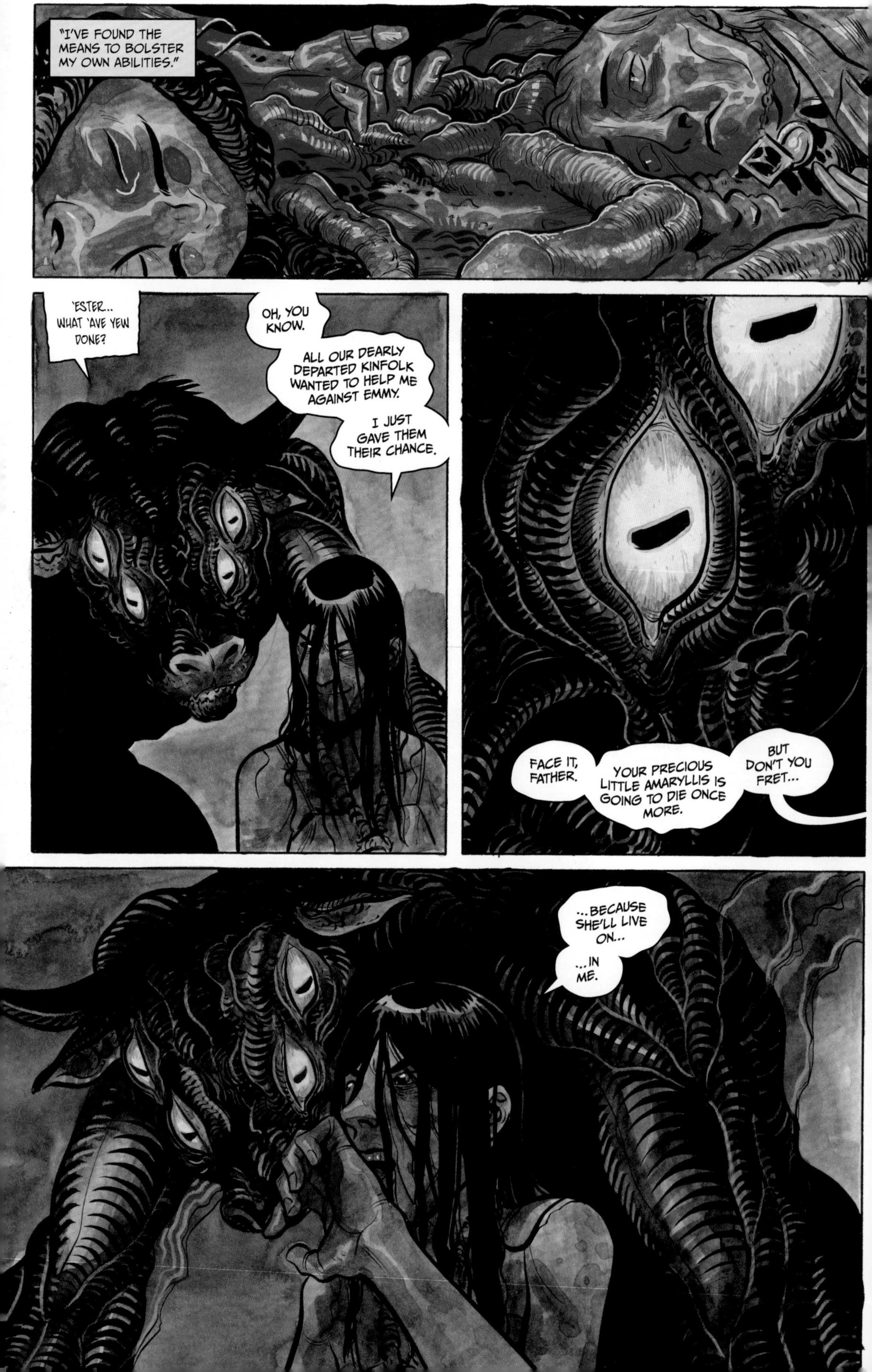
"I'VE FOUND THE MEANS TO BOLSTER MY OWN ABILITIES."
'ESTER... WHAT 'AVE YEW DONE?
OH, YOU KNOW.
ALL OUR DEARLY DEPARTED KINFOLK WANTED TO HELP ME AGAINST EMMY.
I JUST GAVE THEM THEIR CHANCE.
FACE IT, FATHER.
YOUR PRECIOUS LITTLE AMARYLLIS IS GOING TO DIE ONCE MORE.
BUT DON'T YOU FRET...
...BECAUSE SHE'LL LIVE ON...
...IN ME.

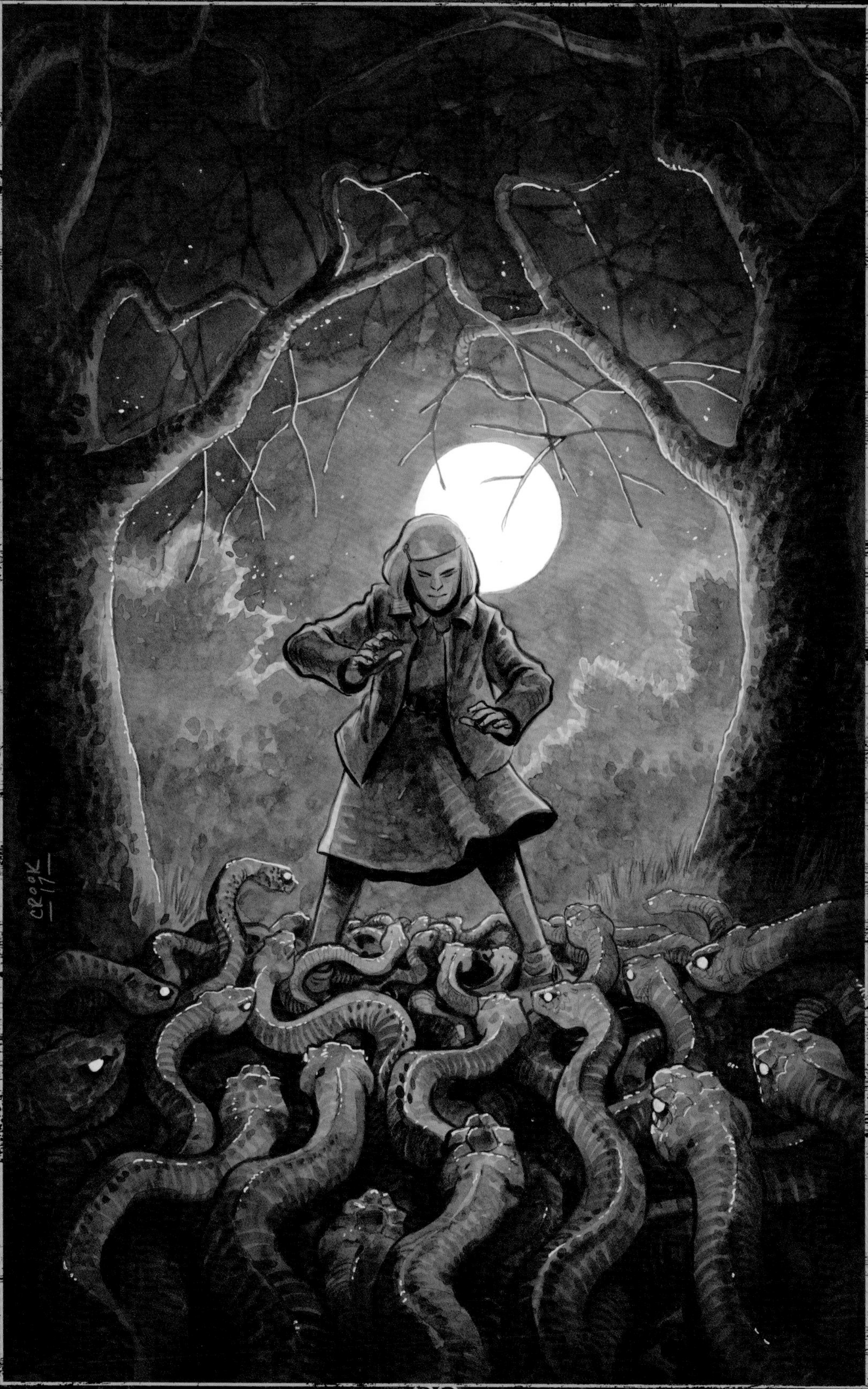
CROOK
17

TWO

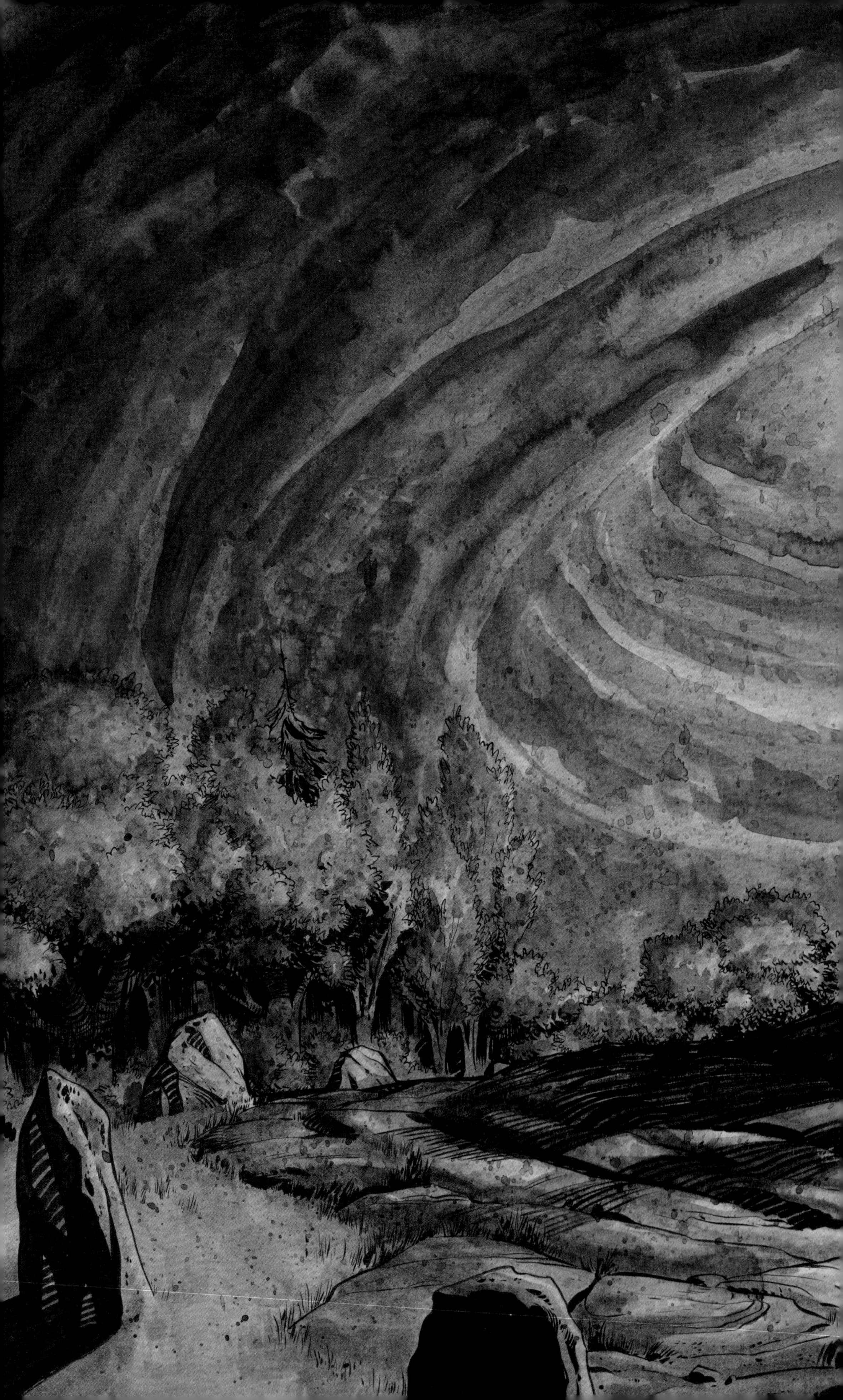

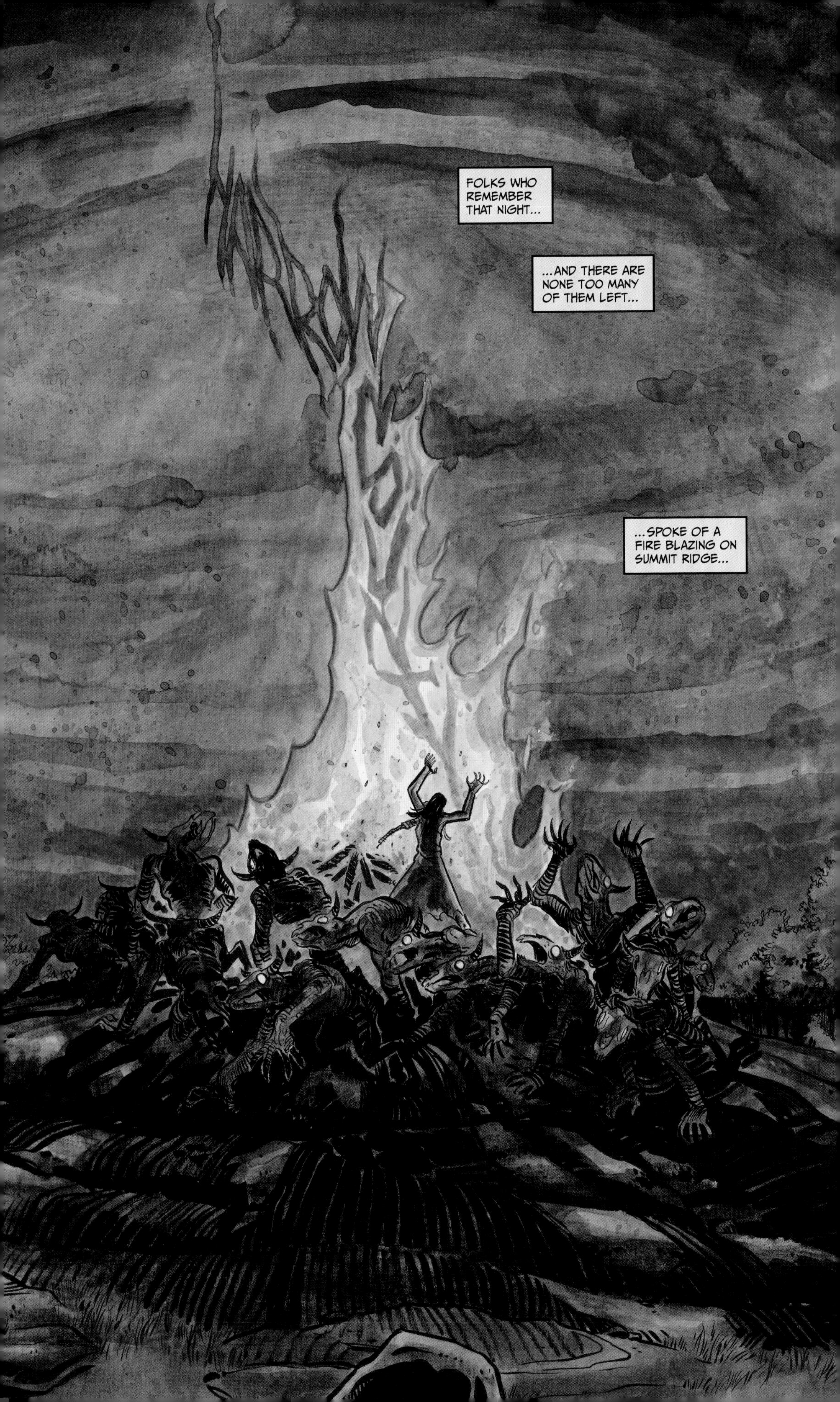
FOLKS WHO REMEMBER THAT NIGHT...
...AND THERE ARE NONE TOO MANY OF THEM LEFT...
...SPOKE OF A FIRE BLAZING ON SUMMIT RIDGE...

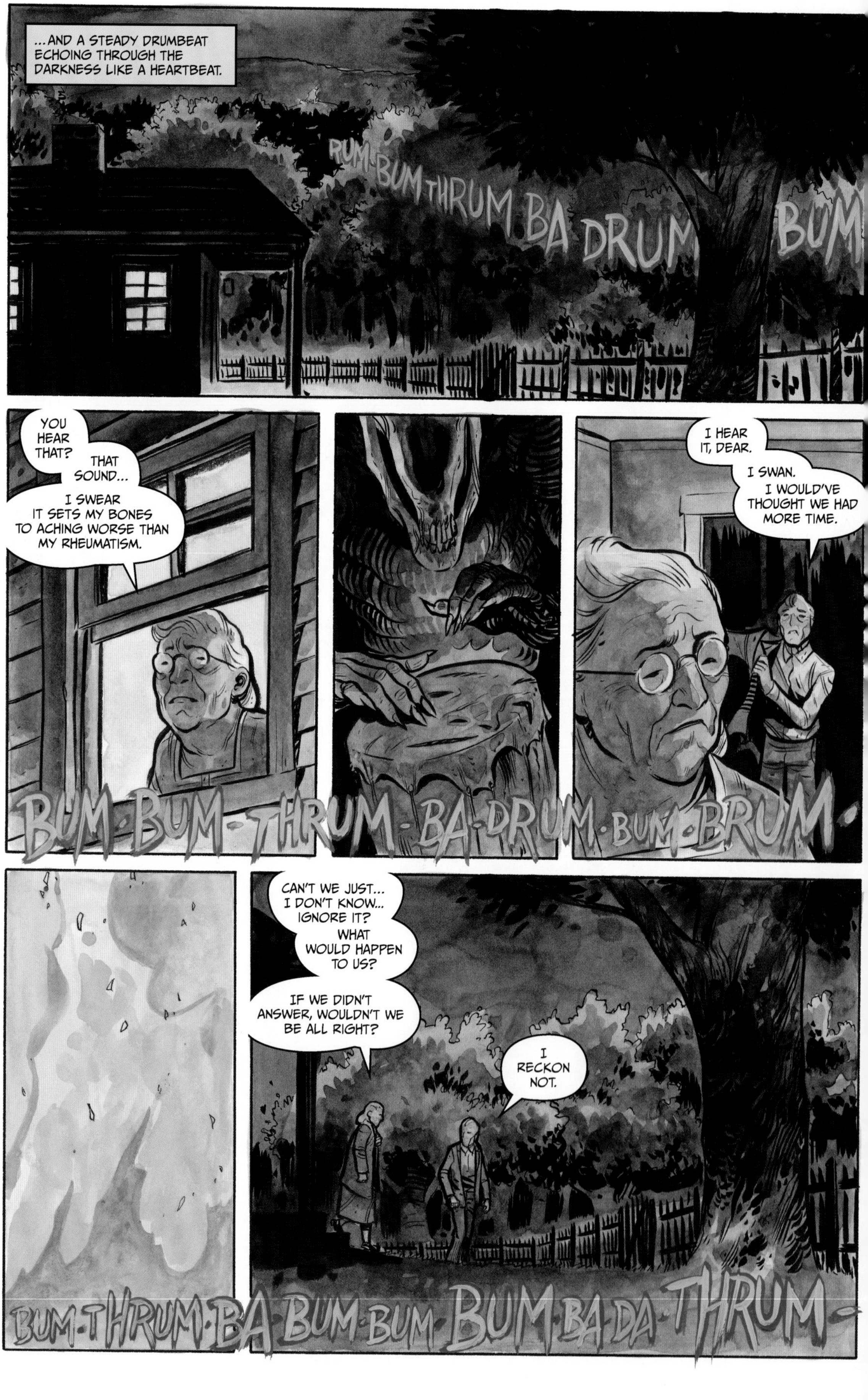
...AND A STEADY DRUMBEAT ECHOING THROUGH THE DARKNESS LIKE A HEARTBEAT.
RUM BUM THRUM BA DRUM BUM
YOU HEAR THAT?
THAT SOUND...
I SWEAR IT SETS MY BONES TO ACHING WORSE THAN MY RHEUMATISM.
I HEAR IT, DEAR.
I SWAN.
I WOULD'VE THOUGHT WE HAD MORE TIME.
BUM BUM THRUM BA DRUM BUM BRUM
CAN'T WE JUST... I DON'T KNOW... IGNORE IT?
WHAT WOULD HAPPEN TO US?
IF WE DIDN'T ANSWER, WOULDN'T WE BE ALL RIGHT?
I RECKON NOT.
BUM THRUM BA BUM BUM BUM BA DA THRUM

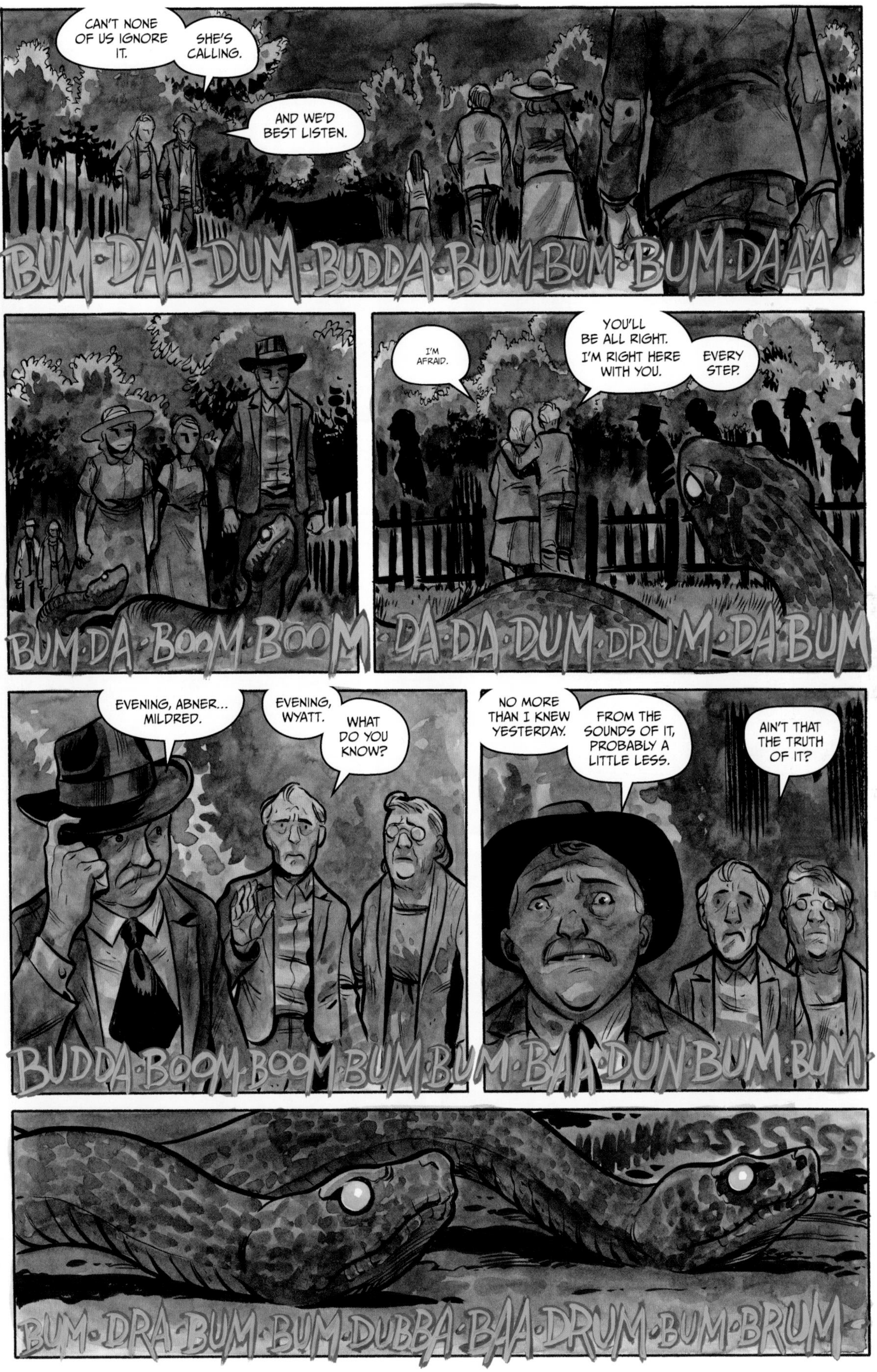
CAN'T NONE OF US IGNORE IT.
SHE'S CALLING.
AND WE'D BEST LISTEN.
BUM·DAA·DUM·BUDDA·BUM·BUM·BUM·DAAA
BUM·DA·BOOM·BOOM
I'M AFRAID.
YOU'LL BE ALL RIGHT. I'M RIGHT HERE WITH YOU.
EVERY STEP.
DA·DA·DUM·DRUM·DA·BUM
EVENING, ABNER... MILDRED.
EVENING, WYATT.
WHAT DO YOU KNOW?
NO MORE THAN I KNEW YESTERDAY.
FROM THE SOUNDS OF IT, PROBABLY A LITTLE LESS.
AIN'T THAT THE TRUTH OF IT?
BUDDA·BOOM·BOOM·BUM·BUM·BAA·DUN·BUM·BUM
SSSSSSS
BUM·DRA·BUM·BUM·DUBBA·BAA·DRUM·BUM·BRUM

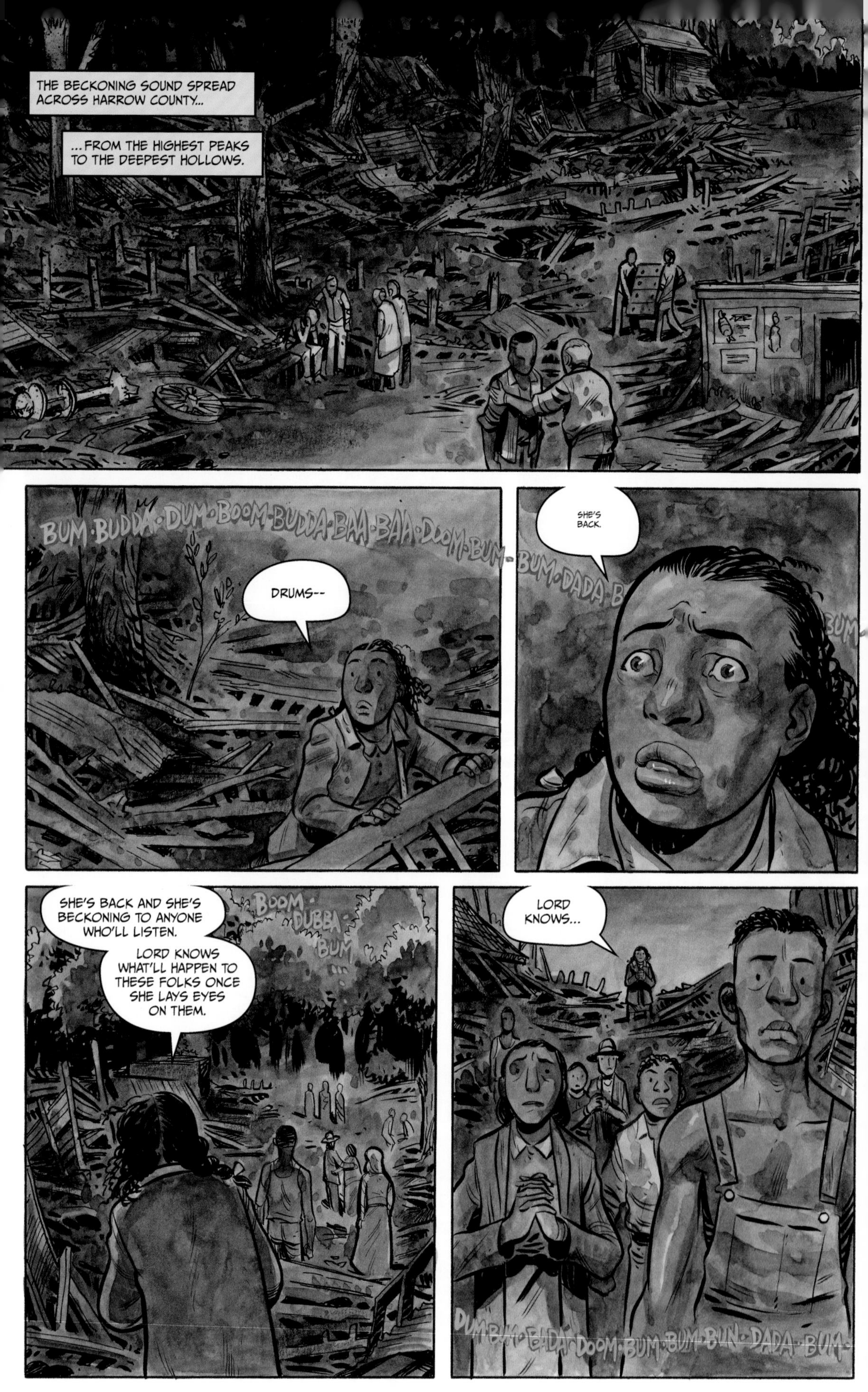
THE BECKONING SOUND SPREAD ACROSS HARROW COUNTY...
...FROM THE HIGHEST PEAKS TO THE DEEPEST HOLLOWS.
BUM·BUDDA·DUM·BOOM·BUDDA·BAA·BAA·DOOM·BUM
DRUMS--
SHE'S BACK.
BUM·DADA·B
BUM
SHE'S BACK AND SHE'S BECKONING TO ANYONE WHO'LL LISTEN.
LORD KNOWS WHAT'LL HAPPEN TO THESE FOLKS ONCE SHE LAYS EYES ON THEM.
BOOM DUBBA BUM
LORD KNOWS...
DUM·BUM·BADA·DOOM·BUM·BUM·BUN·DADA·BUM

BUM BUDA BUM DOOM

I NEED TO FIND EMMY!

WE CAN PUT A STOP TO THIS!

WE JUST NEED TO HELP EACH OTHER!

THIS IS WHAT YOU WERE TALKING ABOUT, ISN'T IT, LOVEY? IT WASN'T KAMMI WHO SCARED YOU SO.

IT WAS THE WITCH-- HESTER!

BADA-DUM-BUM-DOOM-BABA-DUM-BUDA-DOOM

EMMY CAN'T FACE HER ALONE.

SHE THINKS SHE CAN...AFTER WHAT SHE'S DONE... BUT SHE'S WRONG.

DOM BADA

UM DUM BADA BOOM

SHE--

--SHE NEEDS ME.

DUM BUM DABA DOOM BOOM BOOM

NO!

AH--

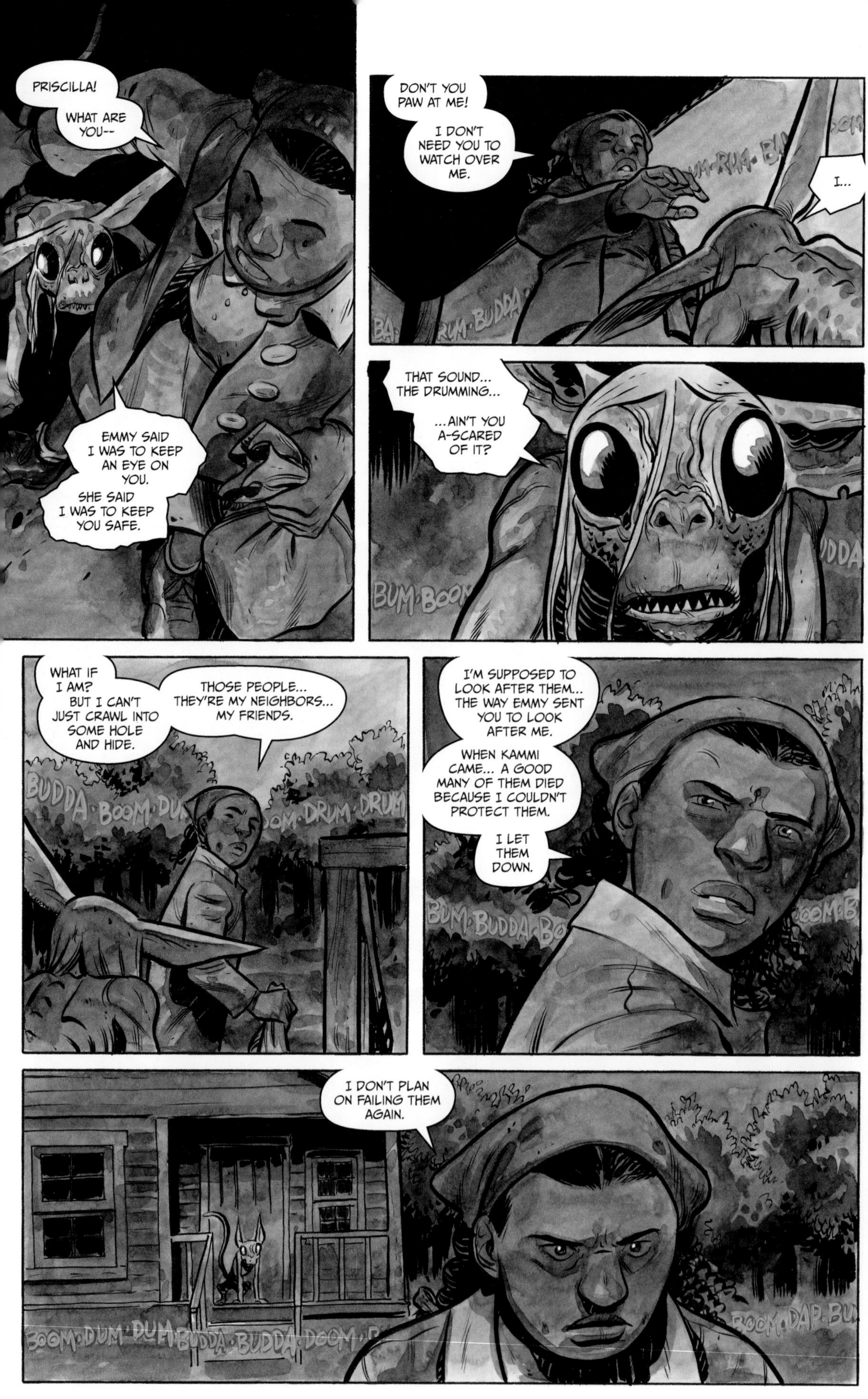
PRISCILLA!
WHAT ARE YOU--
EMMY SAID I WAS TO KEEP AN EYE ON YOU.
SHE SAID I WAS TO KEEP YOU SAFE.
DON'T YOU PAW AT ME!
I DON'T NEED YOU TO WATCH OVER ME.
I...
BA-DRUM-BUDDA
THAT SOUND... THE DRUMMING...
...AIN'T YOU A-SCARED OF IT?
BUM-BOOM
BUDDA
WHAT IF I AM? BUT I CAN'T JUST CRAWL INTO SOME HOLE AND HIDE.
THOSE PEOPLE... THEY'RE MY NEIGHBORS... MY FRIENDS.
BUDDA-BOOM-DUM-BOOM-DRUM-DRUM
I'M SUPPOSED TO LOOK AFTER THEM... THE WAY EMMY SENT YOU TO LOOK AFTER ME.
WHEN KAMMI CAME... A GOOD MANY OF THEM DIED BECAUSE I COULDN'T PROTECT THEM.
I LET THEM DOWN.
BUM-BUDDA-BO
I DON'T PLAN ON FAILING THEM AGAIN.
BOOM-DUM-DUM-BUDDA-BUDDA-DOOM
BOOM-DAP-BU

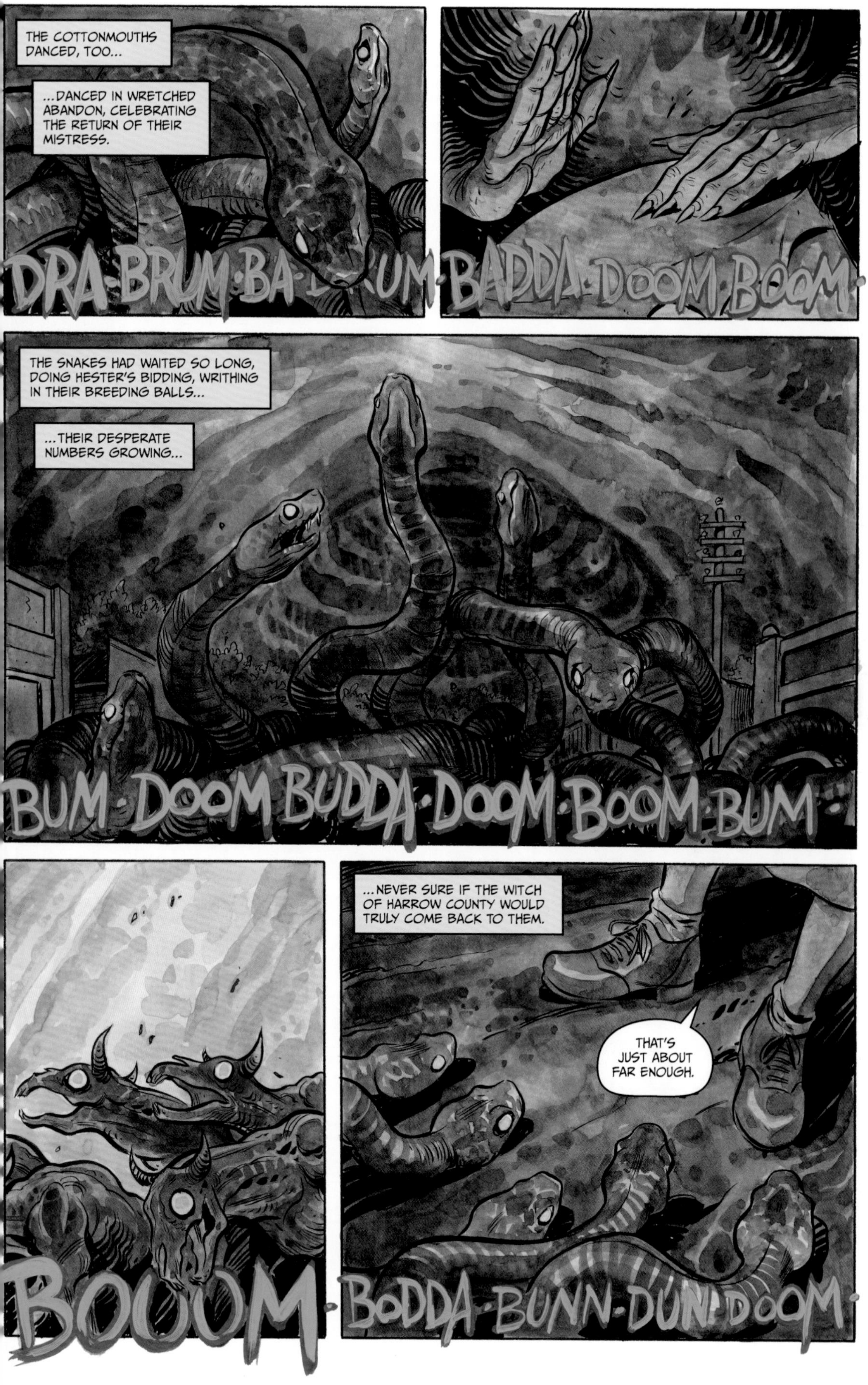
THE COTTONMOUTHS DANCED, TOO...
...DANCED IN WRETCHED ABANDON, CELEBRATING THE RETURN OF THEIR MISTRESS.
DRA·BRUM·BA·
UM·BADDA·DOOM·BOOM·
THE SNAKES HAD WAITED SO LONG, DOING HESTER'S BIDDING, WRITHING IN THEIR BREEDING BALLS...
...THEIR DESPERATE NUMBERS GROWING...
BUM·DOOM·BUDDA·DOOM·BOOM·BUM
...NEVER SURE IF THE WITCH OF HARROW COUNTY WOULD TRULY COME BACK TO THEM.
THAT'S JUST ABOUT FAR ENOUGH.
BOOOM·BODDA·BUNN·DUN·DOOM·

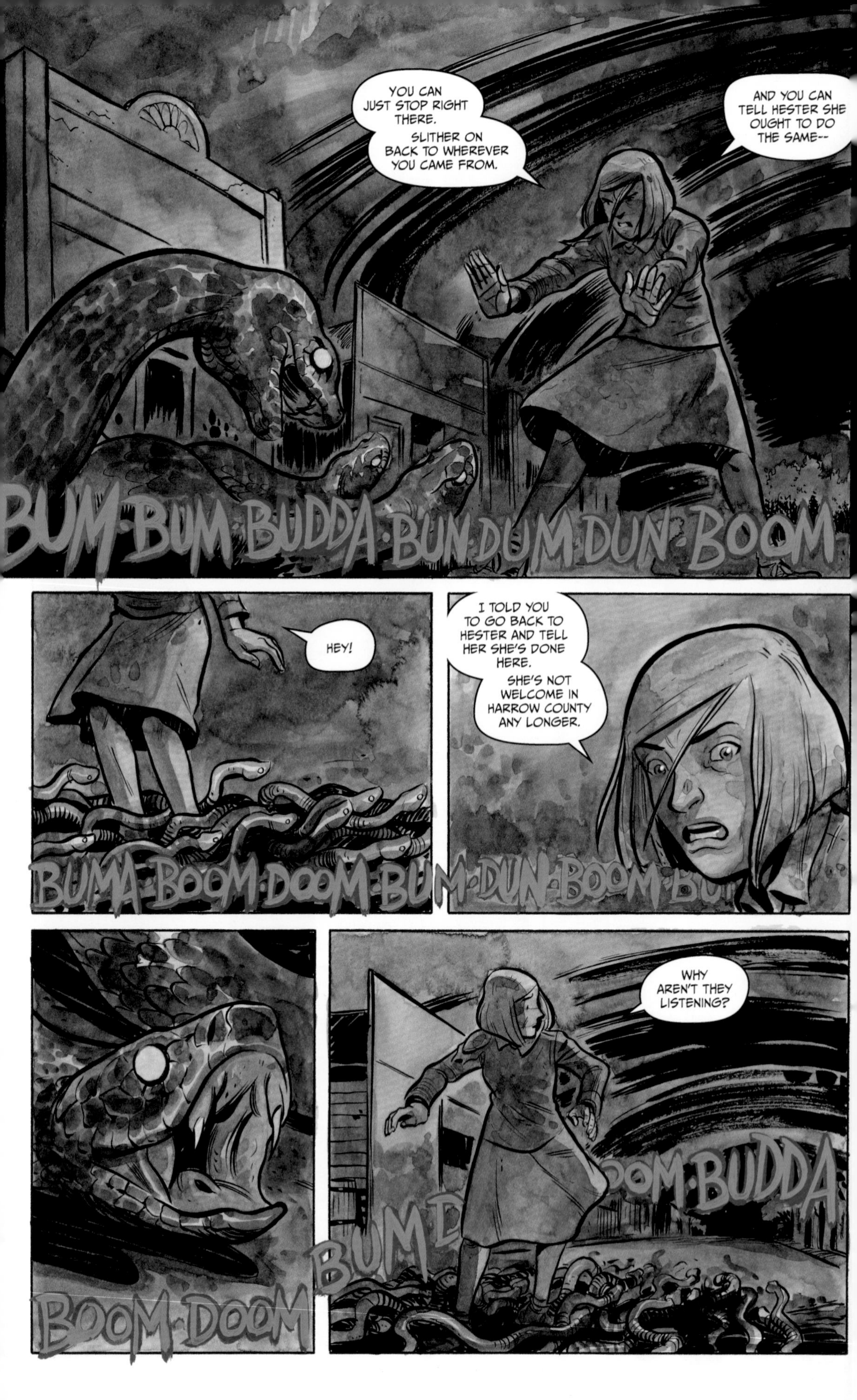
YOU CAN JUST STOP RIGHT THERE.
SLITHER ON BACK TO WHEREVER YOU CAME FROM.
AND YOU CAN TELL HESTER SHE OUGHT TO DO THE SAME--
BUM·BUM·BUDDA·BUN·DUM·DUN·BOOM
HEY!
I TOLD YOU TO GO BACK TO HESTER AND TELL HER SHE'S DONE HERE.
SHE'S NOT WELCOME IN HARROW COUNTY ANY LONGER.
BUMA·BOOM·DOOM·BUM·DUN·BOOM
WHY AREN'T THEY LISTENING?
BOOM·DOOM
OM·BUDDA

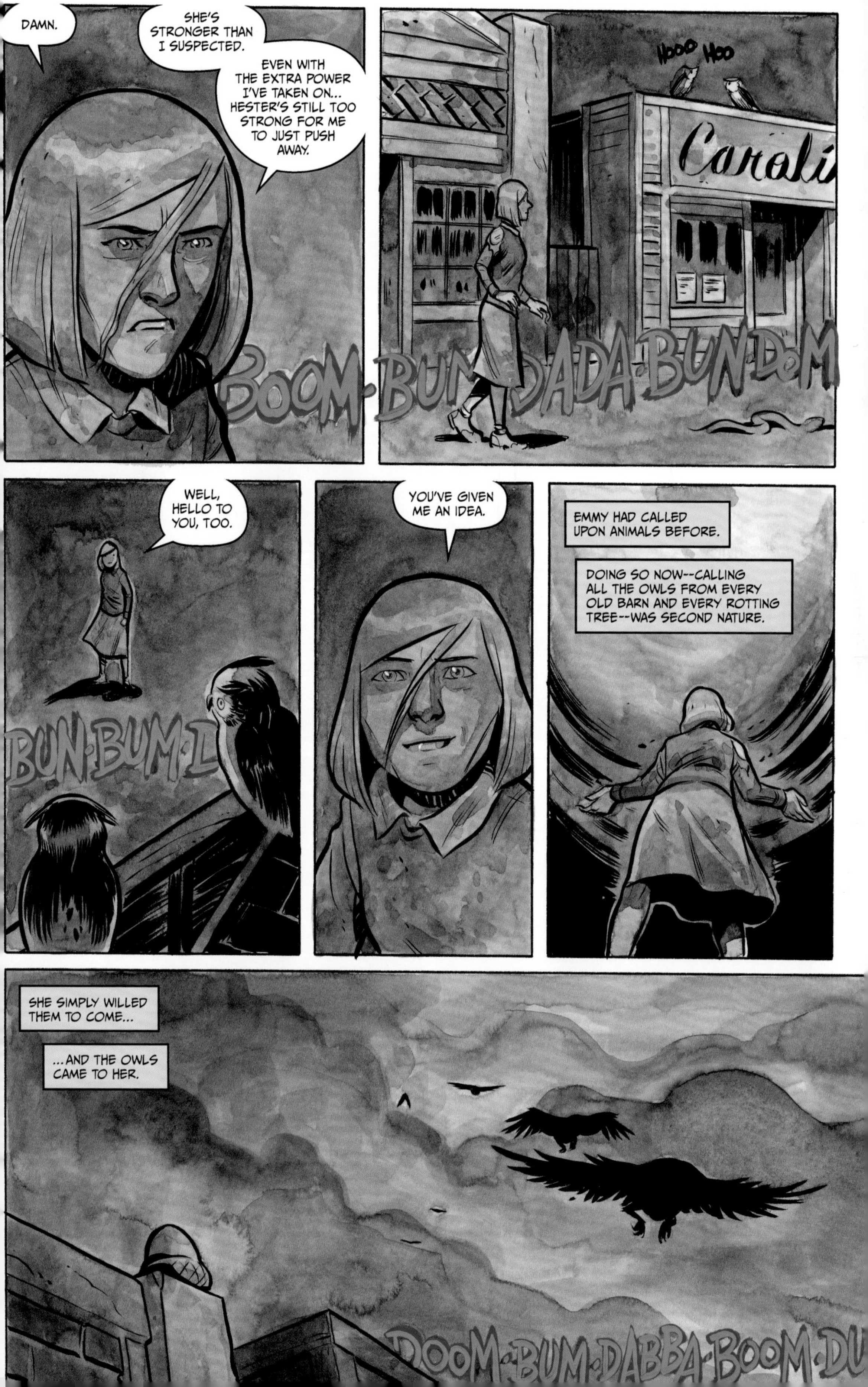
DAMN.
SHE'S STRONGER THAN I SUSPECTED.
EVEN WITH THE EXTRA POWER I'VE TAKEN ON... HESTER'S STILL TOO STRONG FOR ME TO JUST PUSH AWAY.
BOOM-BUM-DADA-BUN-DOM
HOO HOO
Caroli
WELL, HELLO TO YOU, TOO.
BUN-BUM-D
YOU'VE GIVEN ME AN IDEA.
EMMY HAD CALLED UPON ANIMALS BEFORE.
DOING SO NOW--CALLING ALL THE OWLS FROM EVERY OLD BARN AND EVERY ROTTING TREE--WAS SECOND NATURE.
SHE SIMPLY WILLED THEM TO COME...
...AND THE OWLS CAME TO HER.
DOOM-BUM-DABBA-BOOM-DU

ONLY THEY WEREN'T OWLS.

SSKRTEE·RAK

WHAT--

SKREE·LRAK

WHAT DID I CALL DOWN?

SKREEFFFF

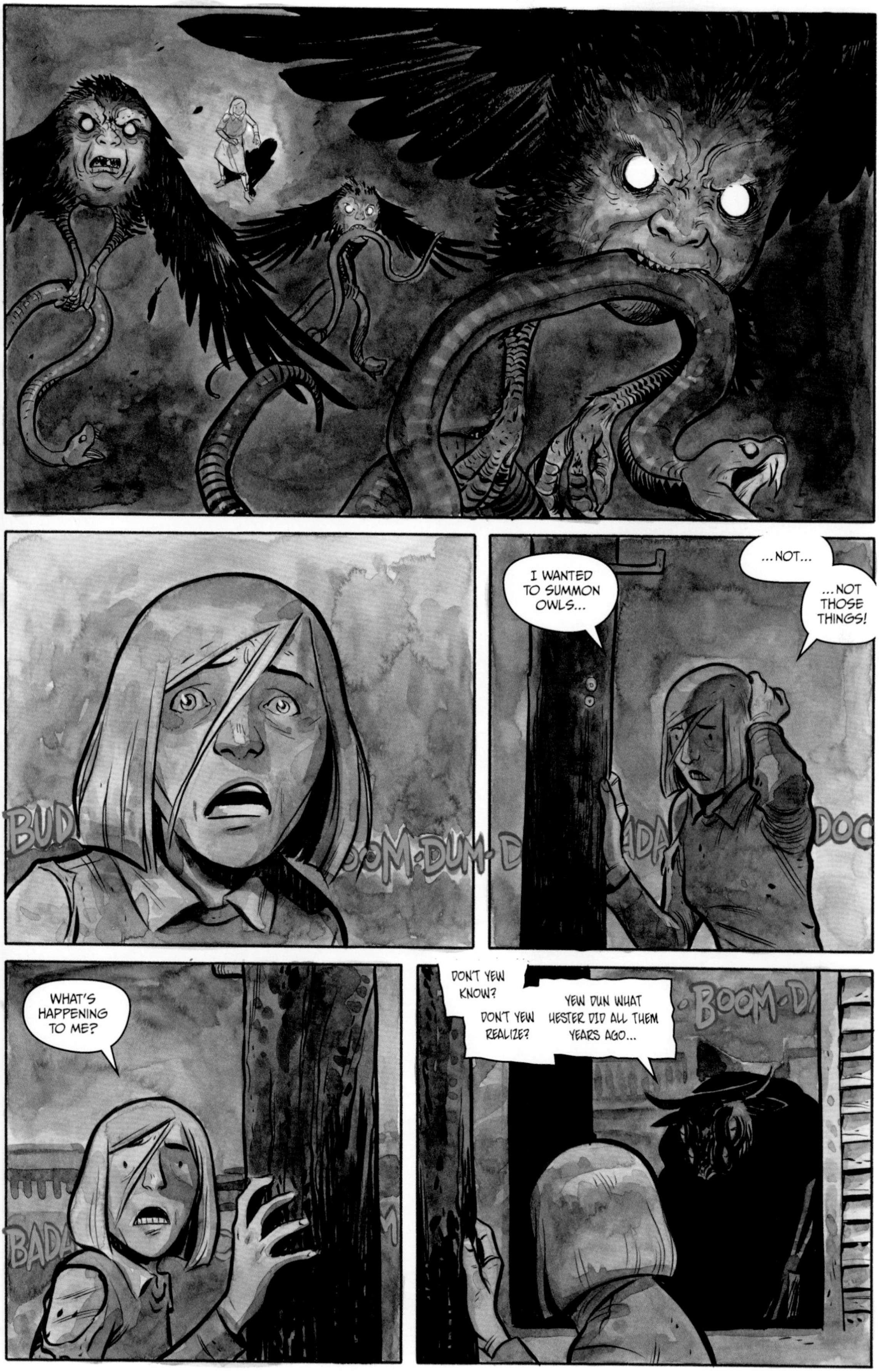
BUD
BOOM-DUM-DA
I WANTED TO SUMMON OWLS...
...NOT...
...NOT THOSE THINGS!
BADA
DOC
WHAT'S HAPPENING TO ME?
BADA
DON'T YEW KNOW?
DON'T YEW REALIZE?
YEW DUN WHAT HESTER DID ALL THEM YEARS AGO...
BOOM-DA

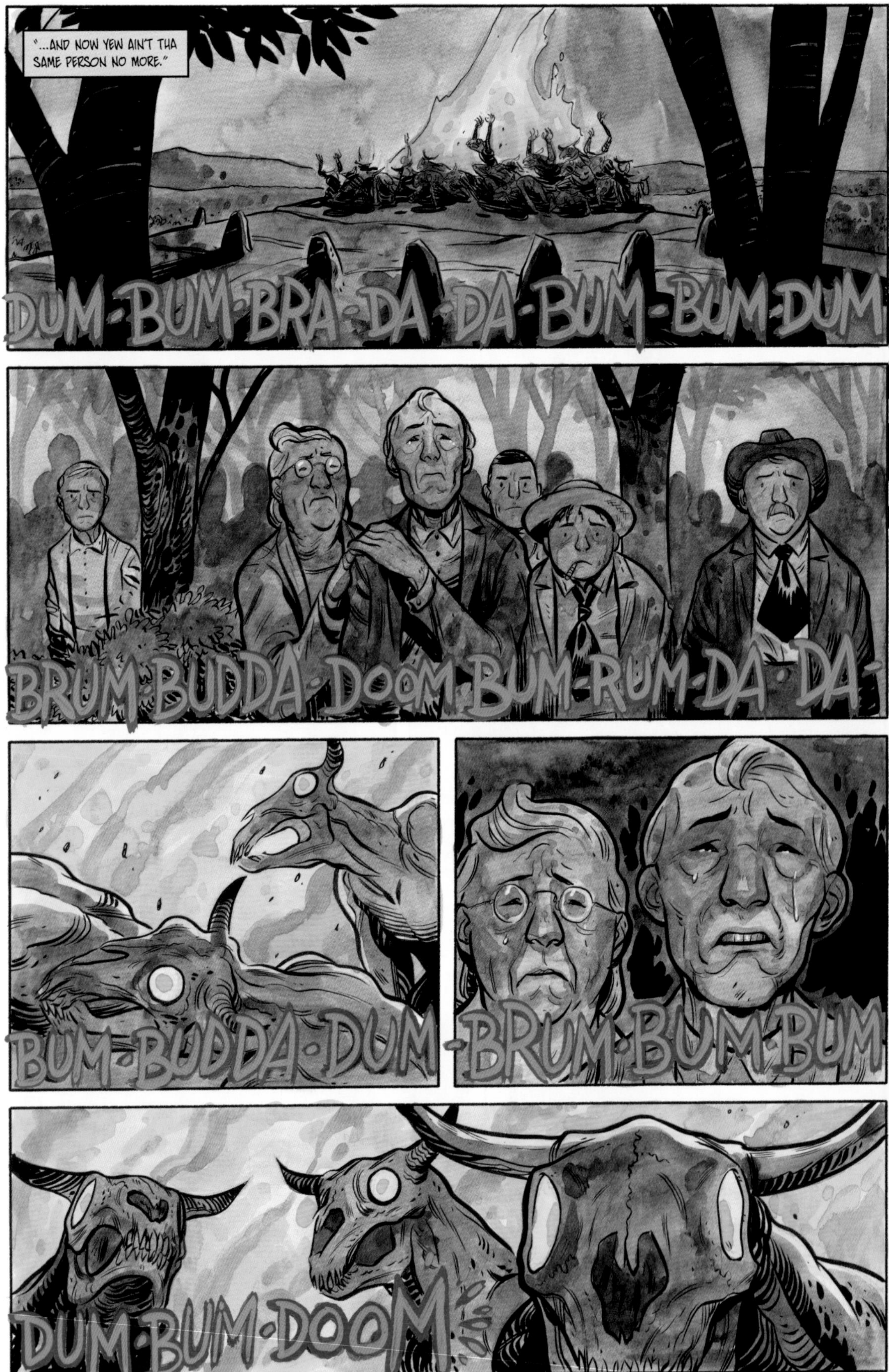
"...AND NOW YEW AIN'T THA SAME PERSON NO MORE."
DUM-BUM-BRA-DA-DA-BUM-BUM-DUM
BRUM-BUDDA-DOOM-BUM-RUM-DA-DA-
BUM-BUDDA-DUM-BRUM-BUM-BUM
DUM-BUM-DOOM

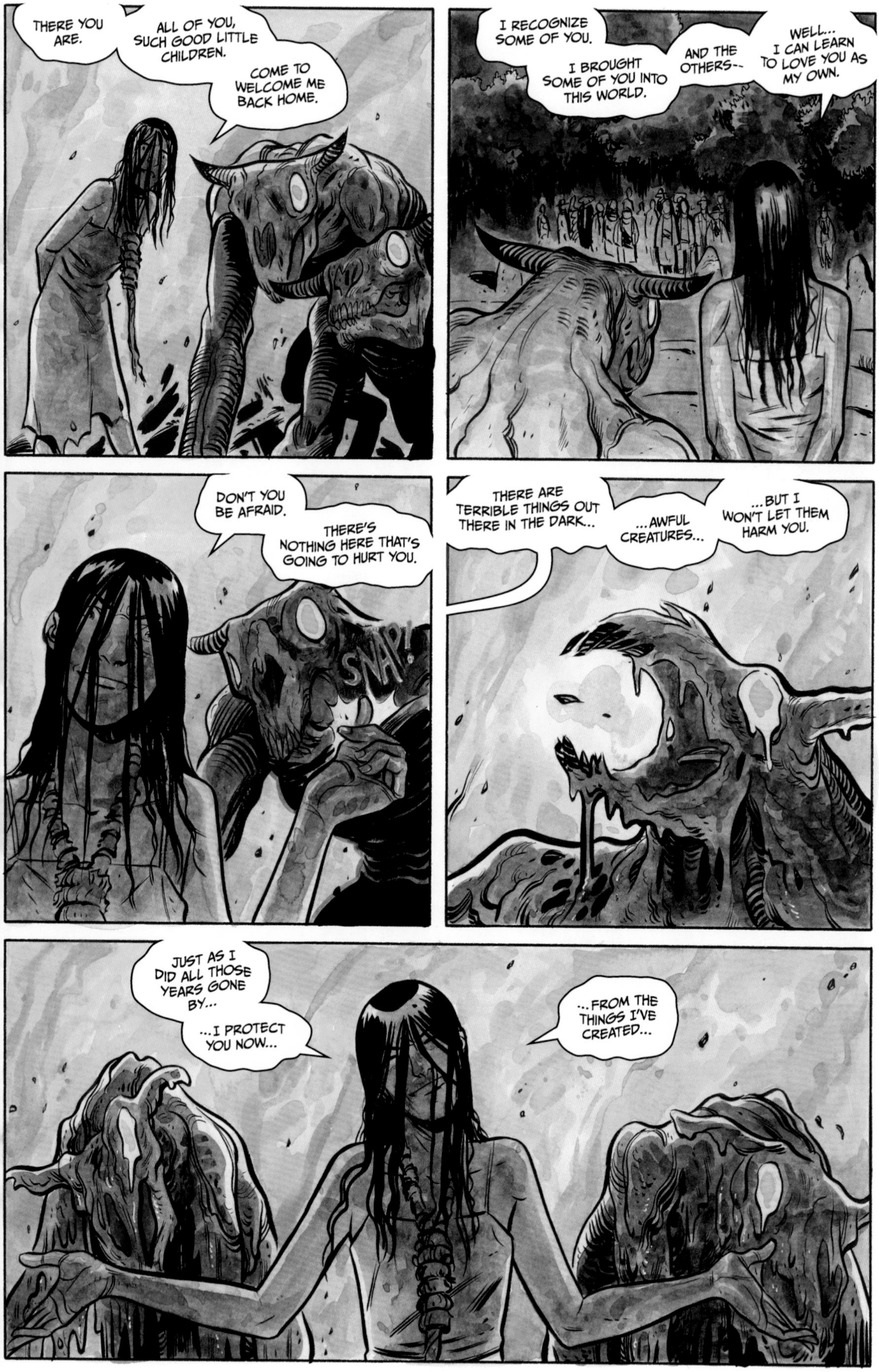
THERE YOU ARE.
ALL OF YOU, SUCH GOOD LITTLE CHILDREN.
COME TO WELCOME ME BACK HOME.
I RECOGNIZE SOME OF YOU.
I BROUGHT SOME OF YOU INTO THIS WORLD.
AND THE OTHERS--
WELL... I CAN LEARN TO LOVE YOU AS MY OWN.
DON'T YOU BE AFRAID.
THERE'S NOTHING HERE THAT'S GOING TO HURT YOU.
SNAP!
THERE ARE TERRIBLE THINGS OUT THERE IN THE DARK...
...AWFUL CREATURES...
...BUT I WON'T LET THEM HARM YOU.
JUST AS I DID ALL THOSE YEARS GONE BY...
...I PROTECT YOU NOW...
...FROM THE THINGS I'VE CREATED...

...AND FROM YOURSELVES...

LOOK AT THEM ALL.

HESTER CREATED SO MANY PEOPLE.

SHE FORMED THEM OUT OF THE MUD... THE SAME WAY SHE MADE ALL HER HAINTS.

I REMEMBER.

YOU BETRAYED ME, THOUGH, DIDN'T YOU?

YOU STRUNG ME UP FROM A TREE AND SET ME ON FIRE.

AND I CAN'T HAVE SOMETHING LIKE THAT HAPPEN AGAIN, NOT AFTER I'VE WORKED SO HARD TO RETURN TO YOU.

SHE DIDN'T MAKE EVERYONE, THOUGH.

AND SHE GAVE THEM FREE WILL.

SHE'S GOING TO FIND A WAY TO CONTROL THEM... THE HAINTS AND THE FLESH AND BLOOD FOLKS ALIKE.

WE SHOULDN'T BE HERE.

WHAT ARE YOU--

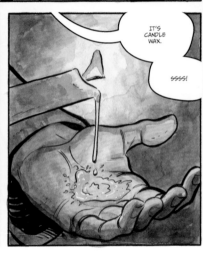

IT'S CANDLE WAX.

SSSS!

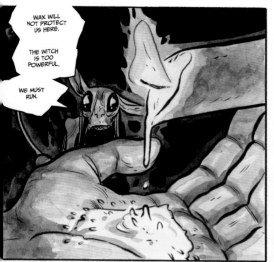

WAX WILL NOT PROTECT US HERE.

THE WITCH IS TOO POWERFUL.

WE MUST RUN.

I MUST ENSURE THAT THIS TIME, YOU'LL BE LOYAL.

SURELY, YOU WON'T FAULT ME FOR THAT.

DON'T FRET.

WE'LL SEE.

WE'LL JUST SEE.

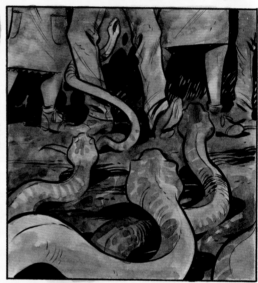

I DON'T SUPPOSE THERE'S ENOUGH WAX TO FILL THOSE BIG EARS OF YOURS.

HERE'S HOPING HESTER'S SNAKES ONLY WORK ON PEOPLE.

THIS WILL ONLY HURT FOR A MOMENT.

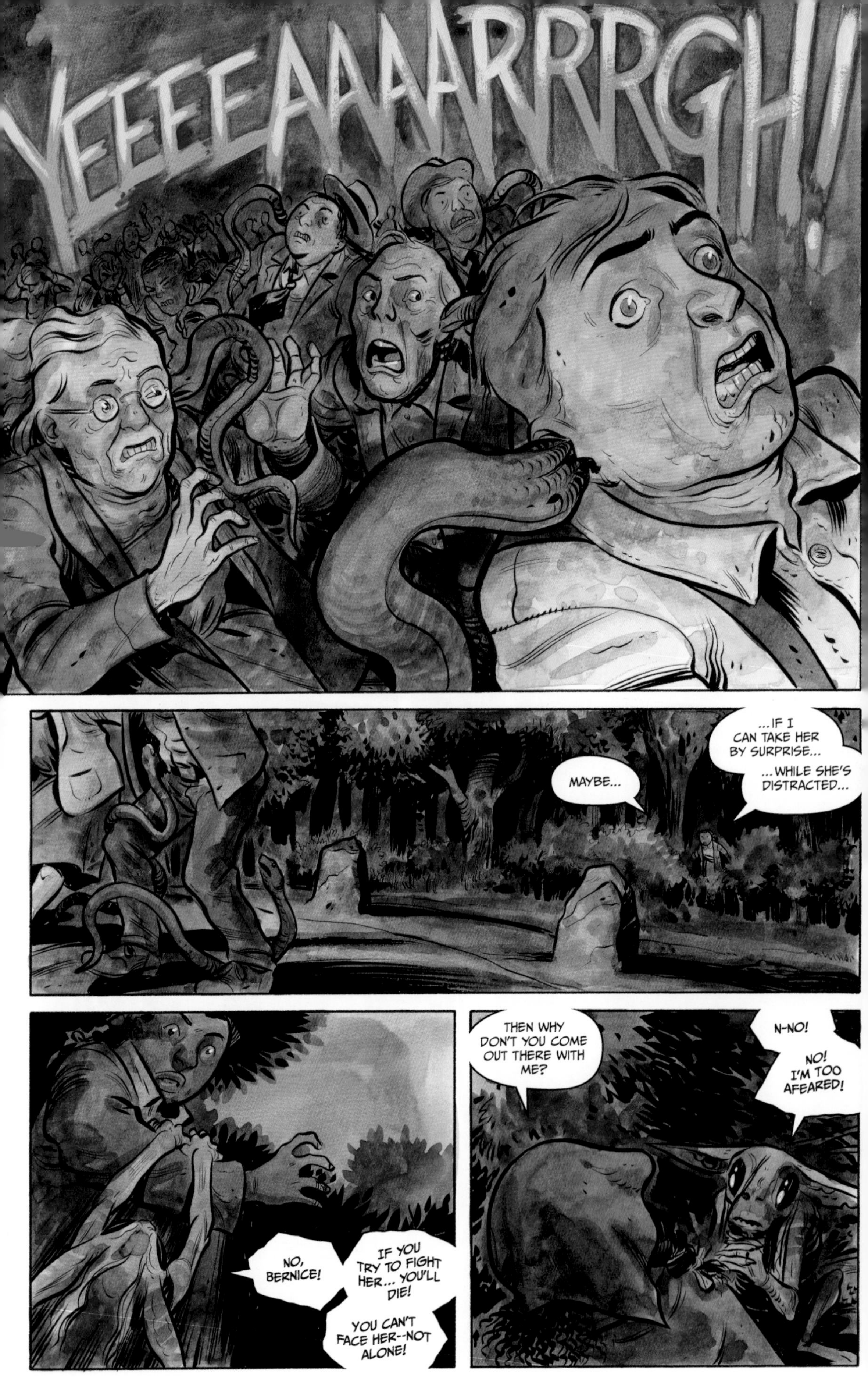
YEEEAAAARRRGH!!
MAYBE...
...IF I CAN TAKE HER BY SURPRISE...
...WHILE SHE'S DISTRACTED...
NO, BERNICE!
IF YOU TRY TO FIGHT HER... YOU'LL DIE!
YOU CAN'T FACE HER--NOT ALONE!
THEN WHY DON'T YOU COME OUT THERE WITH ME?
N-NO!
NO! I'M TOO AFEARED!

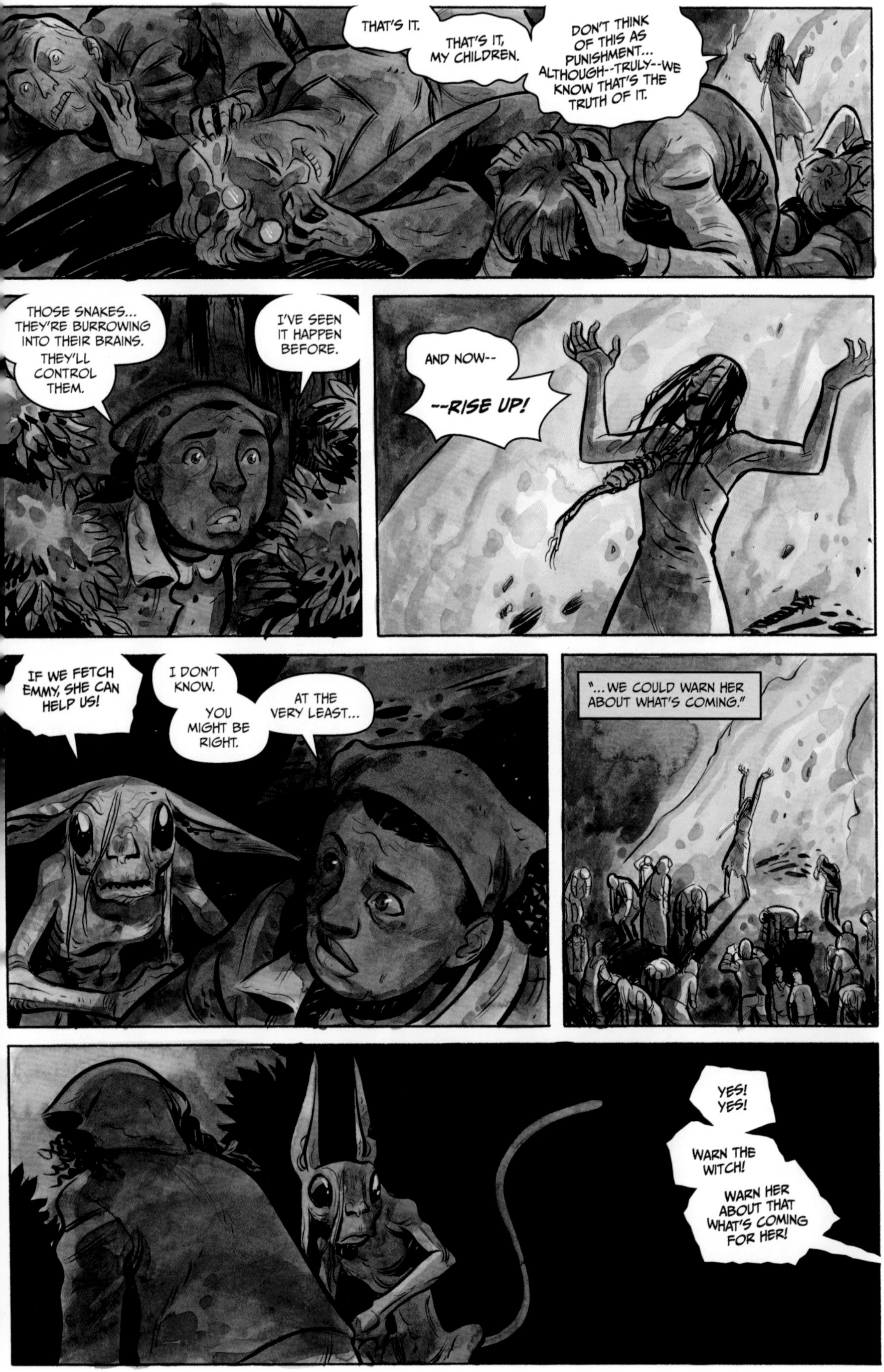
THAT'S IT.
THAT'S IT, MY CHILDREN.
DON'T THINK OF THIS AS PUNISHMENT... ALTHOUGH--TRULY--WE KNOW THAT'S THE TRUTH OF IT.
THOSE SNAKES... THEY'RE BURROWING INTO THEIR BRAINS. THEY'LL CONTROL THEM.
I'VE SEEN IT HAPPEN BEFORE.
AND NOW--
--RISE UP!
IF WE FETCH EMMY, SHE CAN HELP US!
I DON'T KNOW.
YOU MIGHT BE RIGHT.
AT THE VERY LEAST...
"...WE COULD WARN HER ABOUT WHAT'S COMING."
YES! YES!
WARN THE WITCH!
WARN HER ABOUT THAT WHAT'S COMING FOR HER!

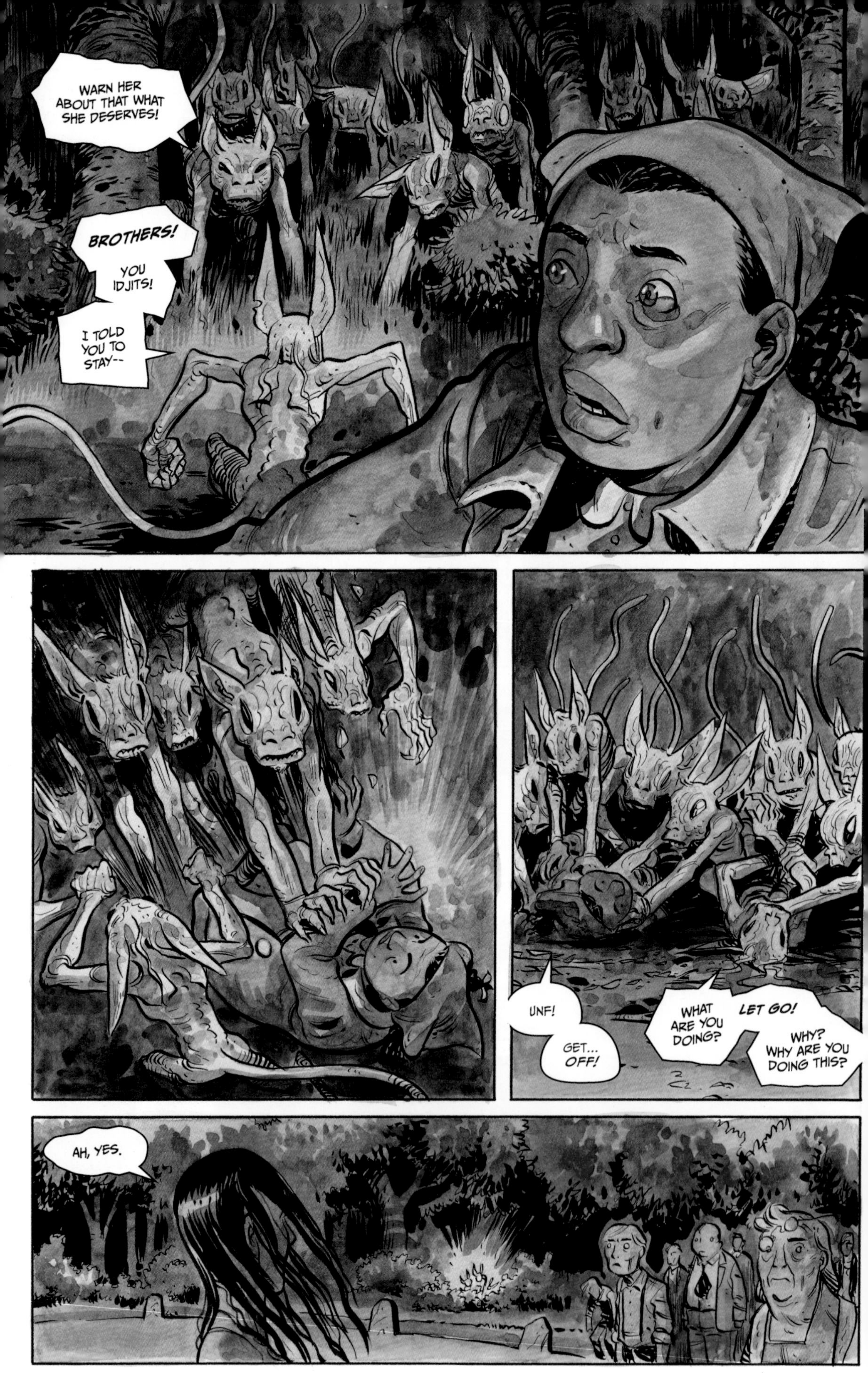
WARN HER ABOUT THAT WHAT SHE DESERVES!
BROTHERS!
YOU IDJITS!
I TOLD YOU TO STAY--
UNF!
GET... OFF!
WHAT ARE YOU DOING?
LET GO!
WHY? WHY ARE YOU DOING THIS?
AH, YES.

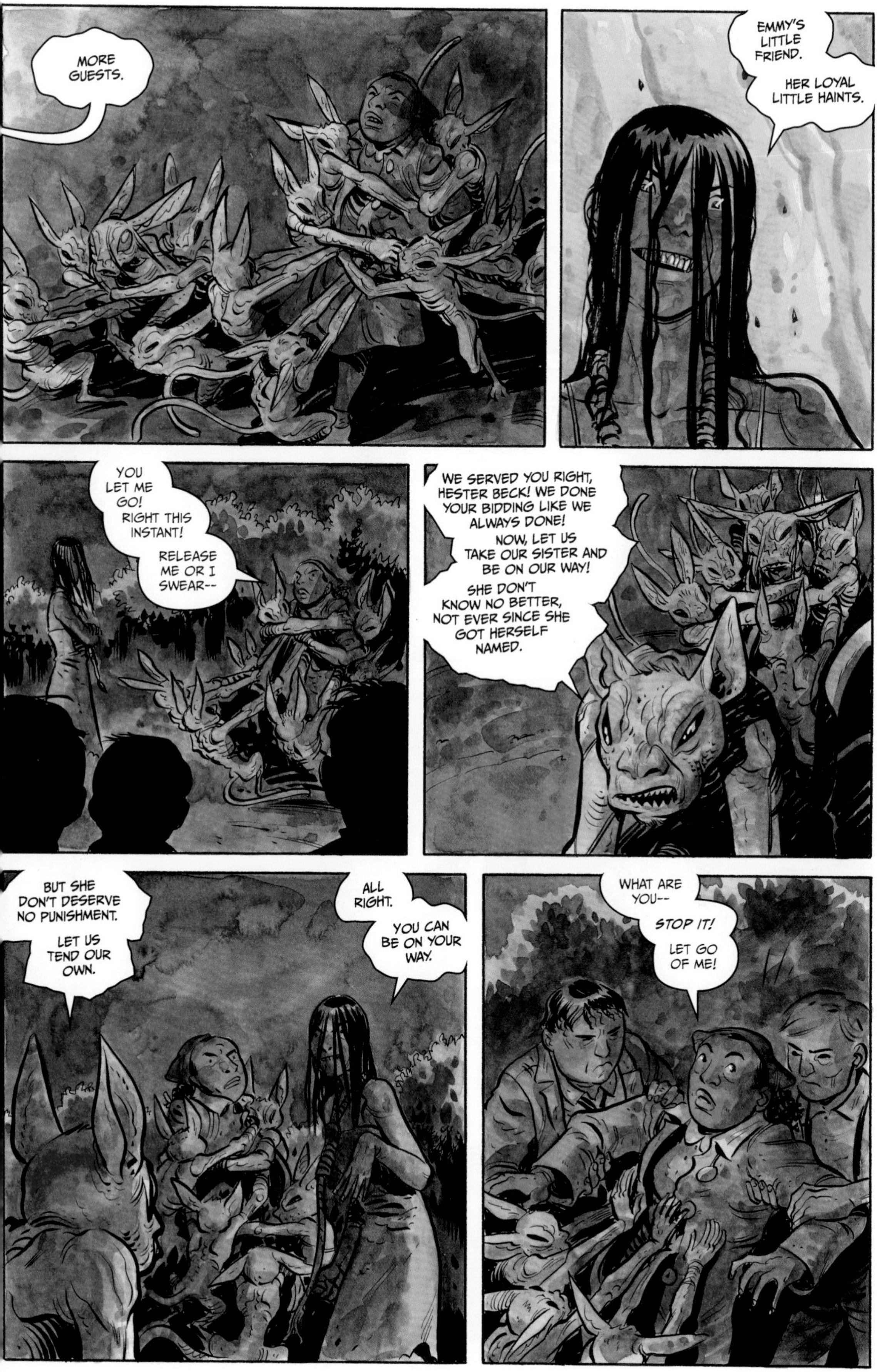
MORE GUESTS.
EMMY'S LITTLE FRIEND.
HER LOYAL LITTLE HAINTS.
YOU LET ME GO! RIGHT THIS INSTANT!
RELEASE ME OR I SWEAR--
WE SERVED YOU RIGHT, HESTER BECK! WE DONE YOUR BIDDING LIKE WE ALWAYS DONE!
NOW, LET US TAKE OUR SISTER AND BE ON OUR WAY!
SHE DON'T KNOW NO BETTER, NOT EVER SINCE SHE GOT HERSELF NAMED.
BUT SHE DON'T DESERVE NO PUNISHMENT.
LET US TEND OUR OWN.
ALL RIGHT.
YOU CAN BE ON YOUR WAY.
WHAT ARE YOU--
STOP IT!
LET GO OF ME!

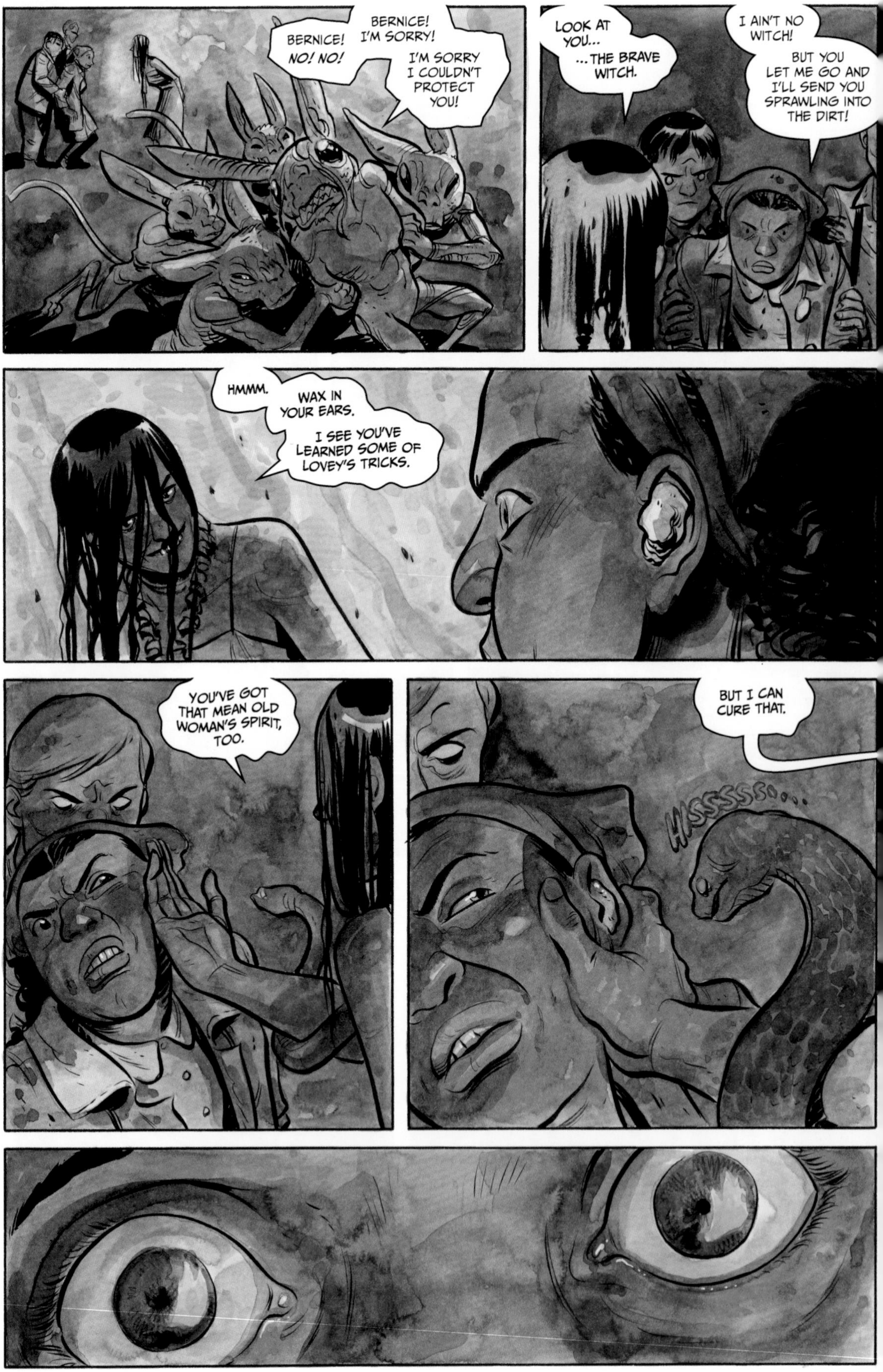
BERNICE!
NO! NO!
BERNICE! I'M SORRY!
I'M SORRY I COULDN'T PROTECT YOU!
LOOK AT YOU...
...THE BRAVE WITCH.
I AIN'T NO WITCH!
BUT YOU LET ME GO AND I'LL SEND YOU SPRAWLING INTO THE DIRT!
HMMM.
WAX IN YOUR EARS.
I SEE YOU'VE LEARNED SOME OF LOVEY'S TRICKS.
YOU'VE GOT THAT MEAN OLD WOMAN'S SPIRIT, TOO.
BUT I CAN CURE THAT.
HISSSSSS...

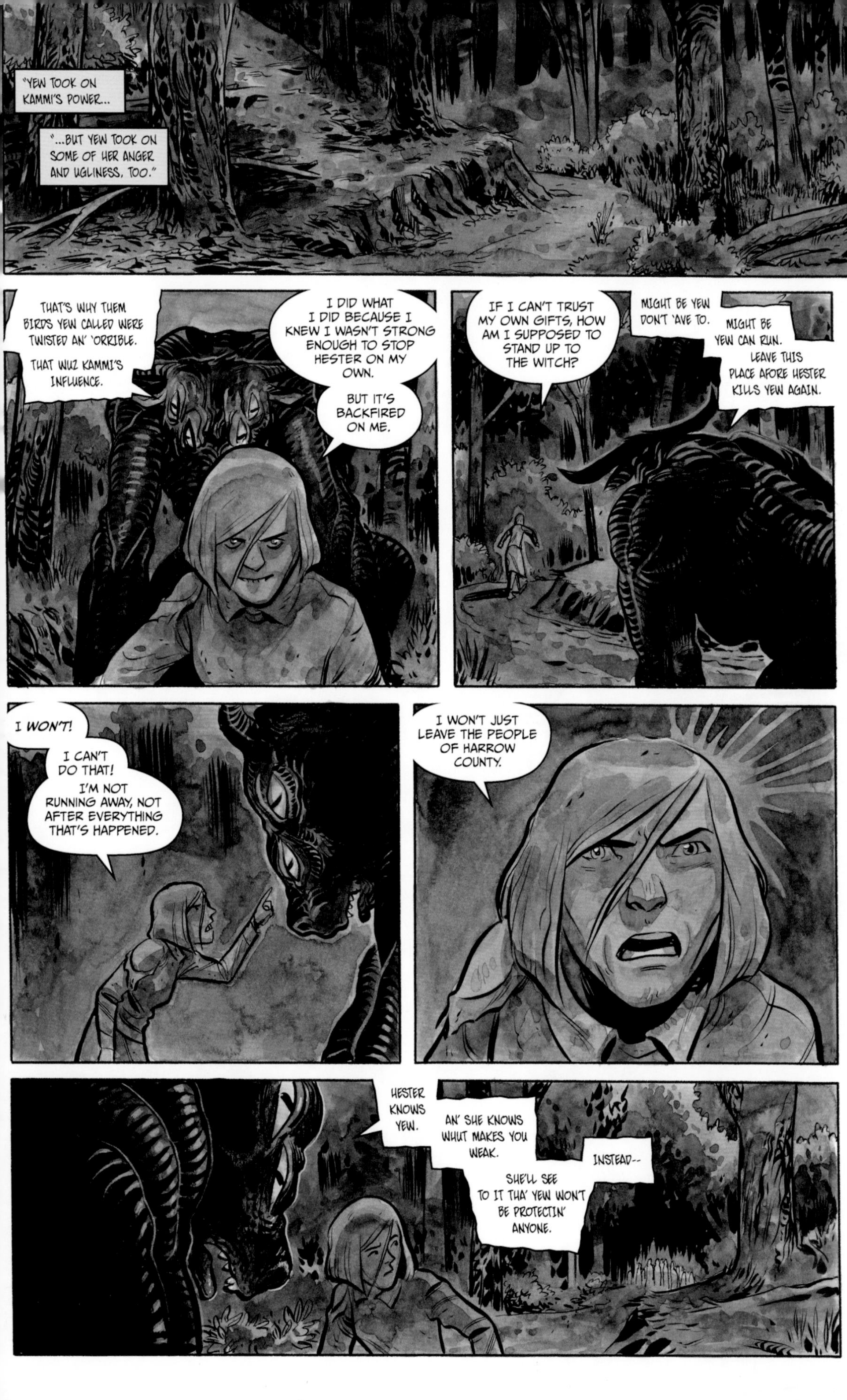
"YEW TOOK ON KAMMI'S POWER...
"...BUT YEW TOOK ON SOME OF HER ANGER AND UGLINESS, TOO."
THAT'S WHY THEM BIRDS YEW CALLED WERE TWISTED AN' 'ORRIBLE.
THAT WUZ KAMMI'S INFLUENCE.
I DID WHAT I DID BECAUSE I KNEW I WASN'T STRONG ENOUGH TO STOP HESTER ON MY OWN.
BUT IT'S BACKFIRED ON ME.
IF I CAN'T TRUST MY OWN GIFTS, HOW AM I SUPPOSED TO STAND UP TO THE WITCH?
MIGHT BE YEW DON'T 'AVE TO.
MIGHT BE YEW CAN RUN.
LEAVE THIS PLACE AFORE HESTER KILLS YEW AGAIN.
I WON'T!
I CAN'T DO THAT!
I'M NOT RUNNING AWAY, NOT AFTER EVERYTHING THAT'S HAPPENED.
I WON'T JUST LEAVE THE PEOPLE OF HARROW COUNTY.
HESTER KNOWS YEW.
AN' SHE KNOWS WHUT MAKES YOU WEAK.
INSTEAD--
SHE'LL SEE TO IT THA' YEW WON'T BE PROTECTIN' ANYONE.

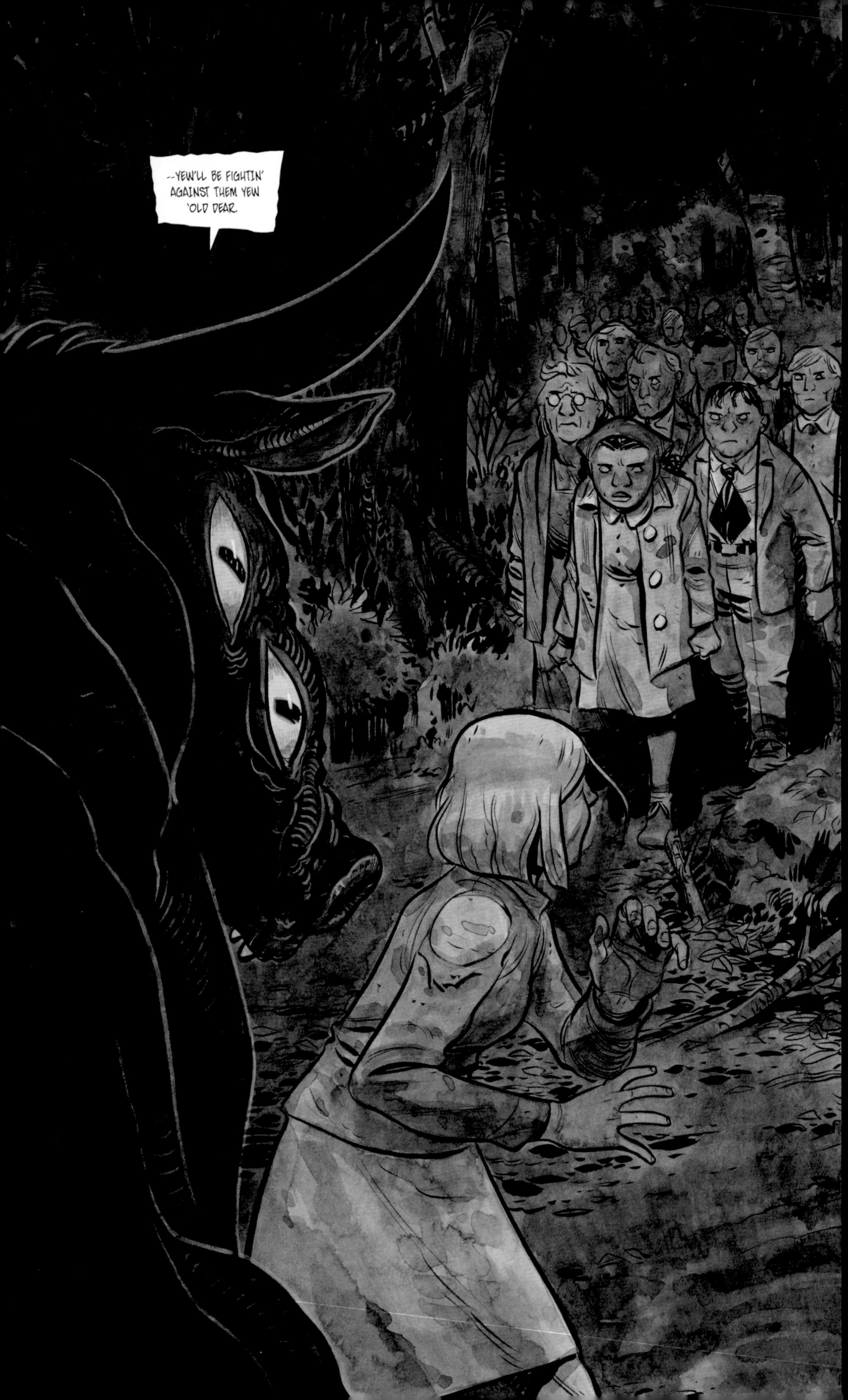
--YEW'LL BE FIGHTIN' AGAINST THEM YEW 'OLD DEAR.

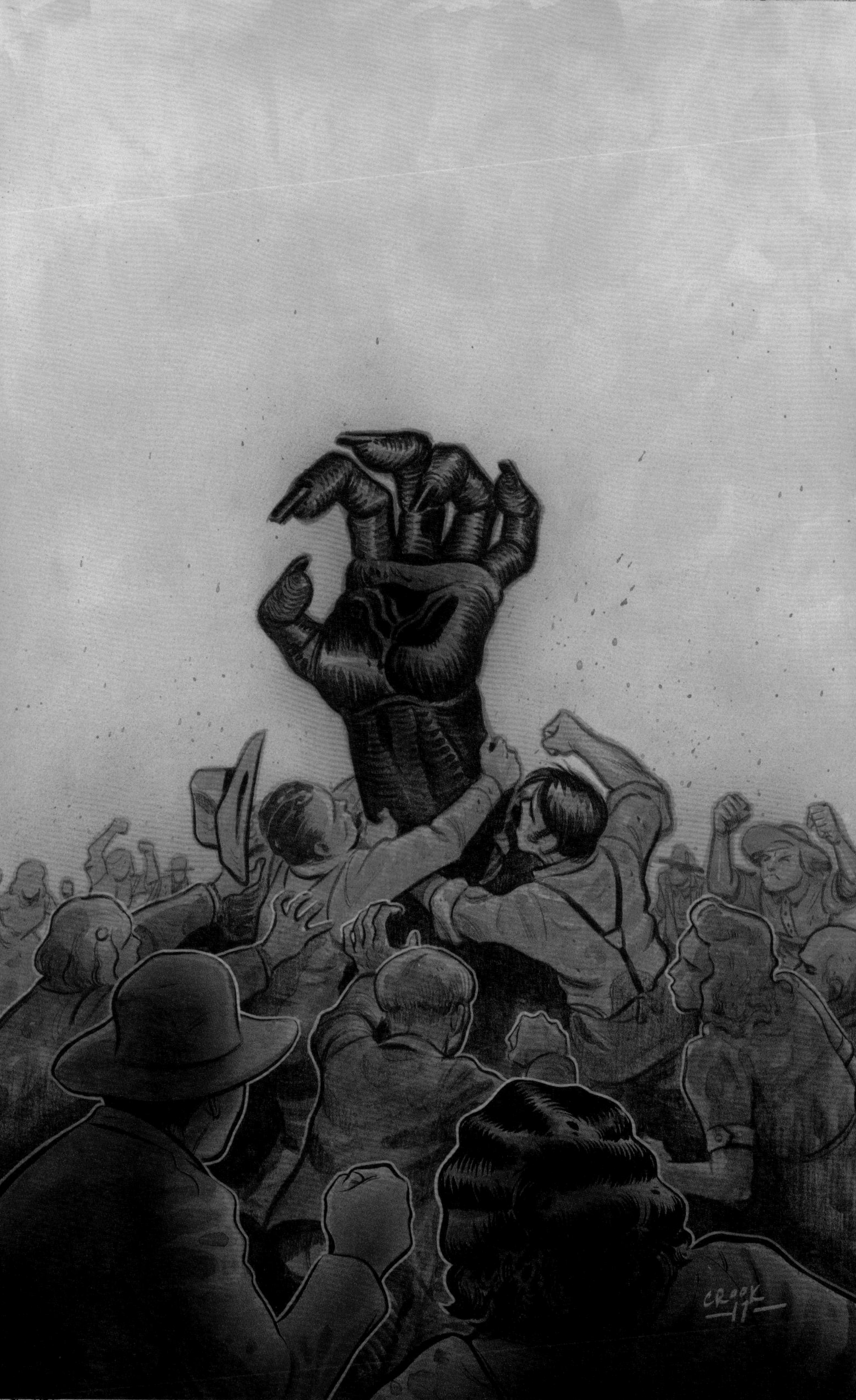
CROOK
11

THREE

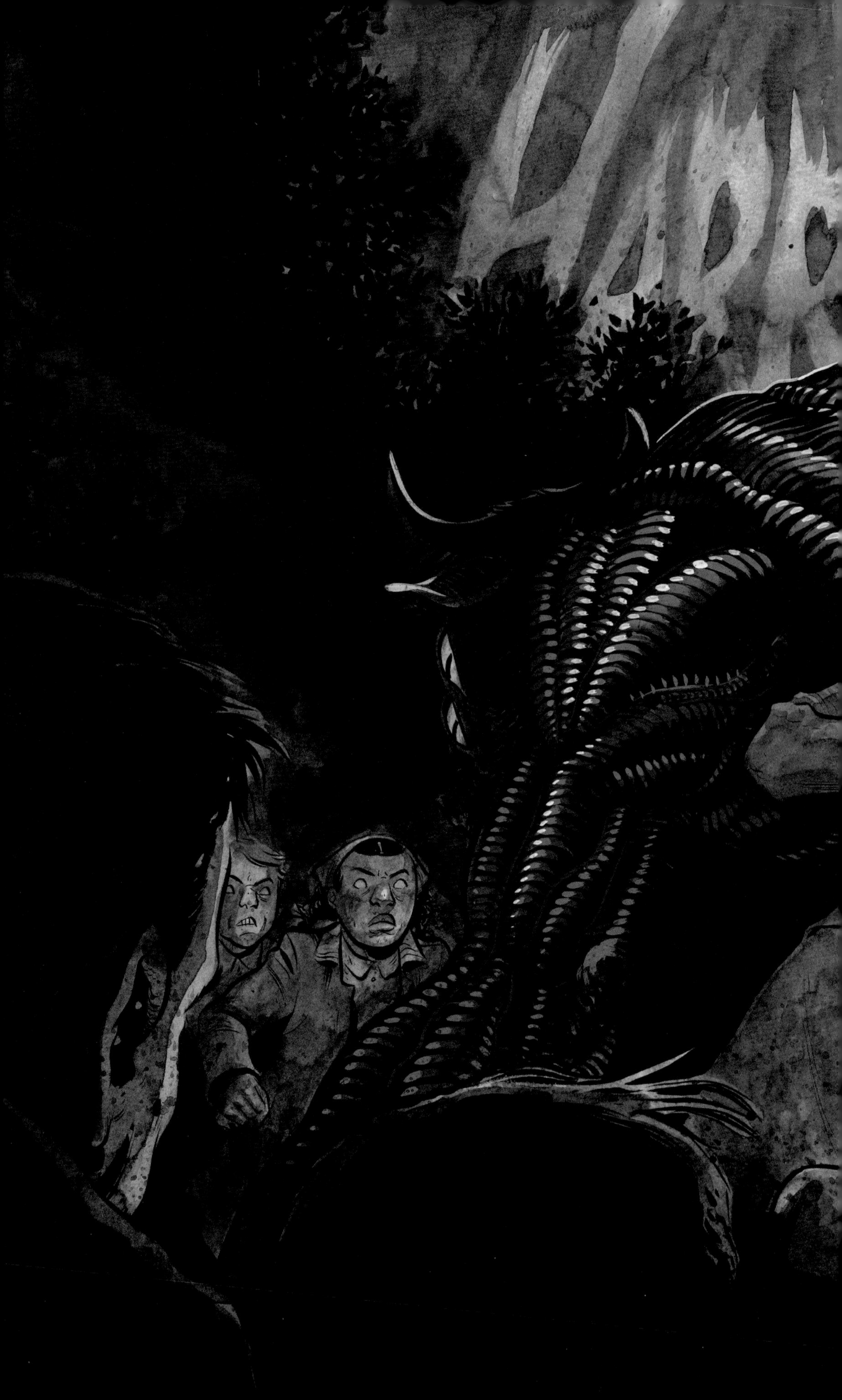

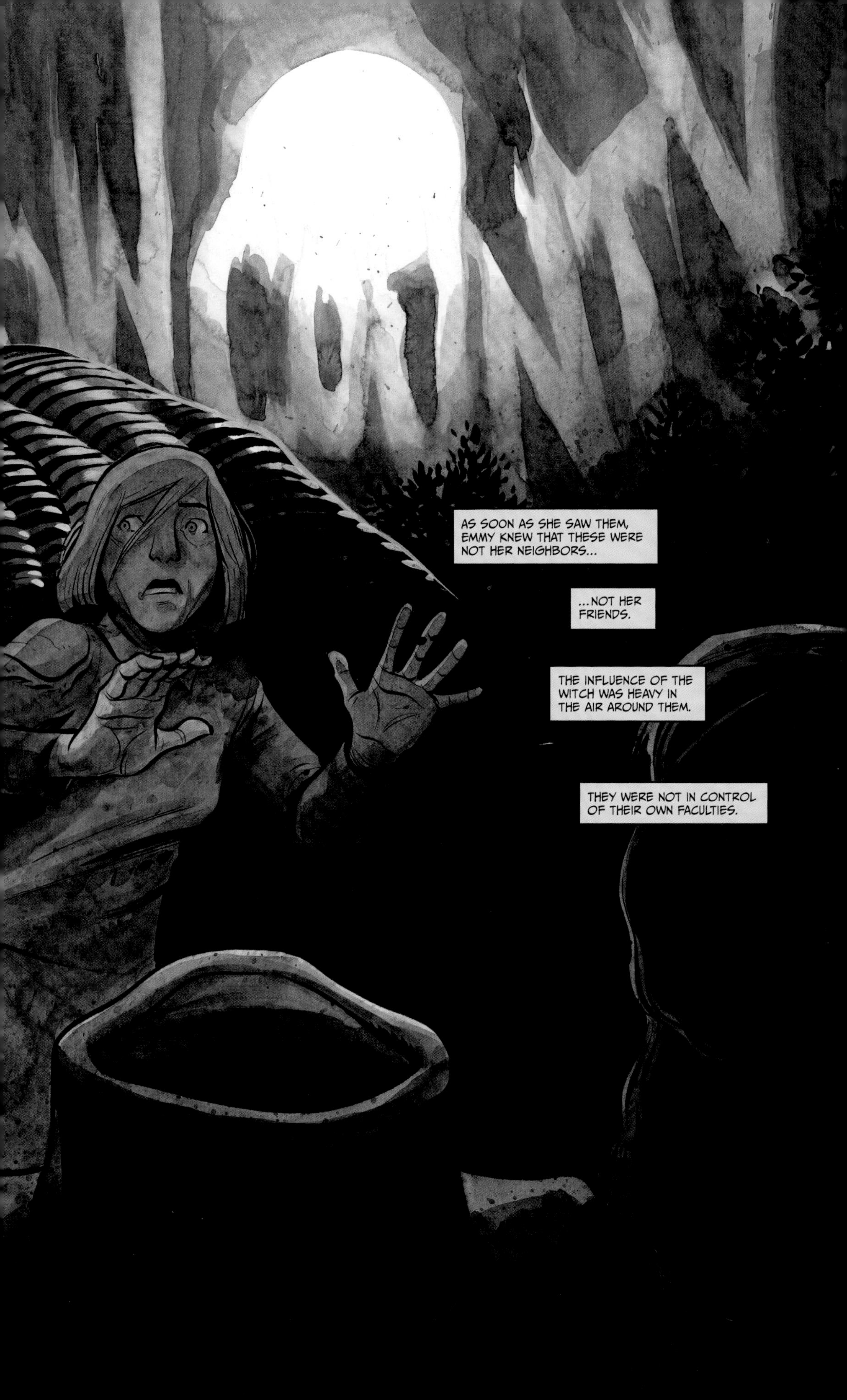
AS SOON AS SHE SAW THEM, EMMY KNEW THAT THESE WERE NOT HER NEIGHBORS...
...NOT HER FRIENDS.
THE INFLUENCE OF THE WITCH WAS HEAVY IN THE AIR AROUND THEM.
THEY WERE NOT IN CONTROL OF THEIR OWN FACULTIES.

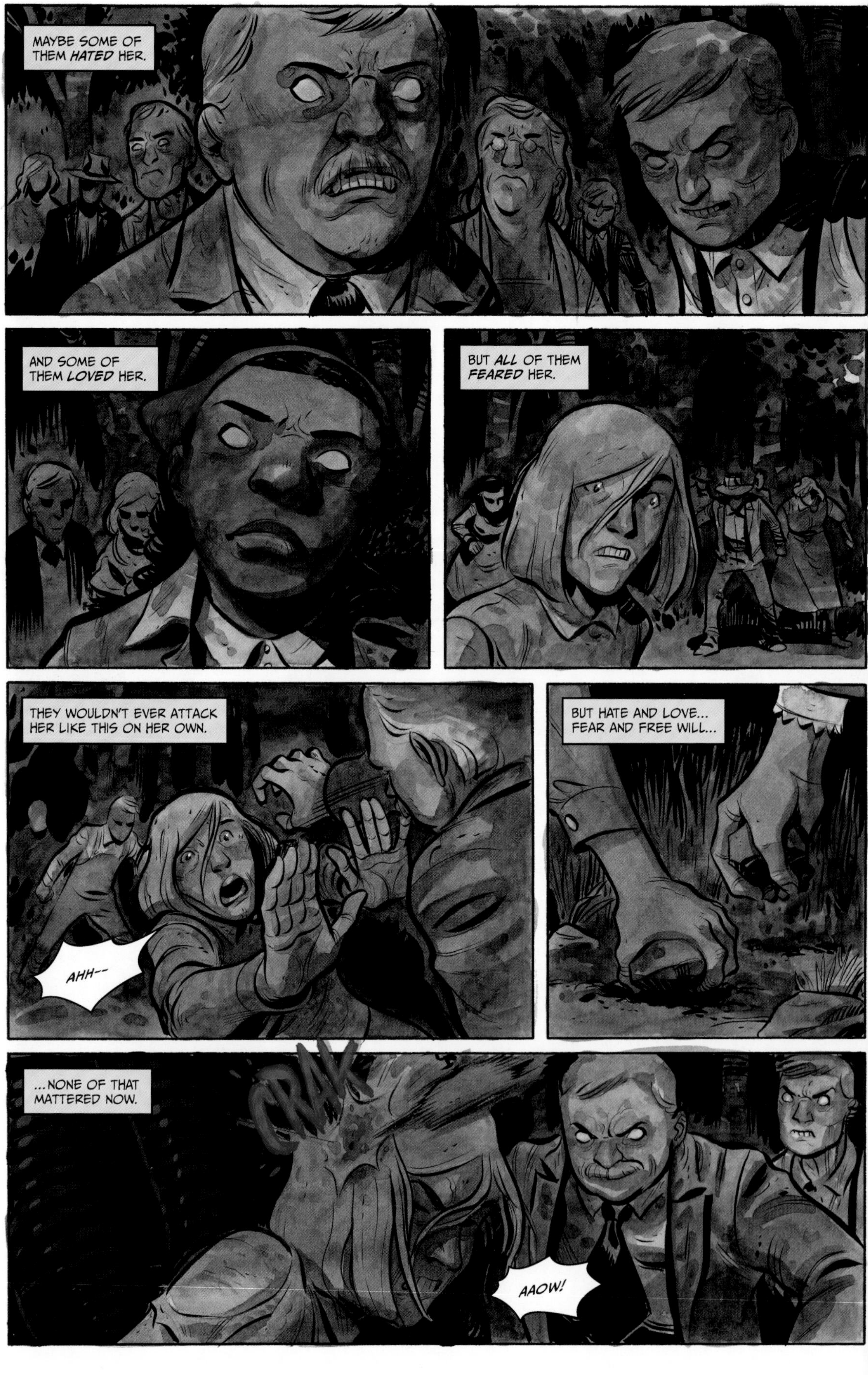
MAYBE SOME OF THEM HATED HER.
AND SOME OF THEM LOVED HER.
BUT ALL OF THEM FEARED HER.
THEY WOULDN'T EVER ATTACK HER LIKE THIS ON HER OWN.
AHH--
BUT HATE AND LOVE... FEAR AND FREE WILL...
...NONE OF THAT MATTERED NOW.
CRAK
AAOW!

...HAVE TO MAKE THEM LISTEN TO ME...

...SEND THEM...

...FAR F-FROM HERE...

PLEASE! ALL OF YOU! LISTEN TO ME!

HESTER'S CONTROLLING YOU! YOU HAVE TO FIGHT HER--

NNN--

LET... LET GO OF ME!

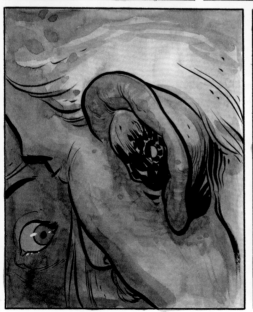

MMMPH!

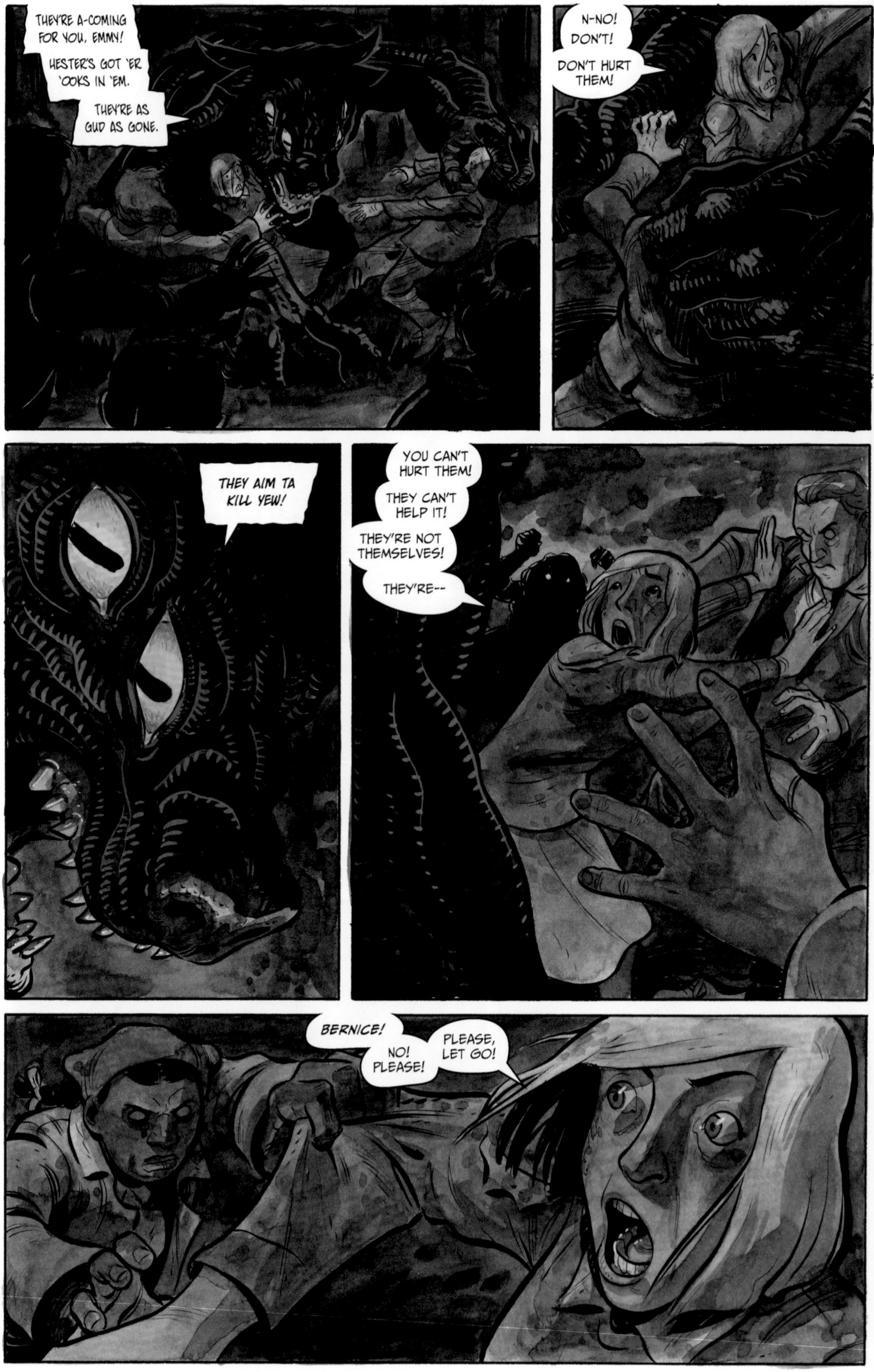

THEY'RE A-COMING FOR YOU, EMMY!
HESTER'S GOT 'ER 'OOKS IN 'EM.
THEY'RE AS GUD AS GONE.
N-NO! DON'T!
DON'T HURT THEM!
THEY AIM TA KILL YEW!
YOU CAN'T HURT THEM!
THEY CAN'T HELP IT!
THEY'RE NOT THEMSELVES!
THEY'RE--
BERNICE!
NO! PLEASE!
PLEASE, LET GO!

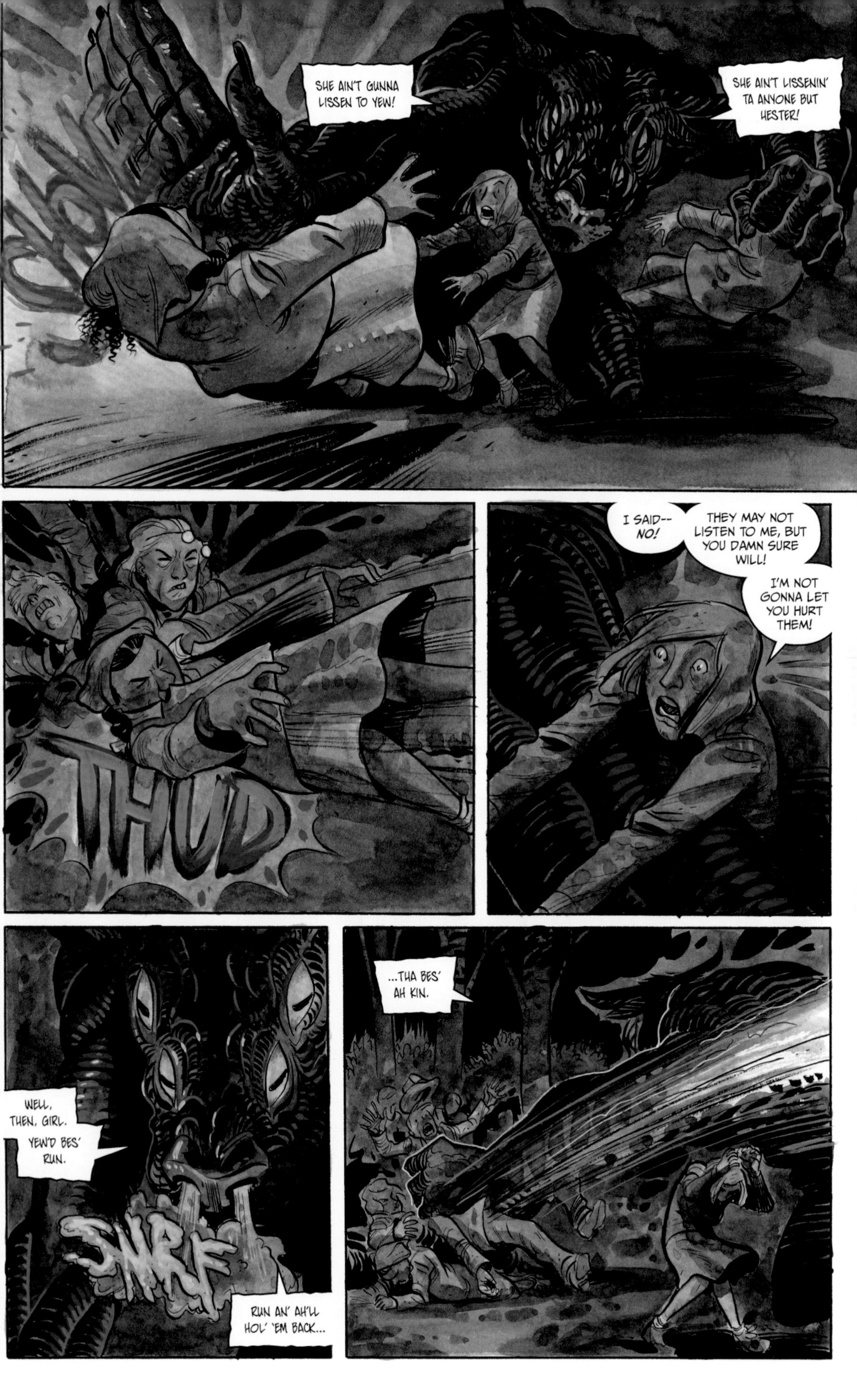
SHE AIN'T GUNNA LISSEN TO YEW!
SHE AIN'T LISSENIN' TA ANYONE BUT HESTER!
THUD
I SAID-- NO!
THEY MAY NOT LISTEN TO ME, BUT YOU DAMN SURE WILL!
I'M NOT GONNA LET YOU HURT THEM!
WELL, THEN, GIRL.
YEW'D BES' RUN.
SNRF
RUN AN' AH'LL HOL' 'EM BACK...
...THA BES' AH KIN.

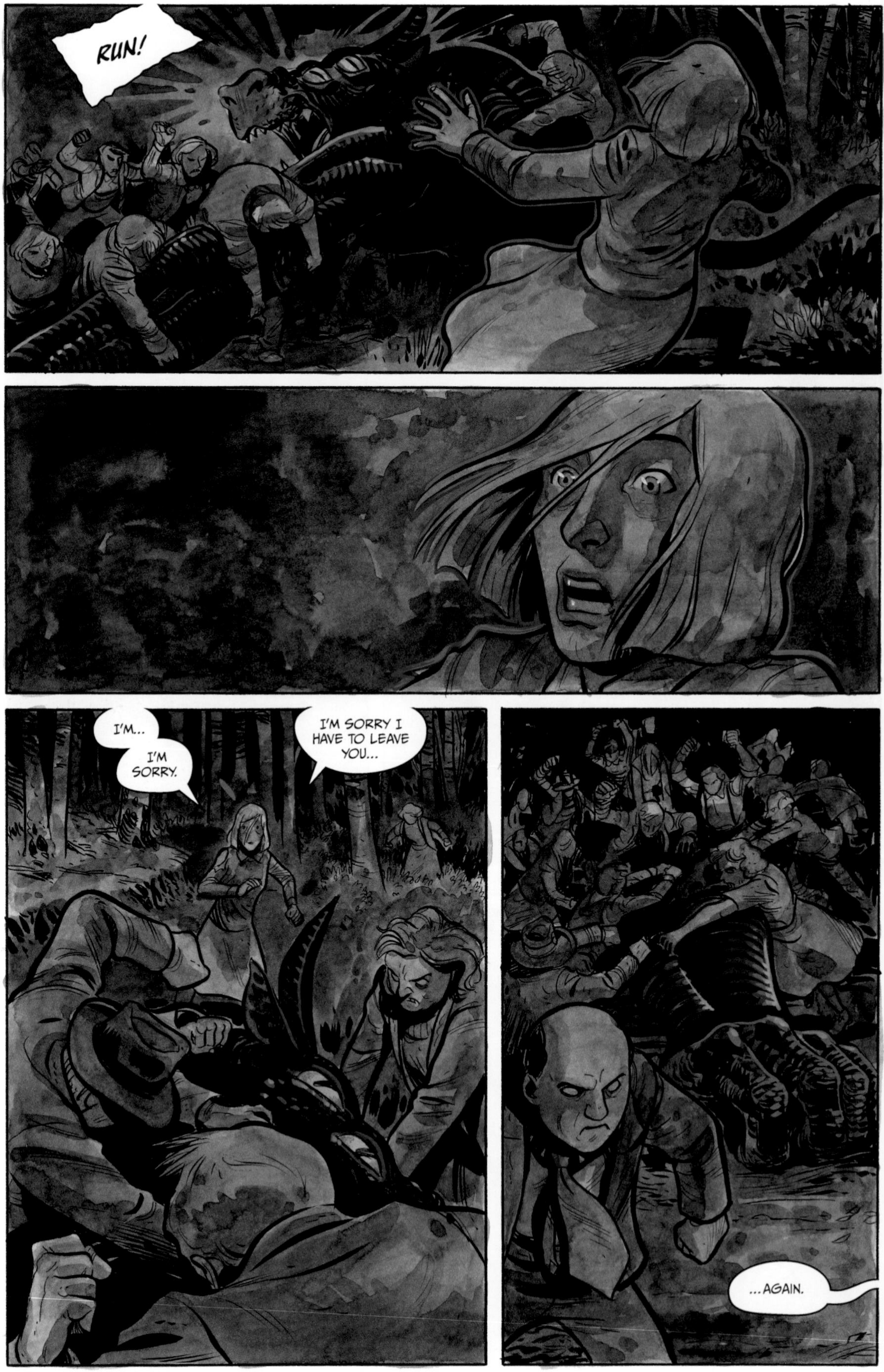
RUN!
I'M...
I'M SORRY.
I'M SORRY I HAVE TO LEAVE YOU...
...AGAIN.

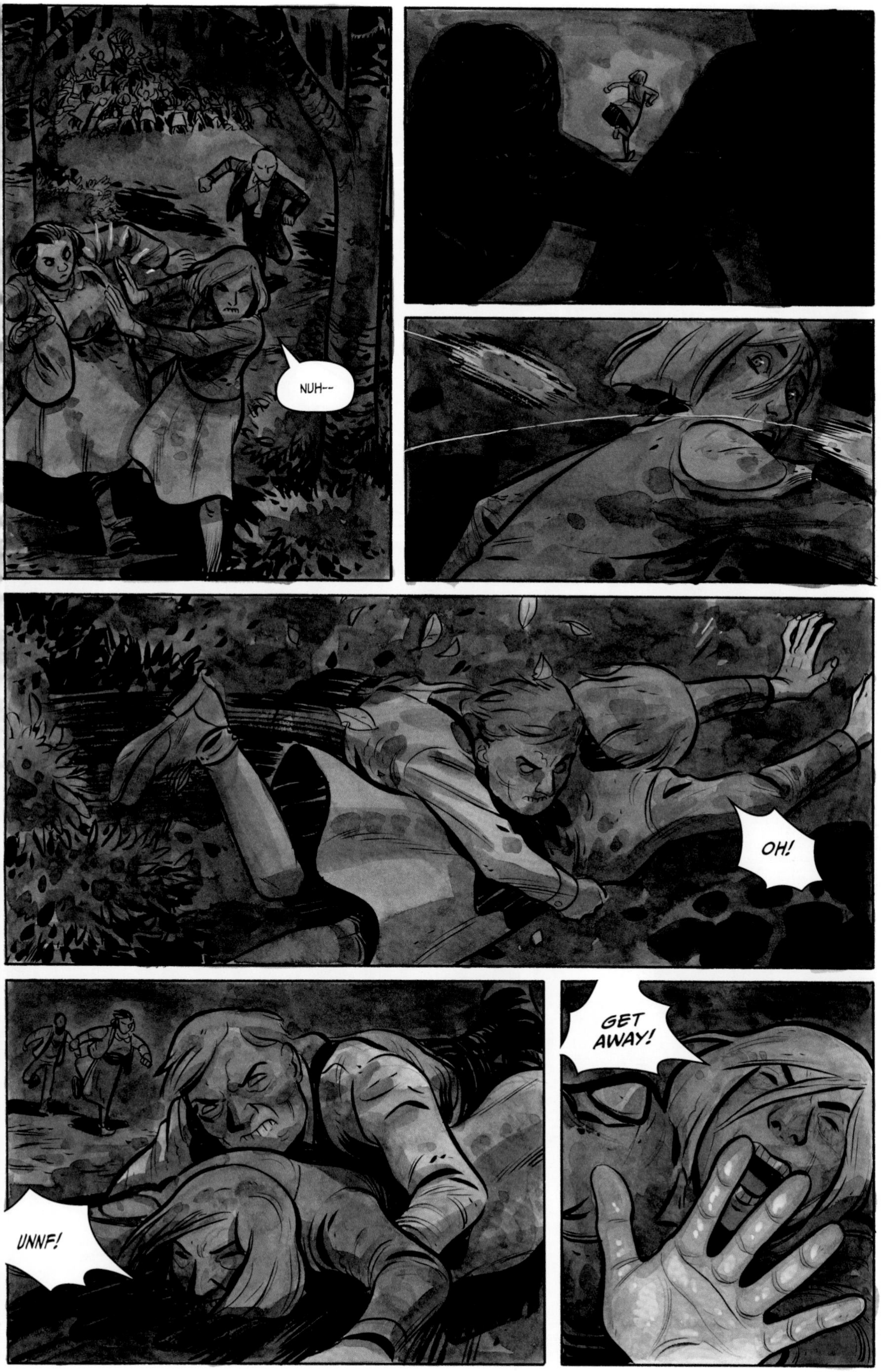
NUH--
OH!
UNNF!
GET AWAY!

N-NO.

I DIDN'T MEAN--

HISSSSSSSSSSS...

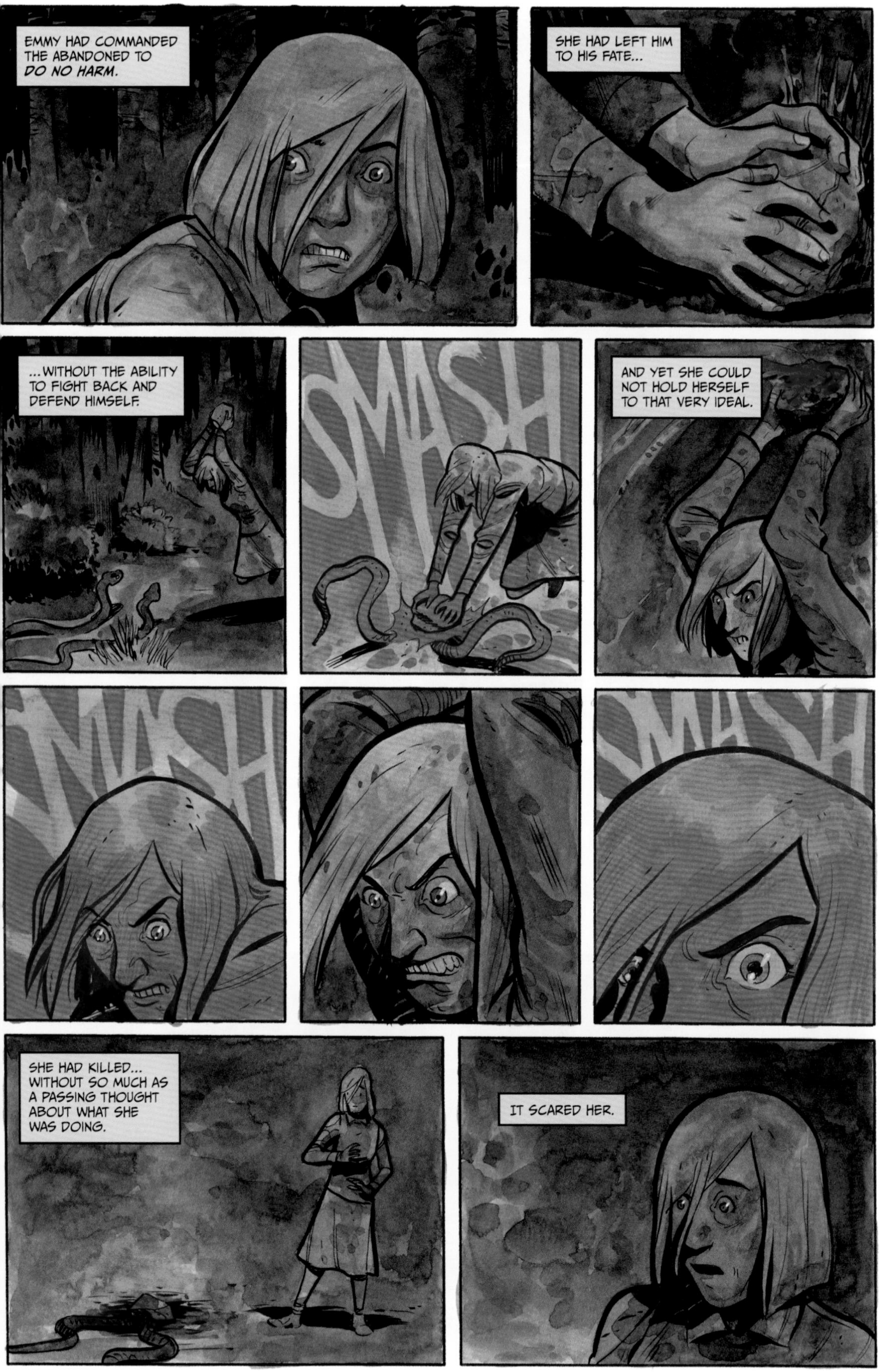
EMMY HAD COMMANDED THE ABANDONED TO DO NO HARM.
SHE HAD LEFT HIM TO HIS FATE...
...WITHOUT THE ABILITY TO FIGHT BACK AND DEFEND HIMSELF.
SMASH
AND YET SHE COULD NOT HOLD HERSELF TO THAT VERY IDEAL.
SMASH
SMASH
SHE HAD KILLED... WITHOUT SO MUCH AS A PASSING THOUGHT ABOUT WHAT SHE WAS DOING.
IT SCARED HER.

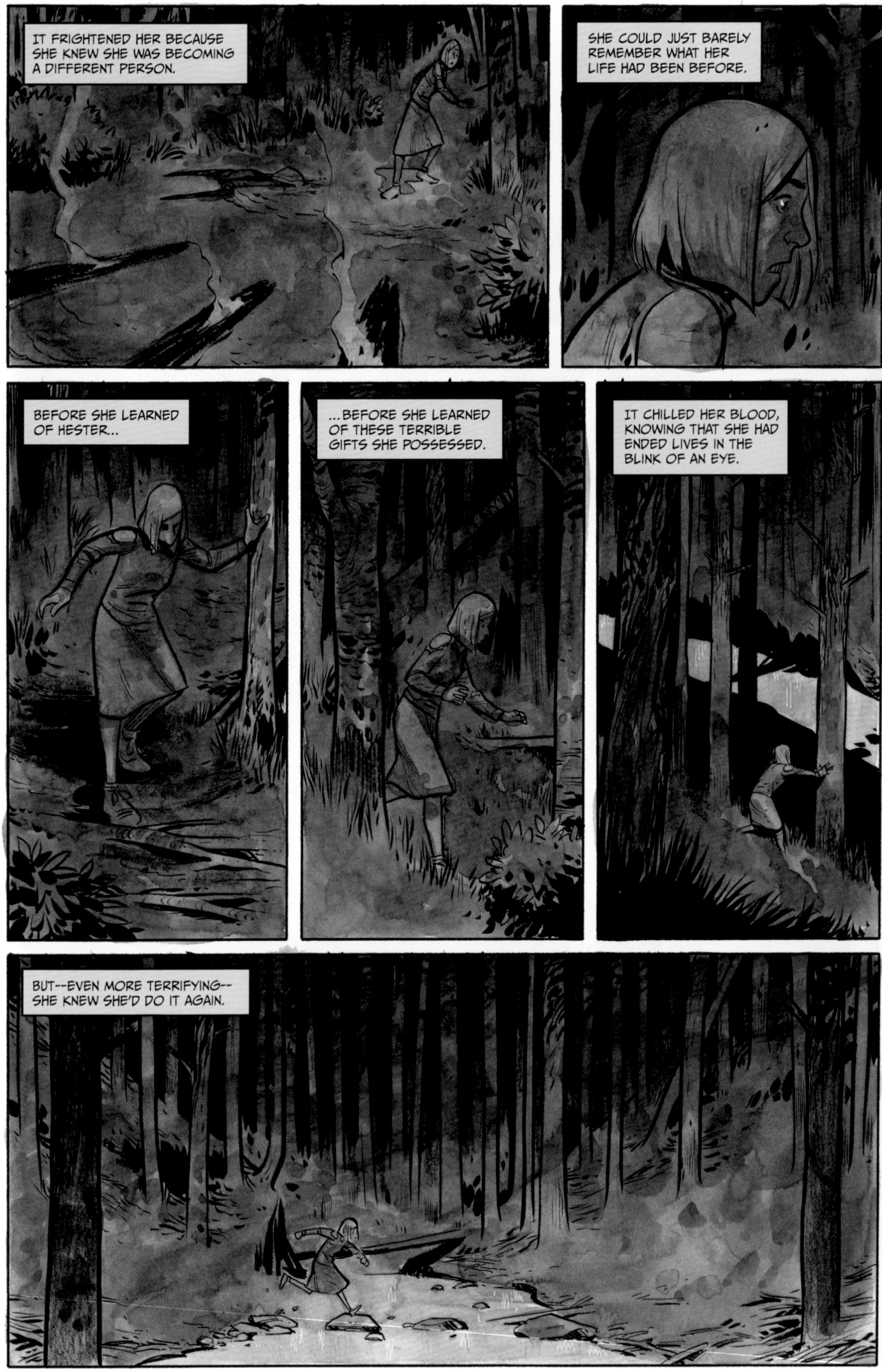
IT FRIGHTENED HER BECAUSE SHE KNEW SHE WAS BECOMING A DIFFERENT PERSON.
SHE COULD JUST BARELY REMEMBER WHAT HER LIFE HAD BEEN BEFORE.
BEFORE SHE LEARNED OF HESTER...
...BEFORE SHE LEARNED OF THESE TERRIBLE GIFTS SHE POSSESSED.
IT CHILLED HER BLOOD, KNOWING THAT SHE HAD ENDED LIVES IN THE BLINK OF AN EYE.
BUT--EVEN MORE TERRIFYING--SHE KNEW SHE'D DO IT AGAIN.

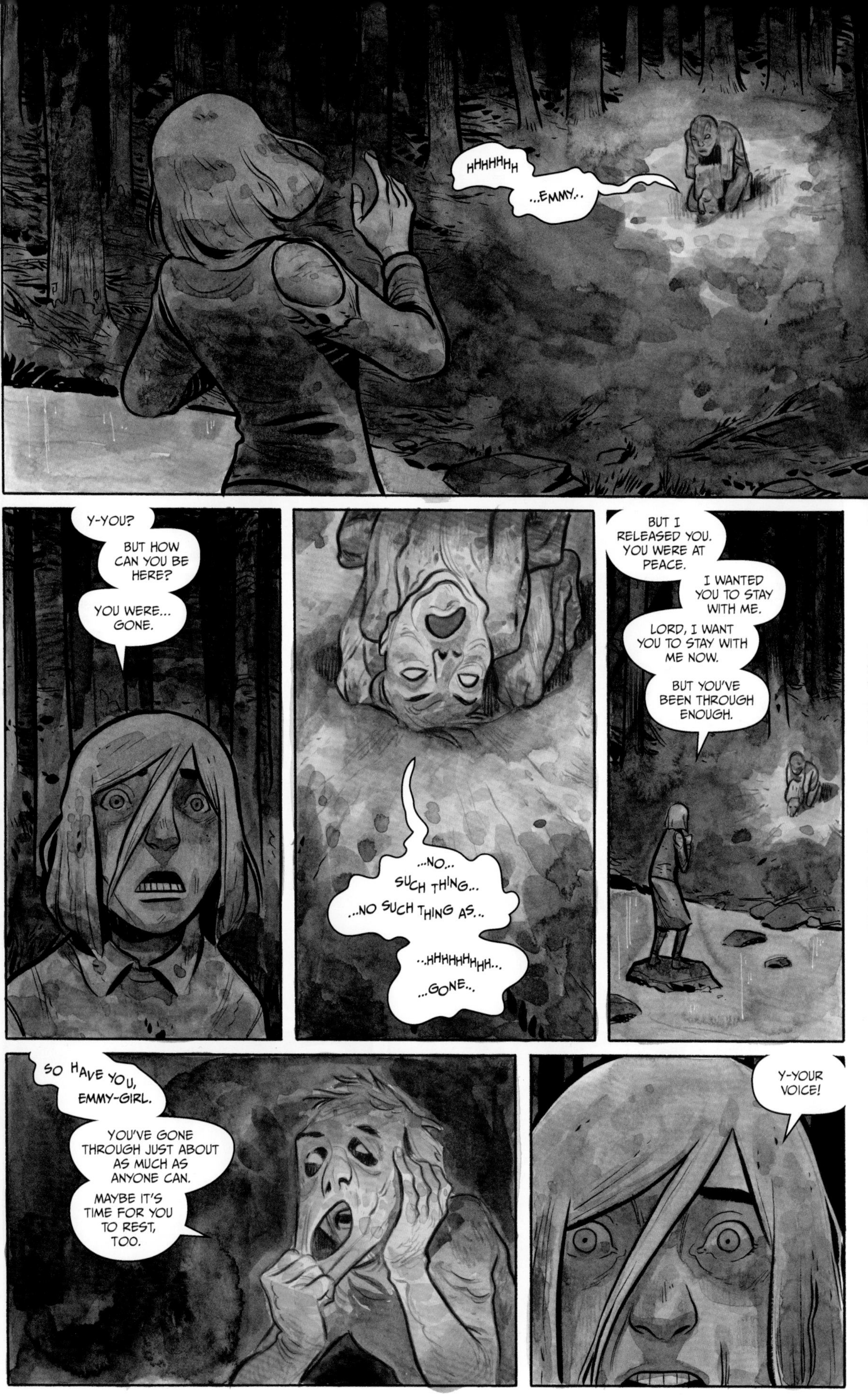
HHHHHHH
...EMMY...
Y-YOU?
BUT HOW CAN YOU BE HERE?
YOU WERE... GONE.
...NO... SUCH THING... ...NO SUCH THING AS...
...HHHHHHHHH... ...GONE...
BUT I RELEASED YOU. YOU WERE AT PEACE.
I WANTED YOU TO STAY WITH ME.
LORD, I WANT YOU TO STAY WITH ME NOW.
BUT YOU'VE BEEN THROUGH ENOUGH.
SO HAVE YOU, EMMY-GIRL.
YOU'VE GONE THROUGH JUST ABOUT AS MUCH AS ANYONE CAN.
MAYBE IT'S TIME FOR YOU TO REST, TOO.
Y-YOUR VOICE!

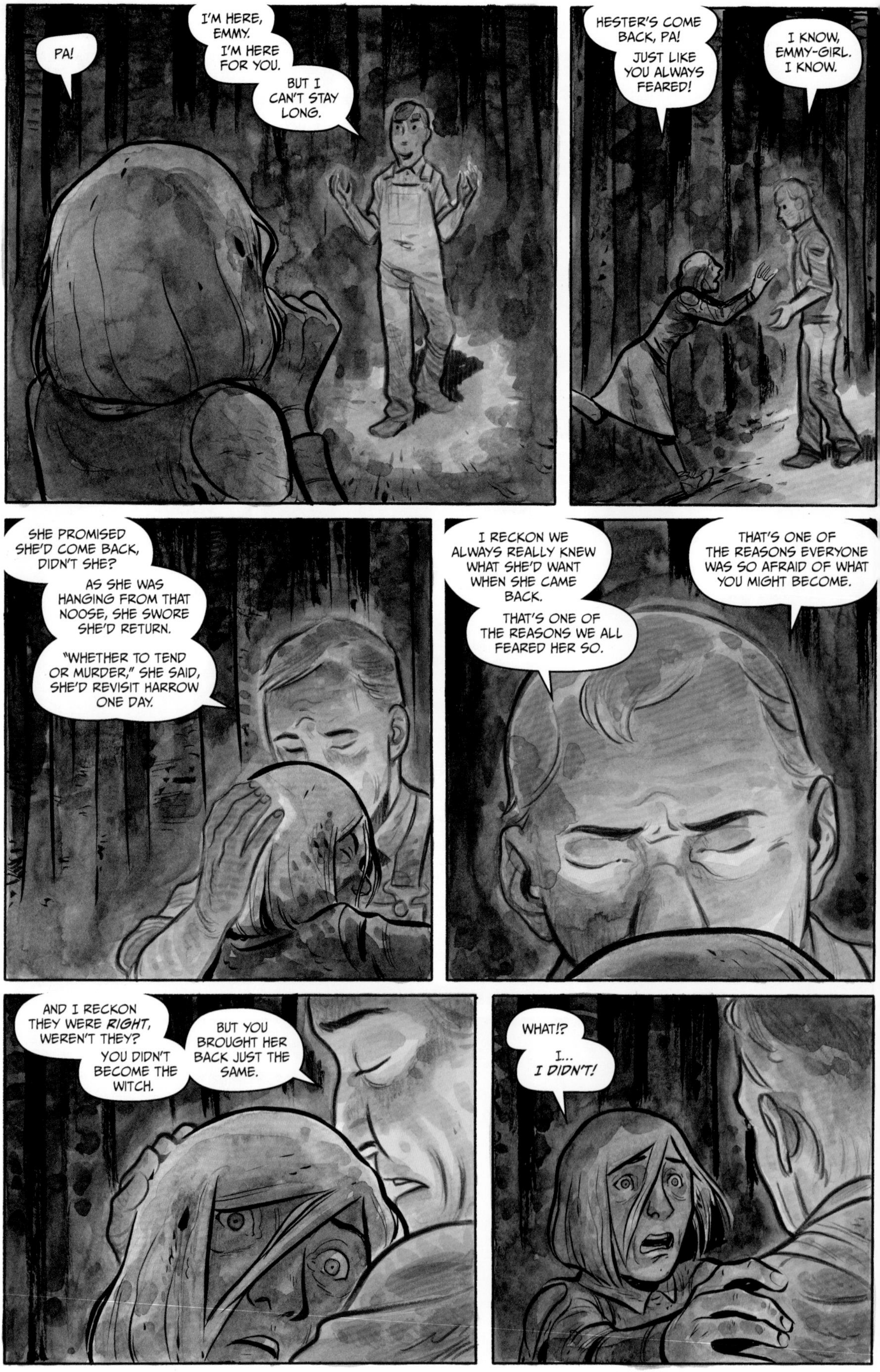
PA!
I'M HERE, EMMY. I'M HERE FOR YOU.
BUT I CAN'T STAY LONG.
HESTER'S COME BACK, PA!
JUST LIKE YOU ALWAYS FEARED!
I KNOW, EMMY-GIRL. I KNOW.
SHE PROMISED SHE'D COME BACK, DIDN'T SHE?
AS SHE WAS HANGING FROM THAT NOOSE, SHE SWORE SHE'D RETURN.
"WHETHER TO TEND OR MURDER," SHE SAID, SHE'D REVISIT HARROW ONE DAY.
I RECKON WE ALWAYS REALLY KNEW WHAT SHE'D WANT WHEN SHE CAME BACK.
THAT'S ONE OF THE REASONS WE ALL FEARED HER SO.
THAT'S ONE OF THE REASONS EVERYONE WAS SO AFRAID OF WHAT YOU MIGHT BECOME.
AND I RECKON THEY WERE *RIGHT*, WEREN'T THEY?
YOU DIDN'T BECOME THE WITCH.
BUT YOU BROUGHT HER BACK JUST THE SAME.
WHAT!?
I... *I DIDN'T!*

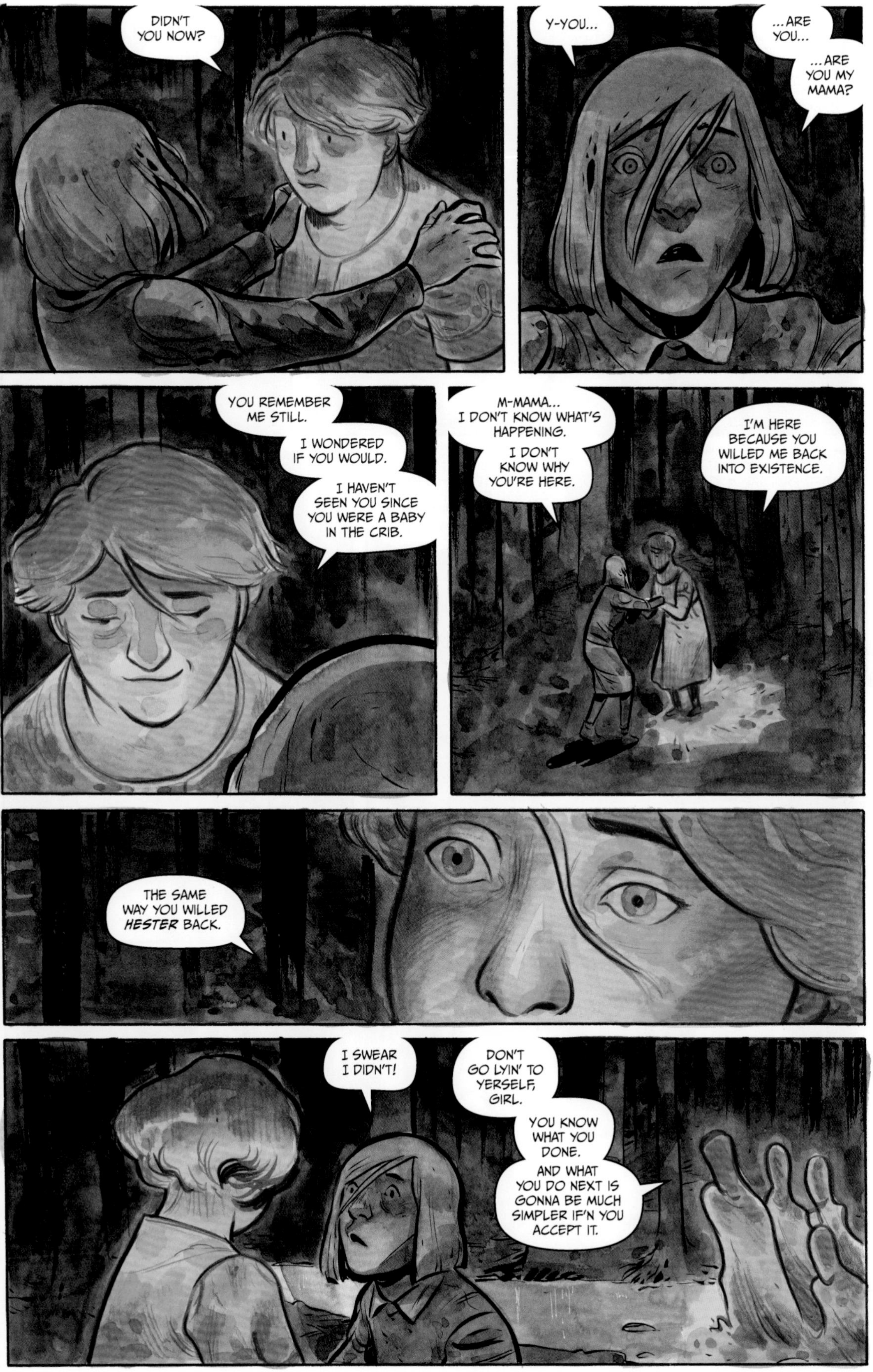
DIDN'T YOU NOW?
Y-YOU...
...ARE YOU...
...ARE YOU MY MAMA?
YOU REMEMBER ME STILL.
I WONDERED IF YOU WOULD.
I HAVEN'T SEEN YOU SINCE YOU WERE A BABY IN THE CRIB.
M-MAMA... I DON'T KNOW WHAT'S HAPPENING.
I DON'T KNOW WHY YOU'RE HERE.
I'M HERE BECAUSE YOU WILLED ME BACK INTO EXISTENCE.
THE SAME WAY YOU WILLED *HESTER* BACK.
I SWEAR I DIDN'T!
DON'T GO LYIN' TO YERSELF, GIRL.
YOU KNOW WHAT YOU DONE.
AND WHAT YOU DO NEXT IS GONNA BE MUCH SIMPLER IF'N YOU ACCEPT IT.

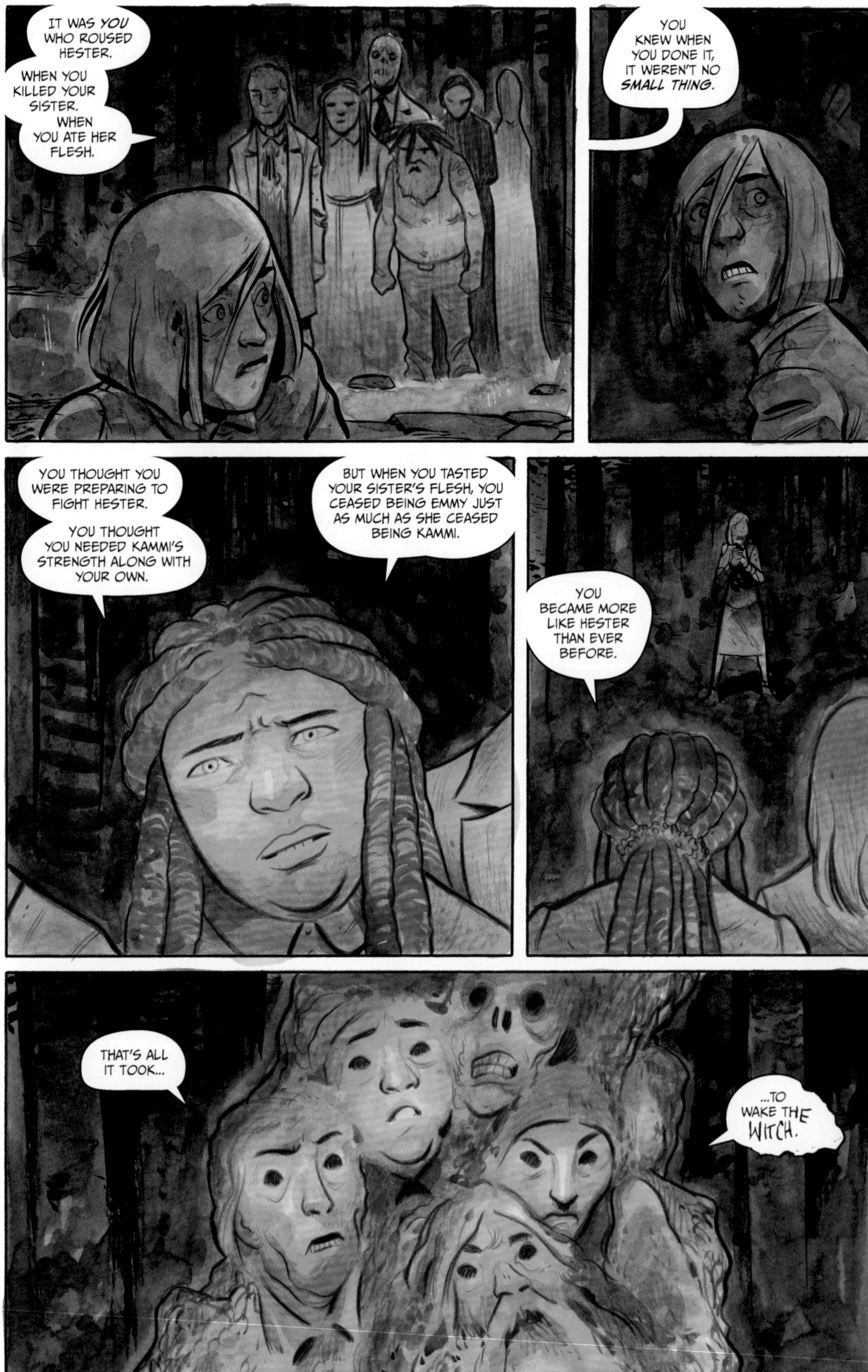
IT WAS YOU WHO ROUSED HESTER.
WHEN YOU KILLED YOUR SISTER.
WHEN YOU ATE HER FLESH.
YOU KNEW WHEN YOU DONE IT, IT WEREN'T NO SMALL THING.
YOU THOUGHT YOU WERE PREPARING TO FIGHT HESTER.
YOU THOUGHT YOU NEEDED KAMMI'S STRENGTH ALONG WITH YOUR OWN.
BUT WHEN YOU TASTED YOUR SISTER'S FLESH, YOU CEASED BEING EMMY JUST AS MUCH AS SHE CEASED BEING KAMMI.
YOU BECAME MORE LIKE HESTER THAN EVER BEFORE.
THAT'S ALL IT TOOK...
...TO WAKE THE WITCH.

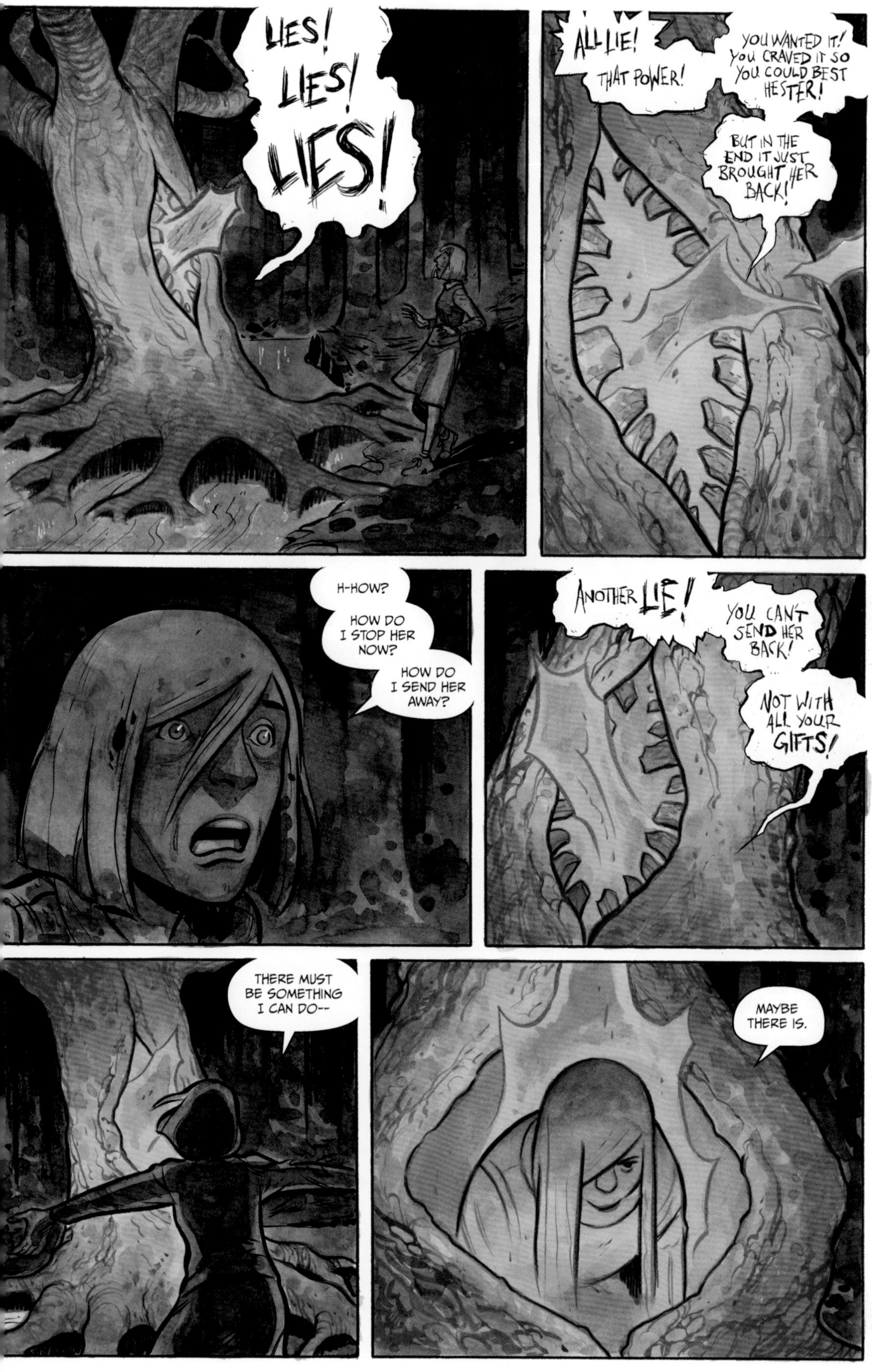
LIES! LIES! LIES!
ALL LIE! THAT POWER!
YOU WANTED IT! YOU CRAVED IT SO YOU COULD BEST HESTER!
BUT IN THE END IT JUST BROUGHT HER BACK!
H-HOW?
HOW DO I STOP HER NOW?
HOW DO I SEND HER AWAY?
ANOTHER LIE!
YOU CAN'T SEND HER BACK!
NOT WITH ALL YOUR GIFTS!
THERE MUST BE SOMETHING I CAN DO--
MAYBE THERE IS.

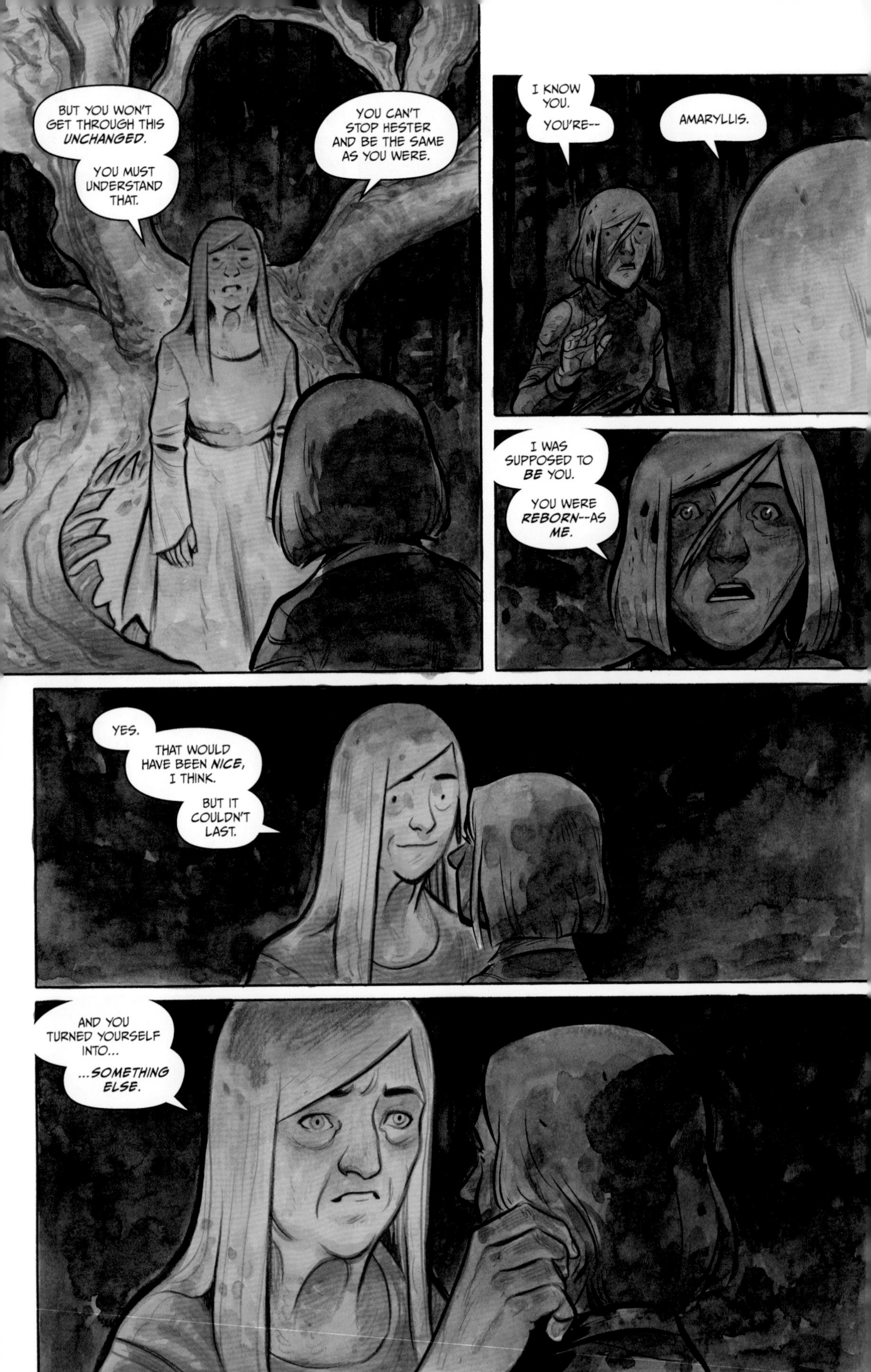
BUT YOU WON'T GET THROUGH THIS *UNCHANGED*.
YOU MUST UNDERSTAND THAT.
YOU CAN'T STOP HESTER AND BE THE SAME AS YOU WERE.
I KNOW YOU.
YOU'RE--
AMARYLLIS.
I WAS SUPPOSED TO *BE* YOU.
YOU WERE *REBORN*--AS *ME*.
YES.
THAT WOULD HAVE BEEN *NICE*, I THINK.
BUT IT COULDN'T LAST.
AND YOU TURNED YOURSELF INTO...
...*SOMETHING ELSE*.

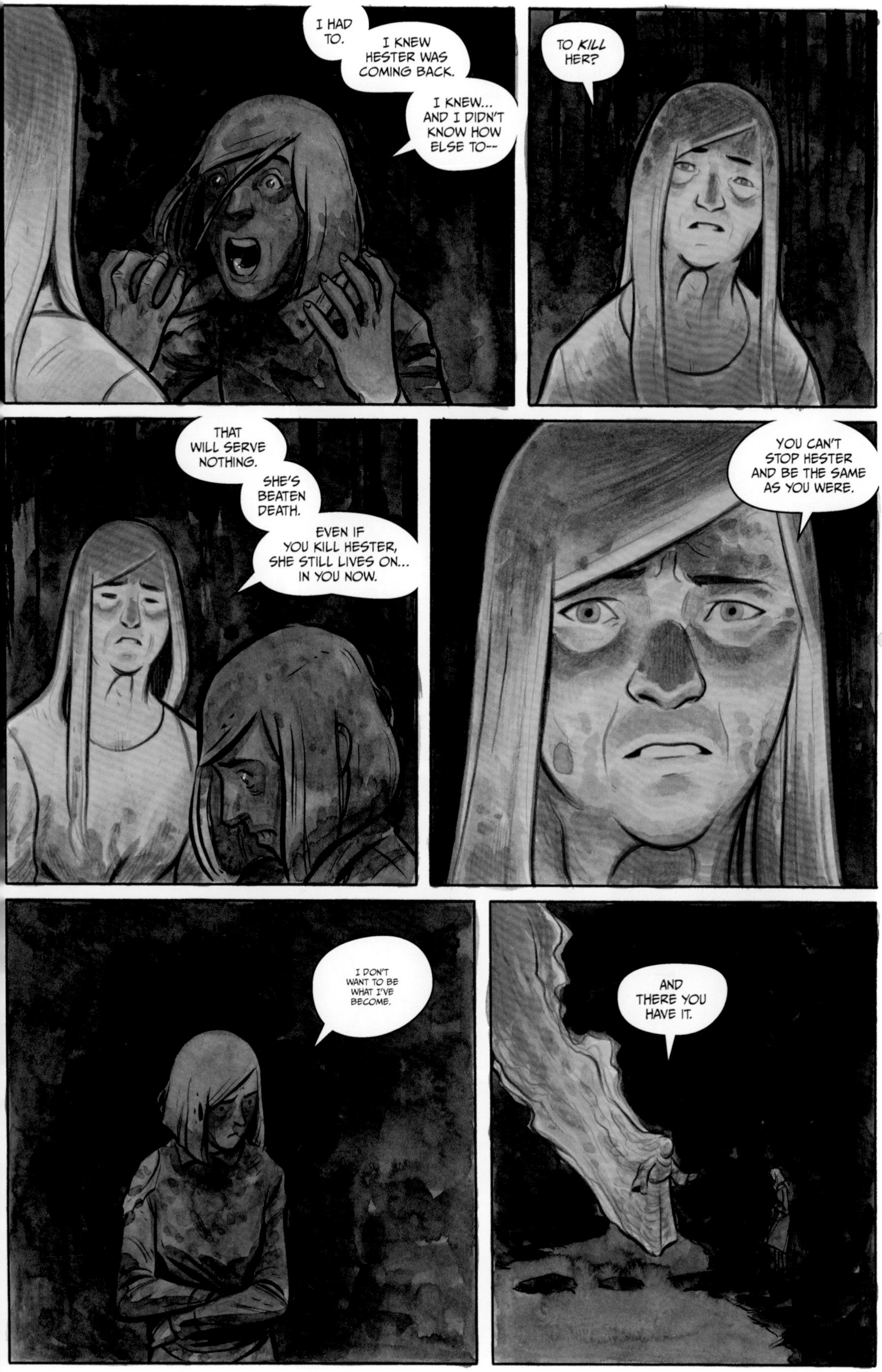
I HAD TO.
I KNEW HESTER WAS COMING BACK.
I KNEW... AND I DIDN'T KNOW HOW ELSE TO--
TO *KILL* HER?
THAT WILL SERVE NOTHING.
SHE'S BEATEN DEATH.
EVEN IF YOU KILL HESTER, SHE STILL LIVES ON... IN YOU NOW.
YOU CAN'T STOP HESTER AND BE THE SAME AS YOU WERE.
I DON'T WANT TO BE WHAT I'VE BECOME.
AND THERE YOU HAVE IT.

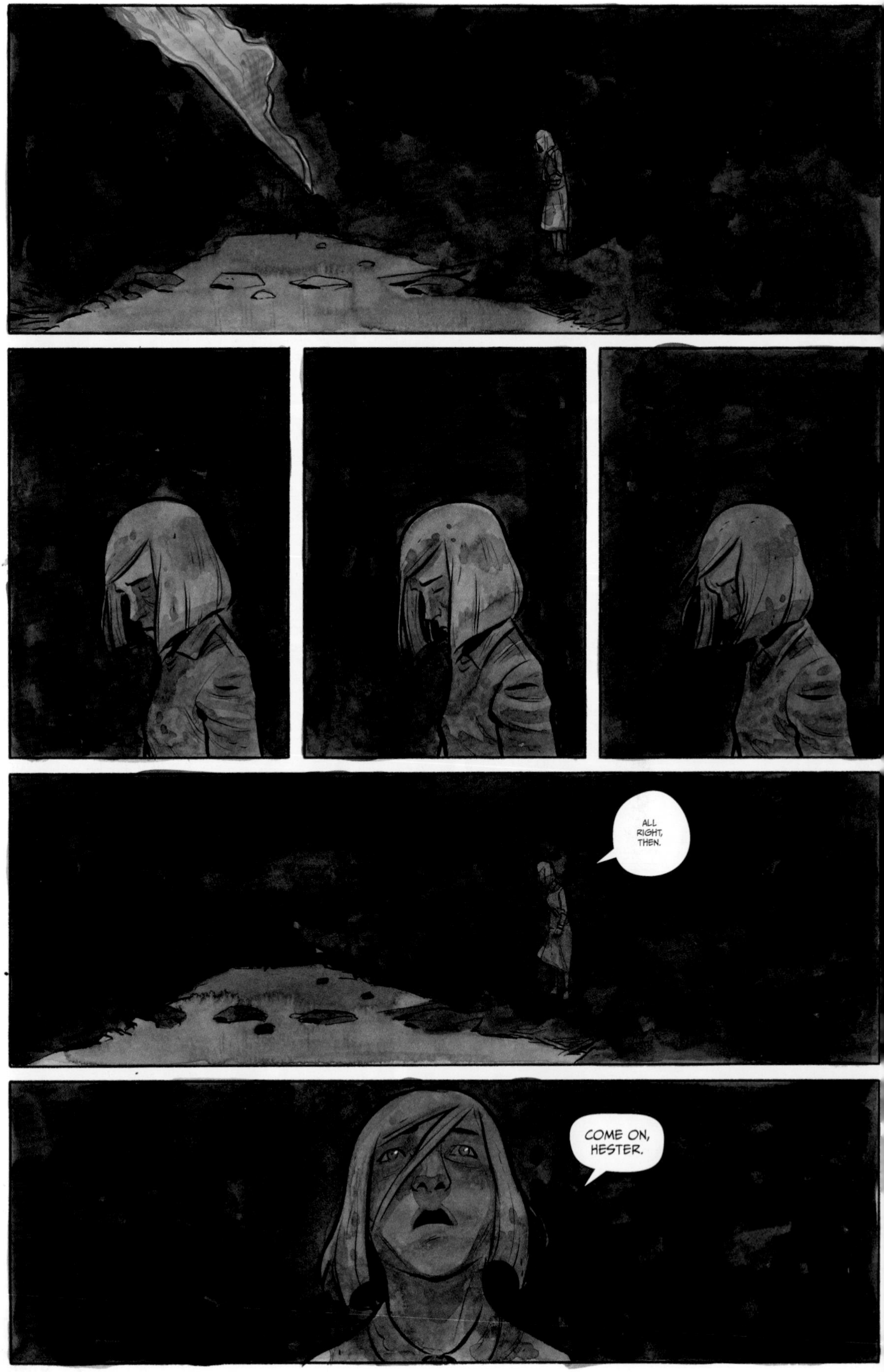
ALL RIGHT, THEN.
COME ON, HESTER.

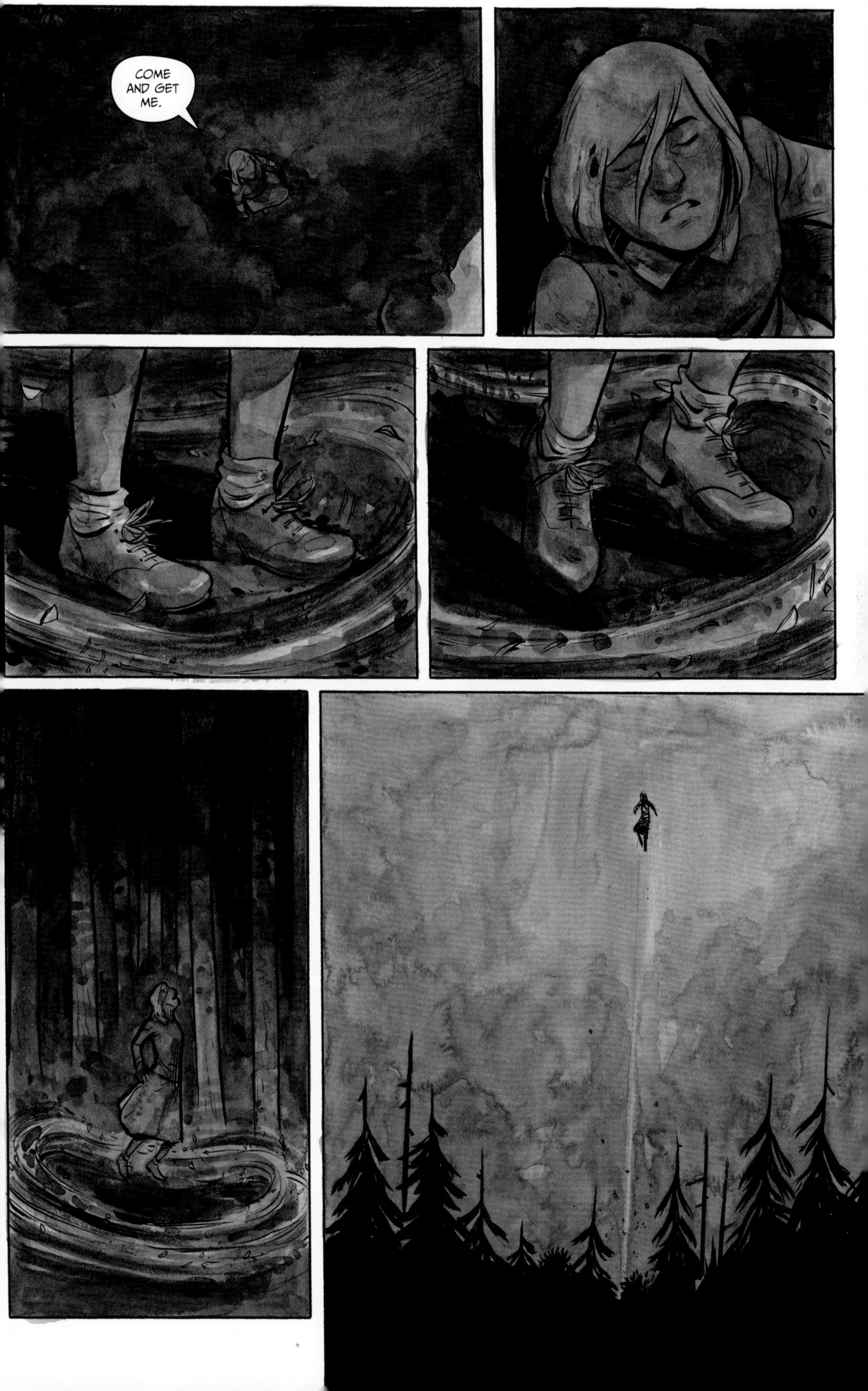
COME AND GET ME.

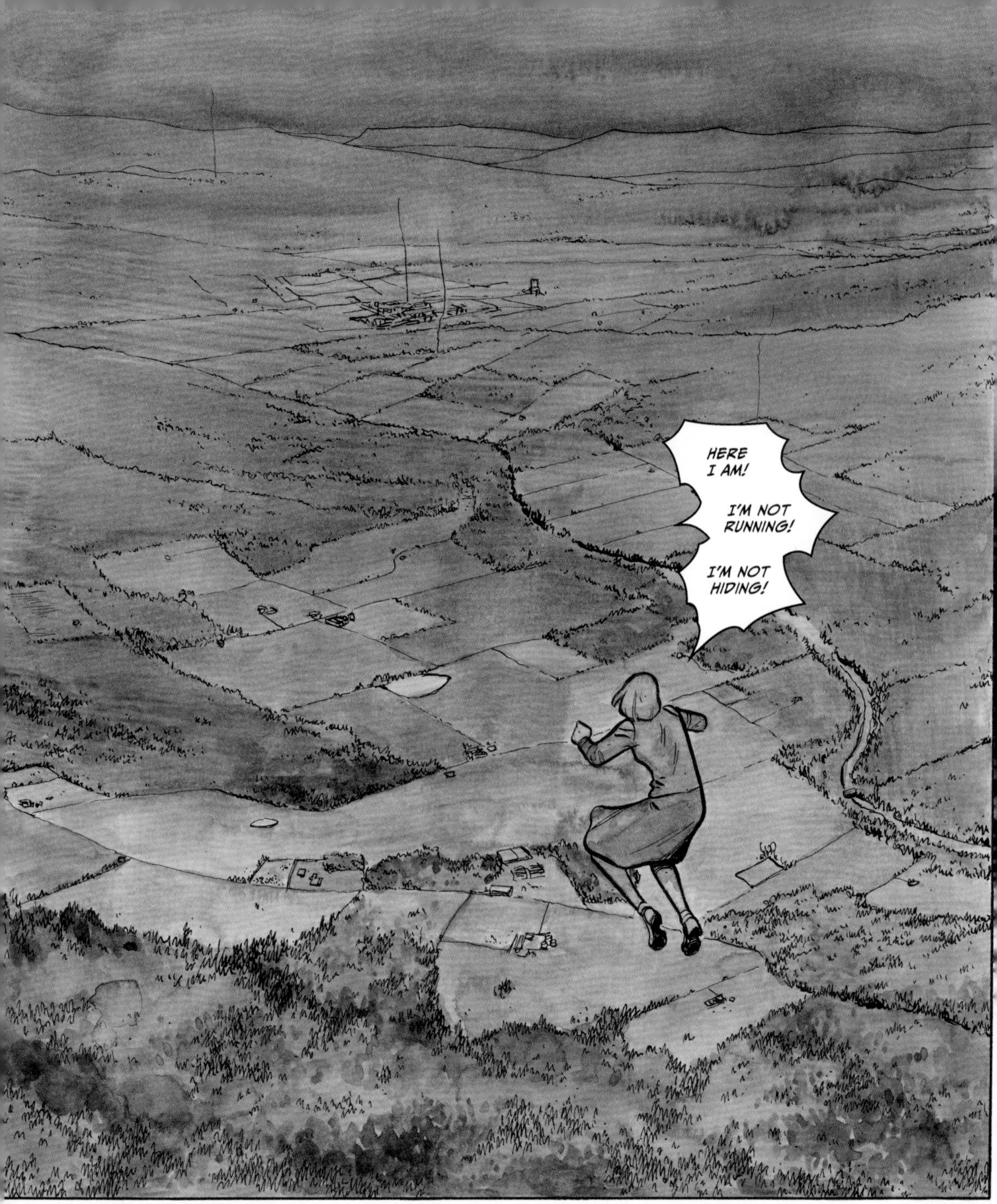
HERE I AM!
I'M NOT RUNNING!
I'M NOT HIDING!

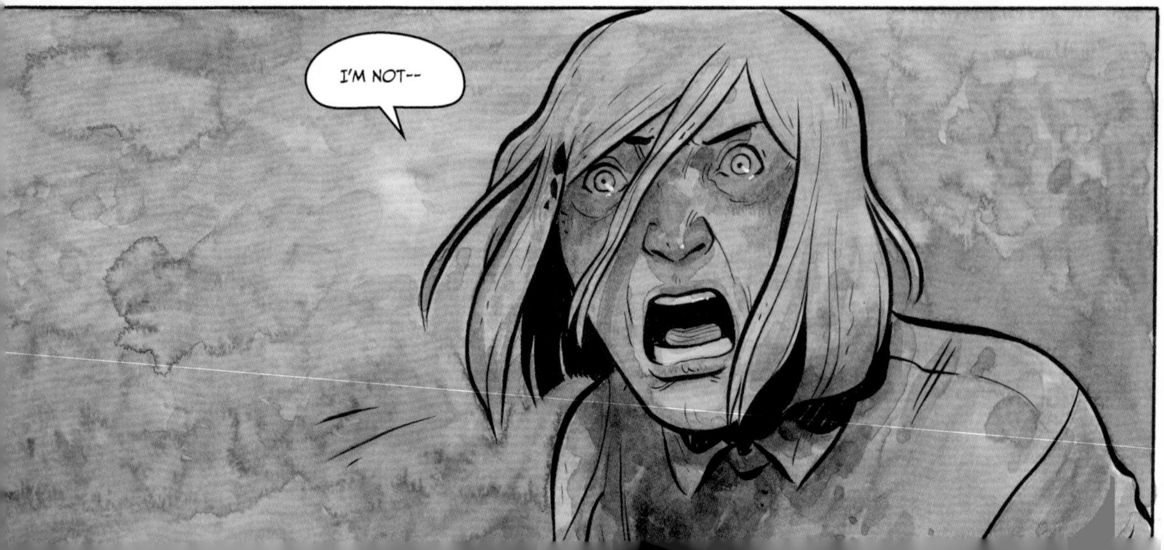
I'M NOT--

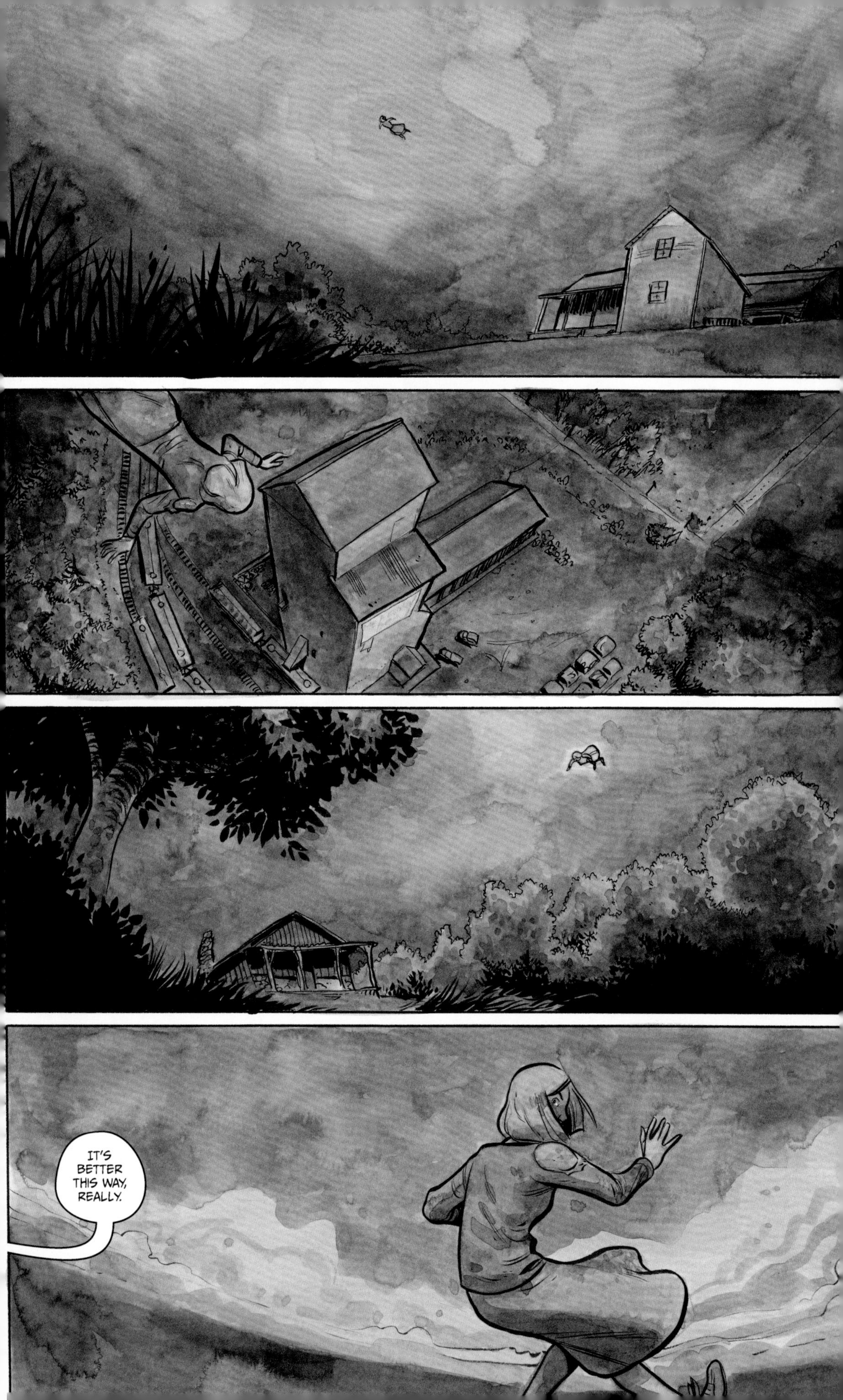
IT'S BETTER THIS WAY, REALLY.

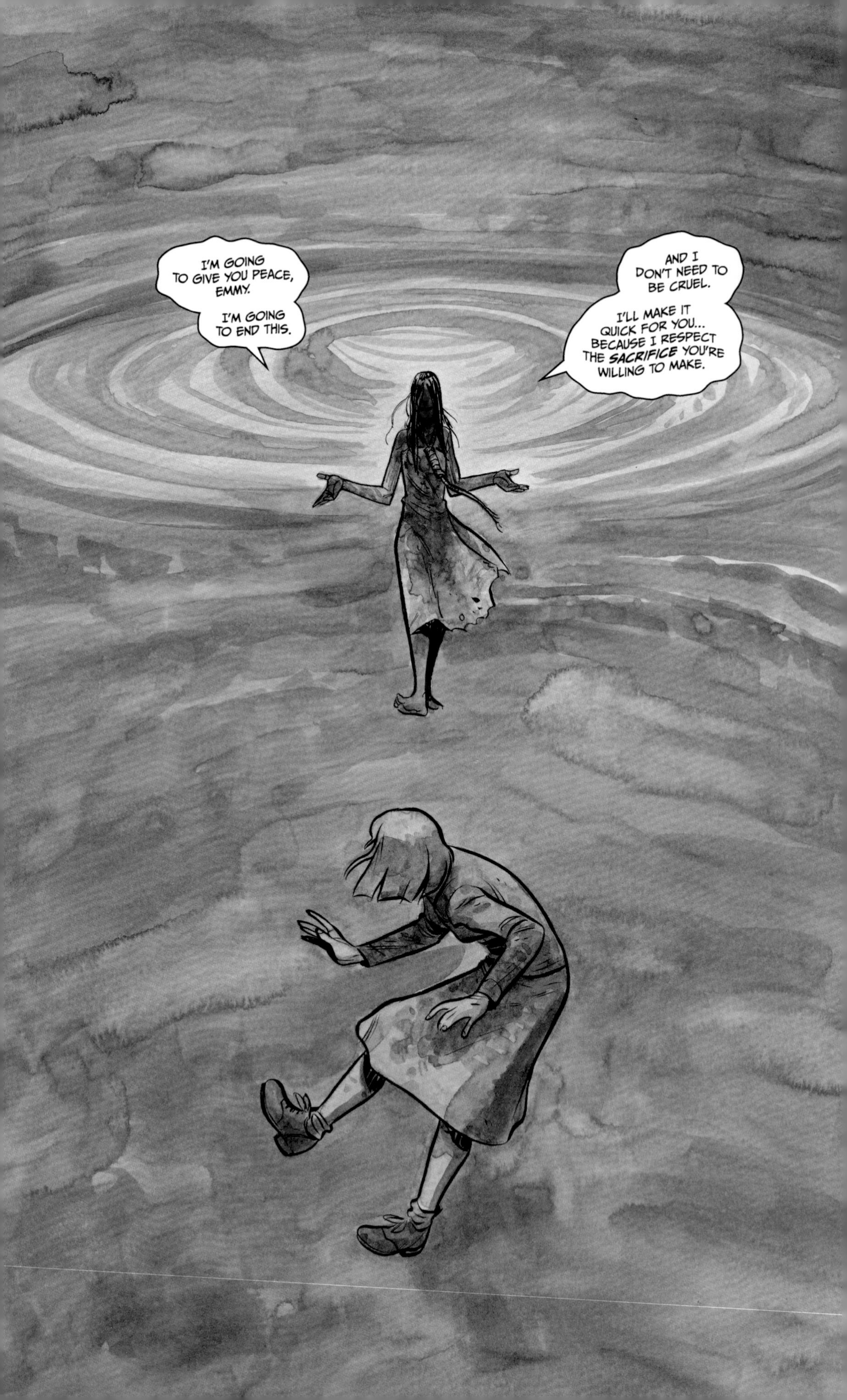
I'M GOING TO GIVE YOU PEACE, EMMY.
I'M GOING TO END THIS.
AND I DON'T NEED TO BE CRUEL.
I'LL MAKE IT QUICK FOR YOU... BECAUSE I RESPECT THE SACRIFICE YOU'RE WILLING TO MAKE.

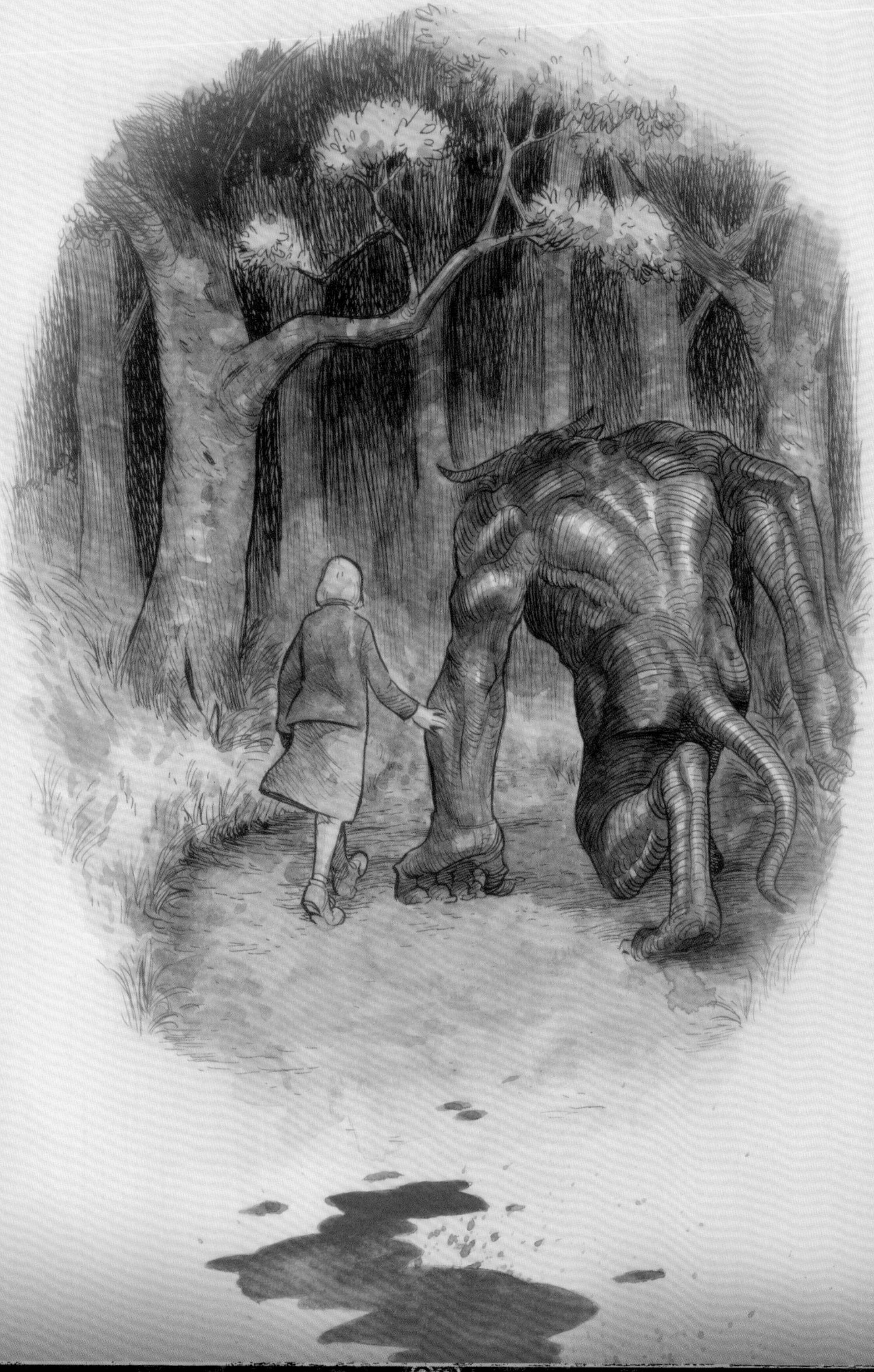

FOUR

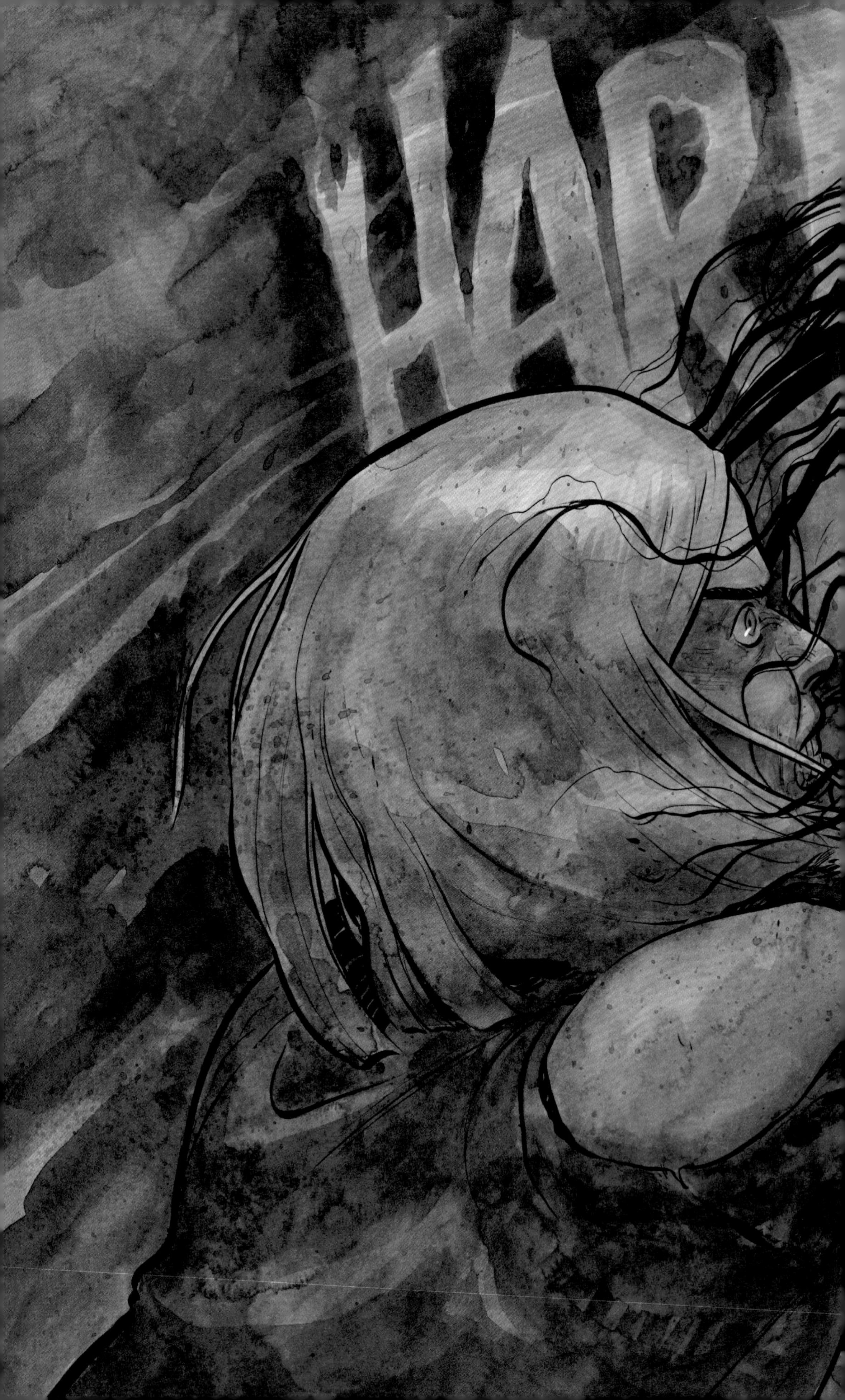
HAP

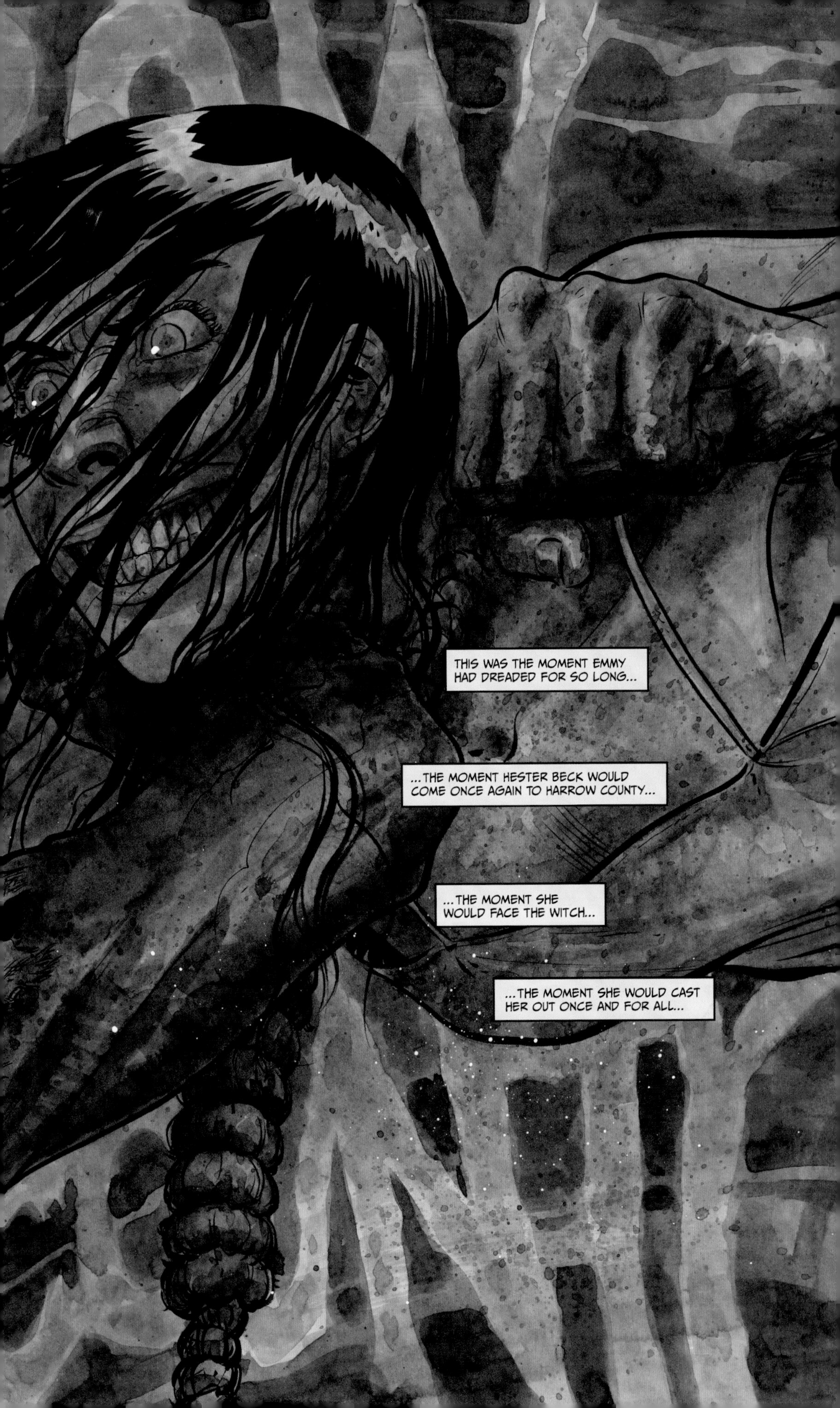
THIS WAS THE MOMENT EMMY HAD DREADED FOR SO LONG...
...THE MOMENT HESTER BECK WOULD COME ONCE AGAIN TO HARROW COUNTY...
...THE MOMENT SHE WOULD FACE THE WITCH...
...THE MOMENT SHE WOULD CAST HER OUT ONCE AND FOR ALL...

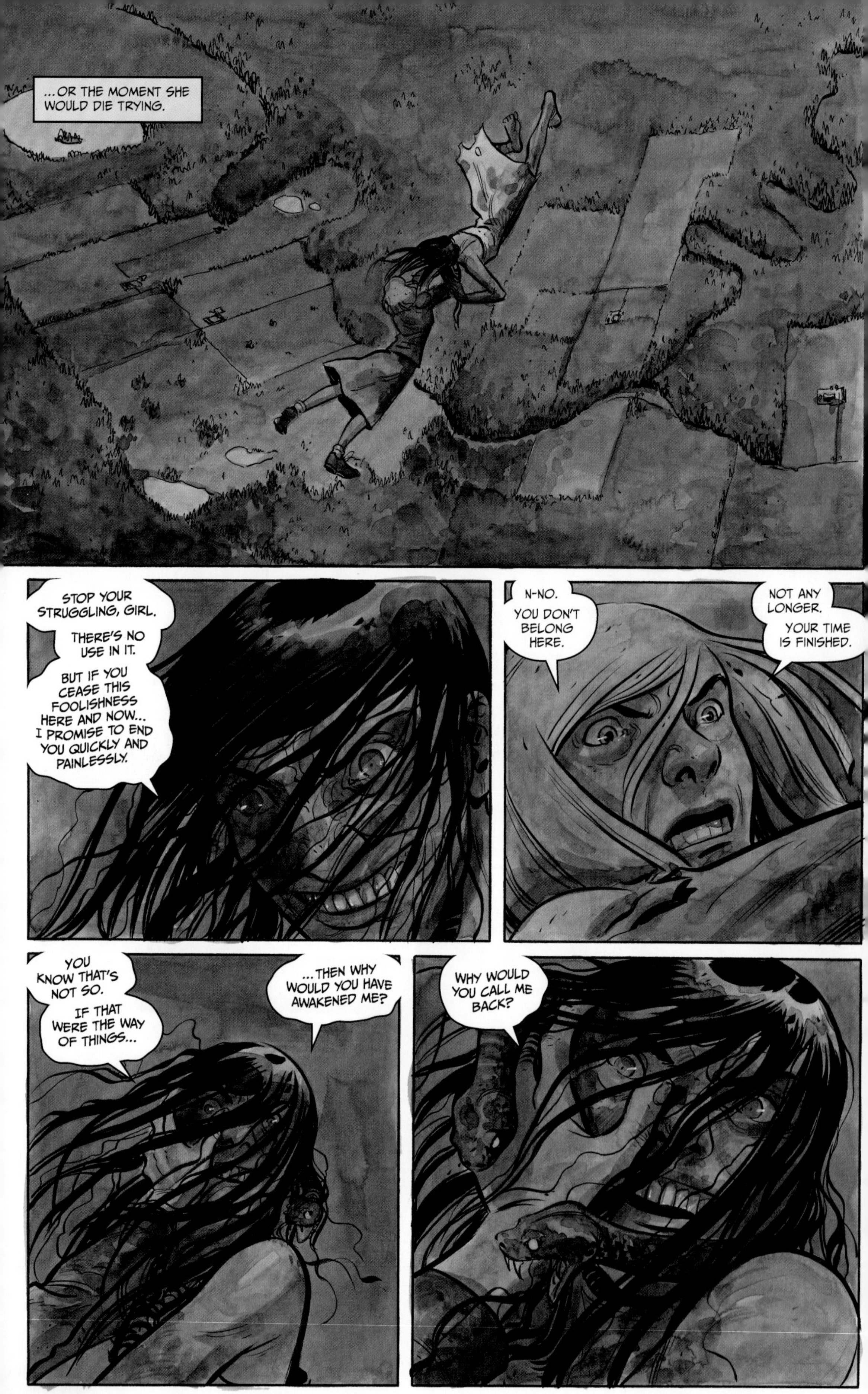
...OR THE MOMENT SHE WOULD DIE TRYING.
STOP YOUR STRUGGLING, GIRL.
THERE'S NO USE IN IT.
BUT IF YOU CEASE THIS FOOLISHNESS HERE AND NOW... I PROMISE TO END YOU QUICKLY AND PAINLESSLY.
N-NO.
YOU DON'T BELONG HERE.
NOT ANY LONGER.
YOUR TIME IS FINISHED.
YOU KNOW THAT'S NOT SO.
IF THAT WERE THE WAY OF THINGS...
...THEN WHY WOULD YOU HAVE AWAKENED ME?
WHY WOULD YOU CALL ME BACK?

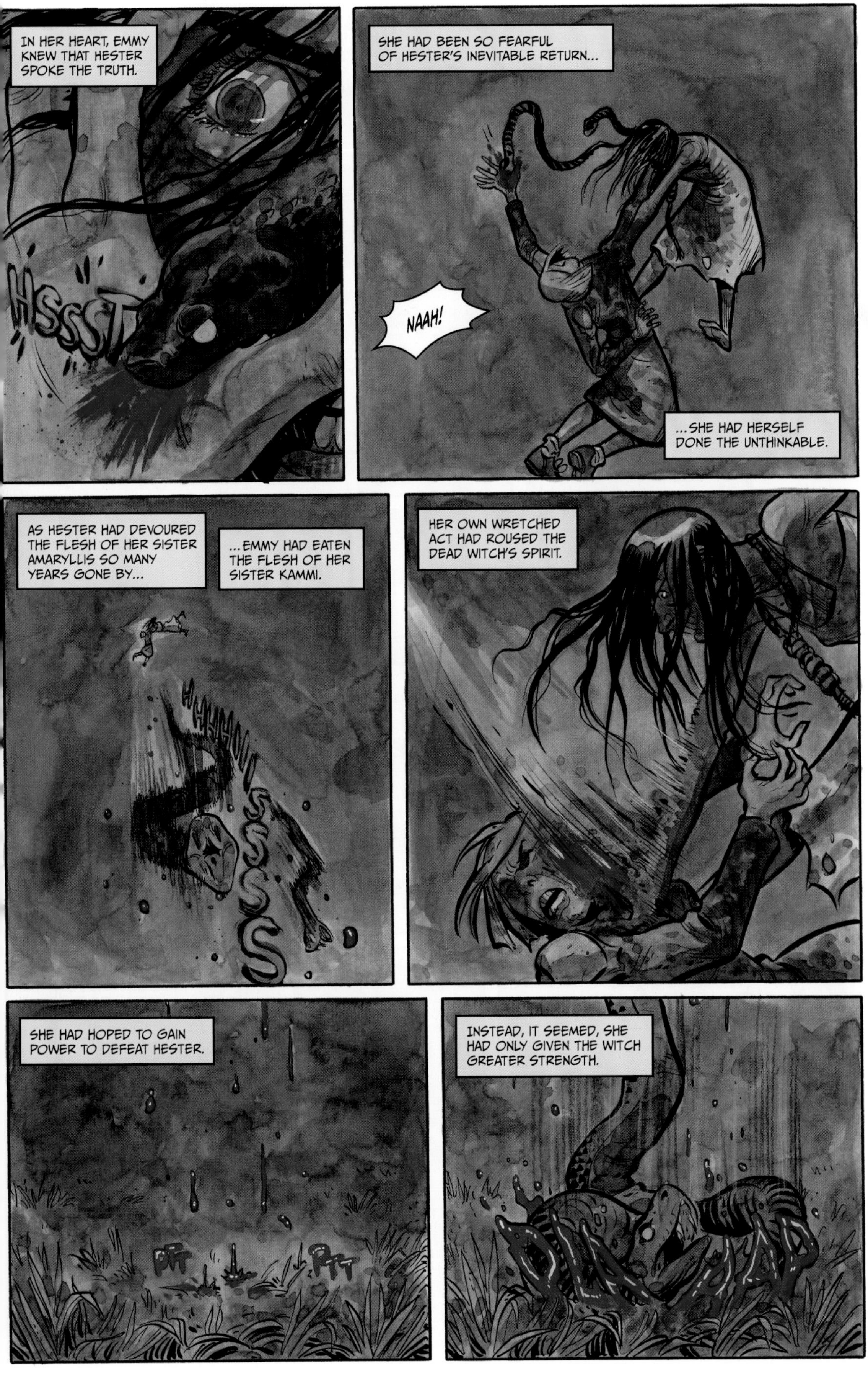
IN HER HEART, EMMY KNEW THAT HESTER SPOKE THE TRUTH.
HSSST
SHE HAD BEEN SO FEARFUL OF HESTER'S INEVITABLE RETURN...
NAAH!
...SHE HAD HERSELF DONE THE UNTHINKABLE.
AS HESTER HAD DEVOURED THE FLESH OF HER SISTER AMARYLLIS SO MANY YEARS GONE BY...
...EMMY HAD EATEN THE FLESH OF HER SISTER KAMMI.
HER OWN WRETCHED ACT HAD ROUSED THE DEAD WITCH'S SPIRIT.
SHE HAD HOPED TO GAIN POWER TO DEFEAT HESTER.
INSTEAD, IT SEEMED, SHE HAD ONLY GIVEN THE WITCH GREATER STRENGTH.

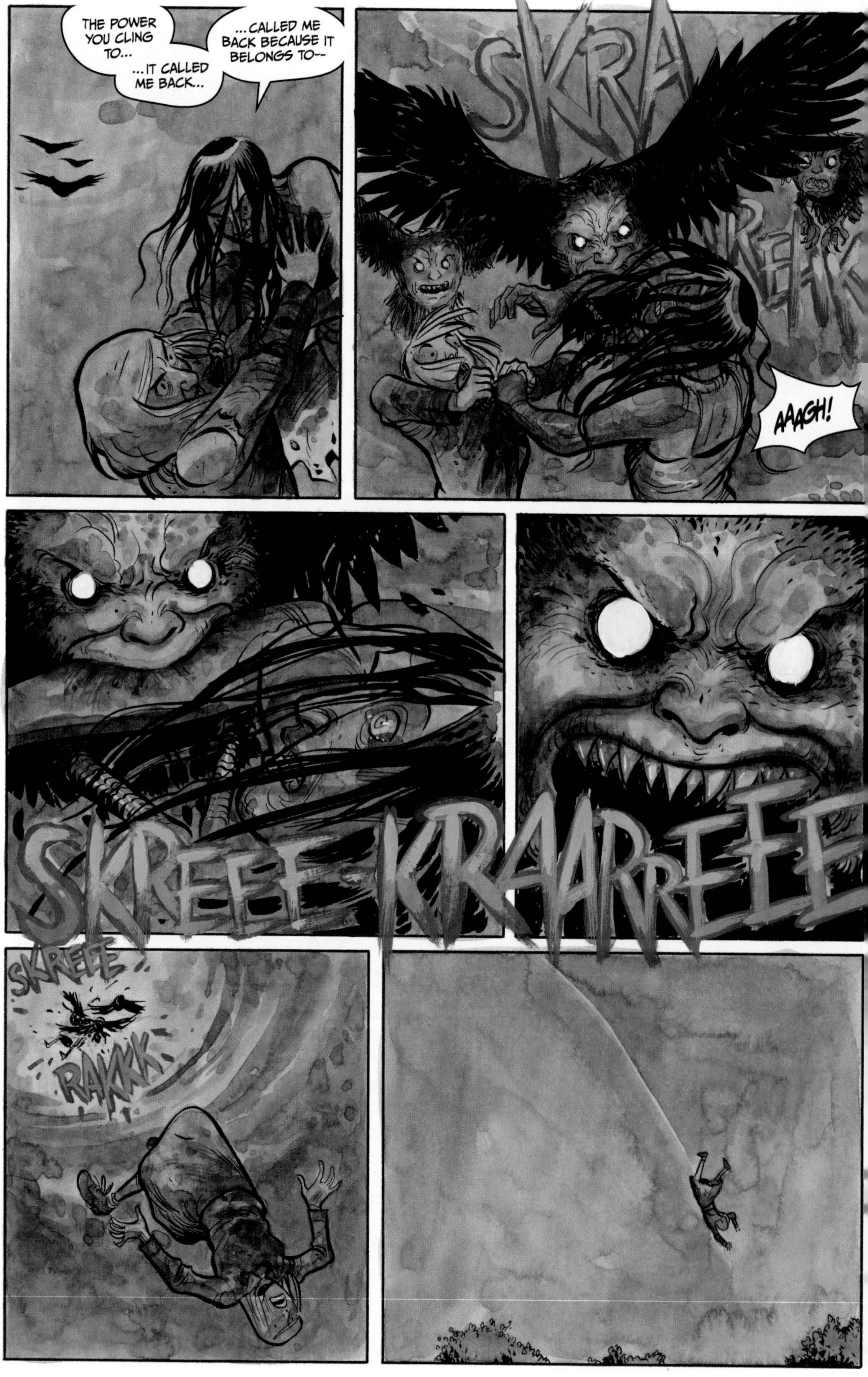
THE POWER YOU CLING TO...
...IT CALLED ME BACK...
...CALLED ME BACK BECAUSE IT BELONGS TO--
SKRA
AAAGH!
SKREEE KRAARREEE
SKREEE
RAKKK

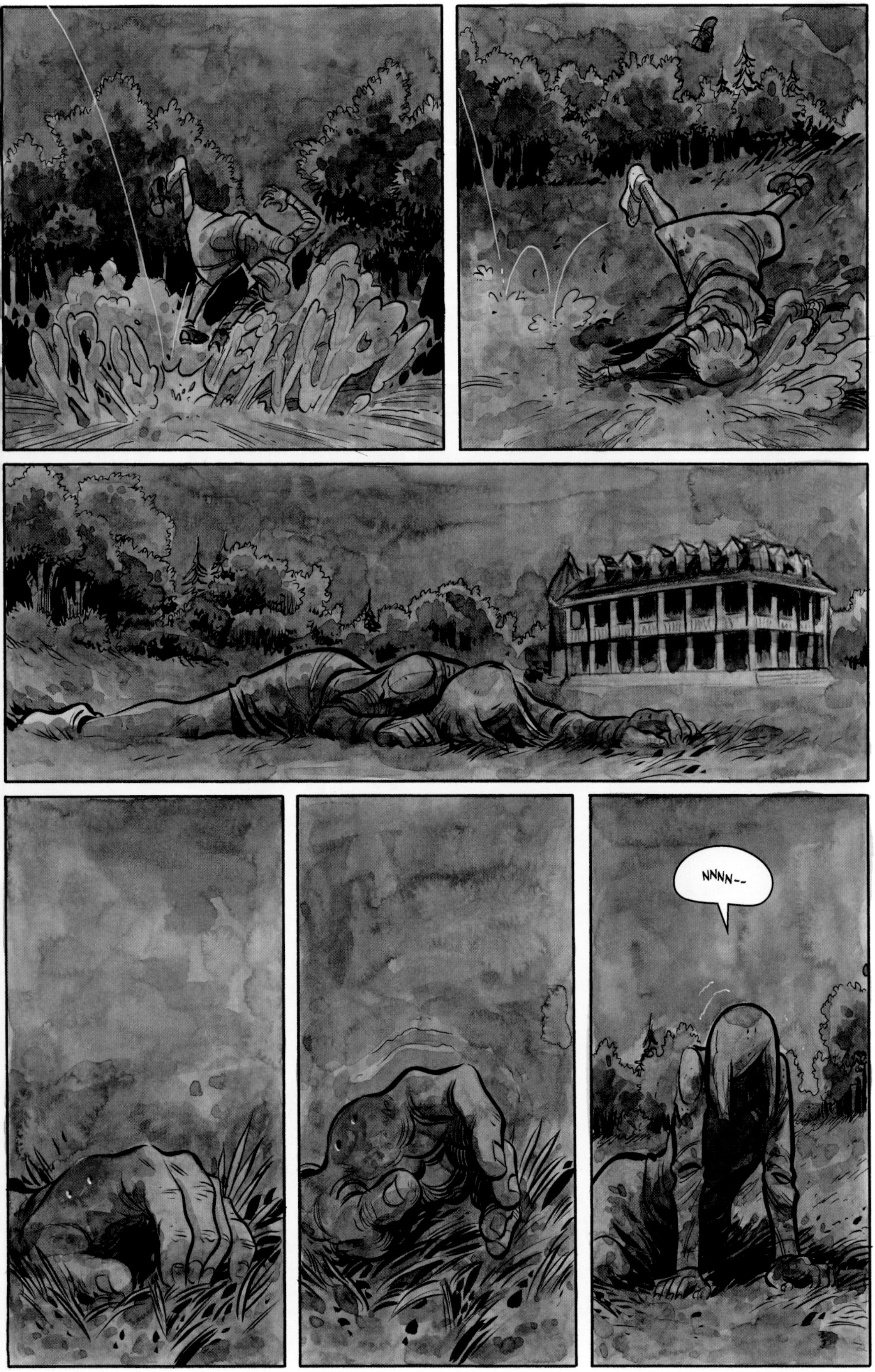
NNNN--

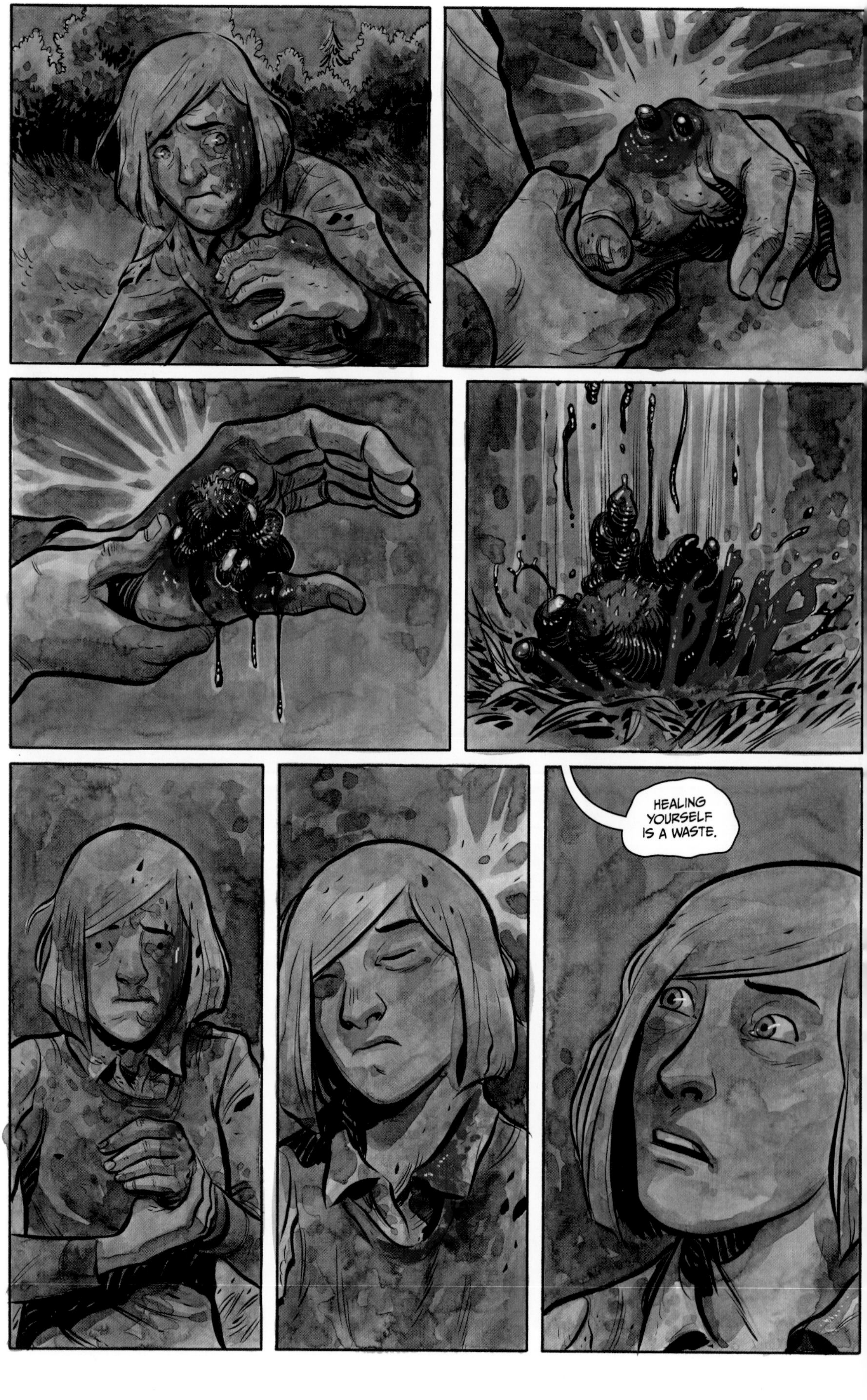
PLIP
HEALING YOURSELF IS A WASTE.

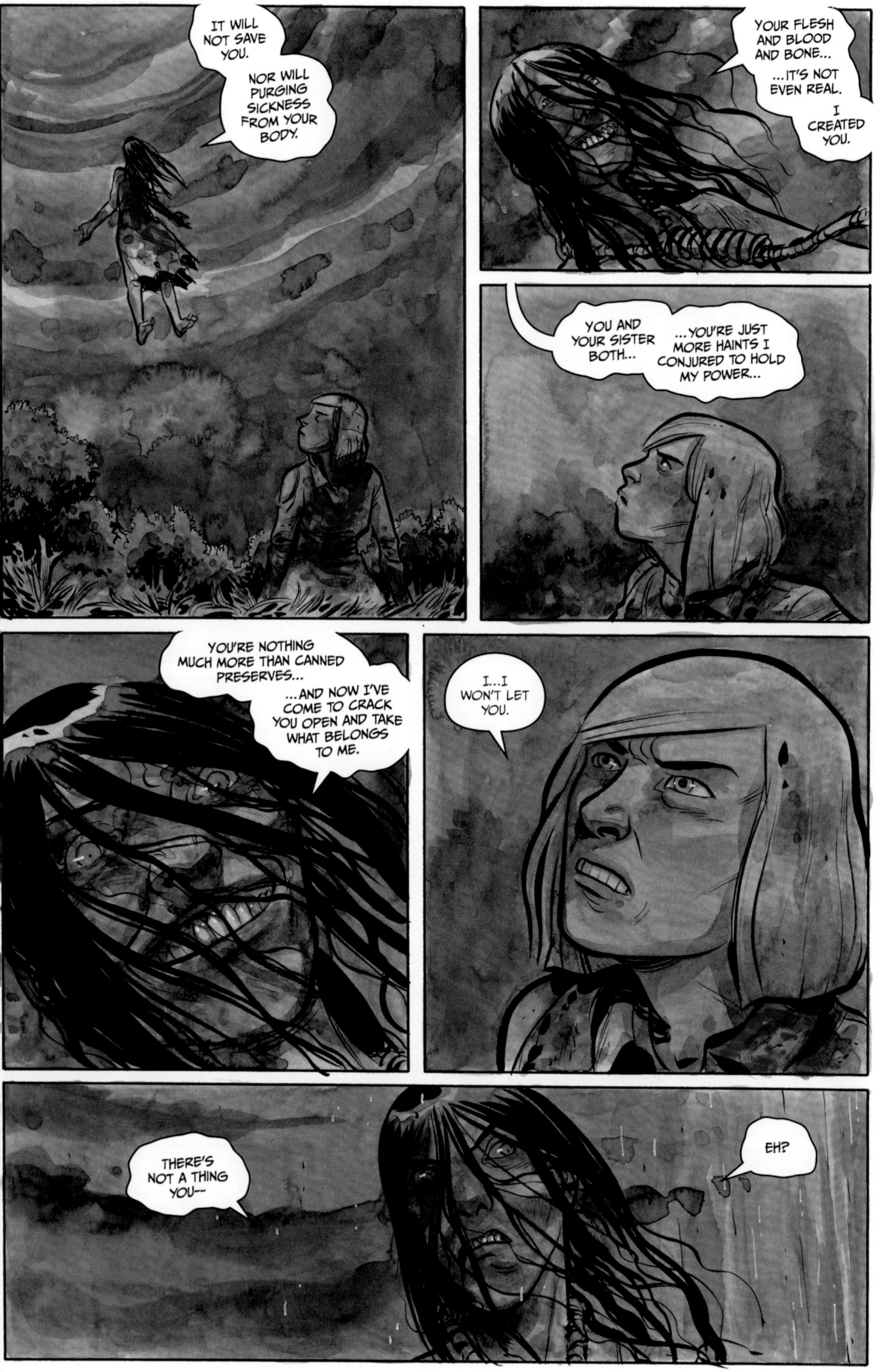
IT WILL NOT SAVE YOU.
NOR WILL PURGING SICKNESS FROM YOUR BODY.
YOUR FLESH AND BLOOD AND BONE...
...IT'S NOT EVEN REAL.
I CREATED YOU.
YOU AND YOUR SISTER BOTH...
...YOU'RE JUST MORE HAINTS I CONJURED TO HOLD MY POWER...
YOU'RE NOTHING MUCH MORE THAN CANNED PRESERVES...
...AND NOW I'VE COME TO CRACK YOU OPEN AND TAKE WHAT BELONGS TO ME.
I...I WON'T LET YOU.
THERE'S NOT A THING YOU--
EH?

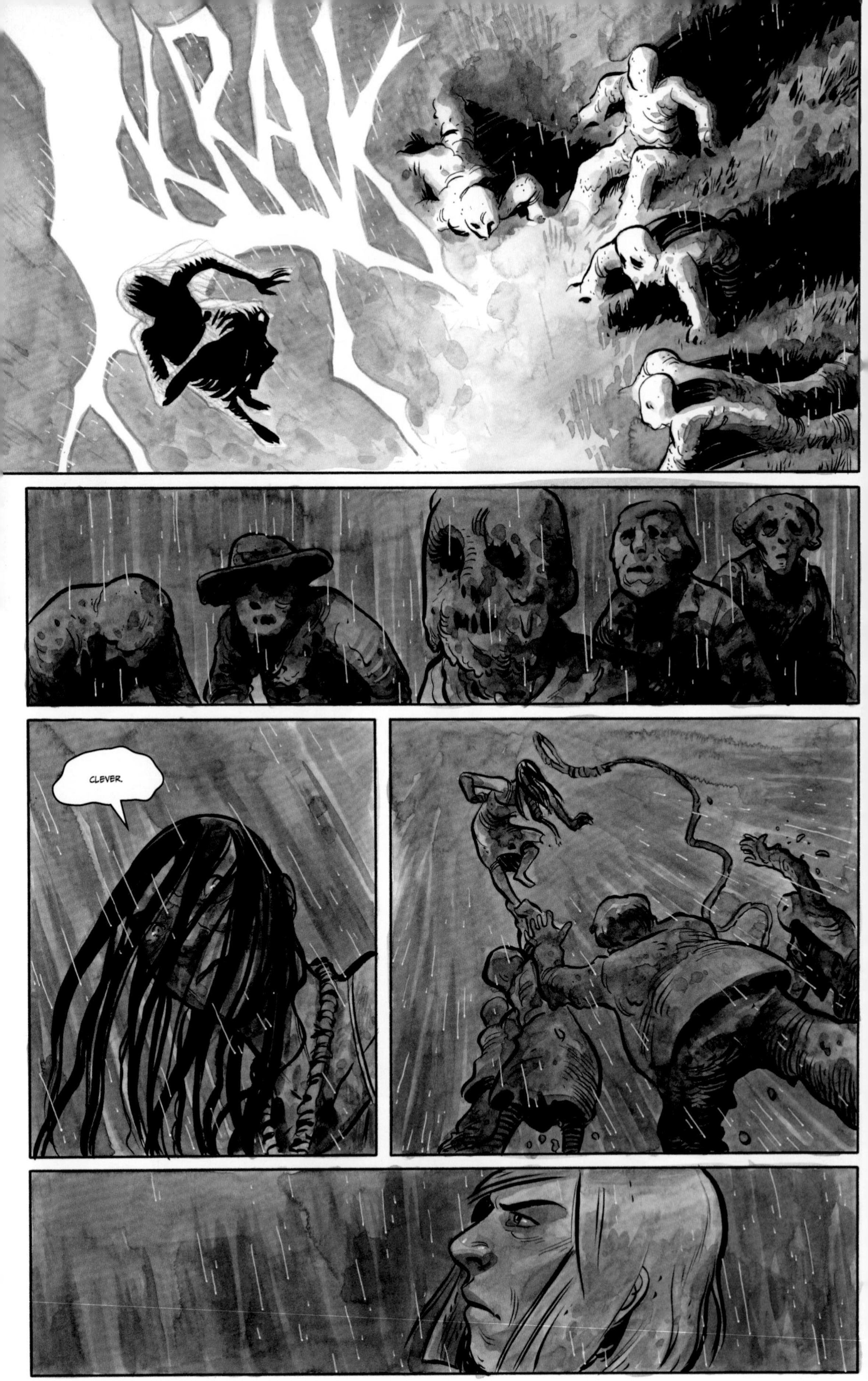
KRAK
CLEVER.

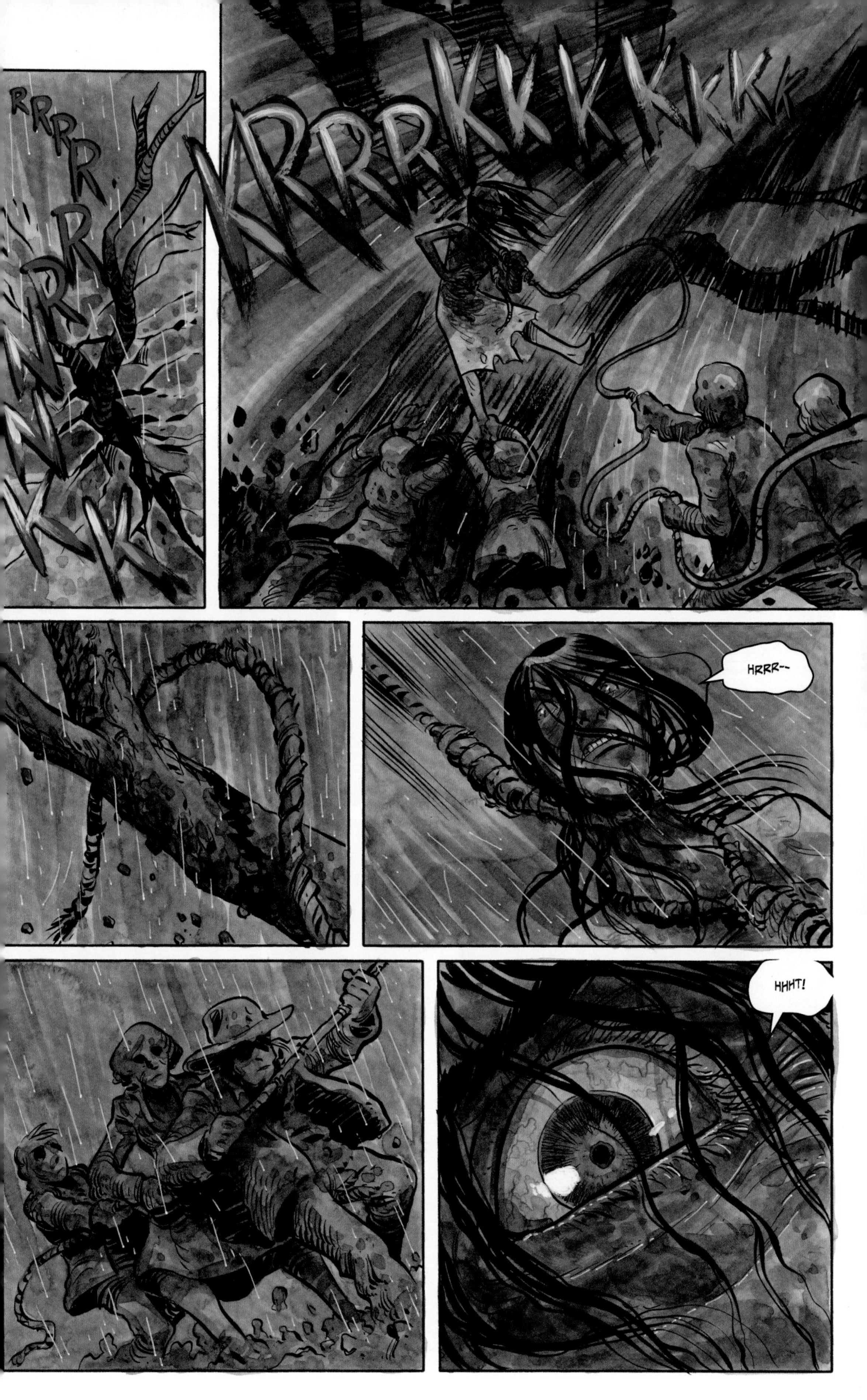
RRRRRRRNNKKK
KRRRRKKKKKKKK
HRRR--
HHHT!

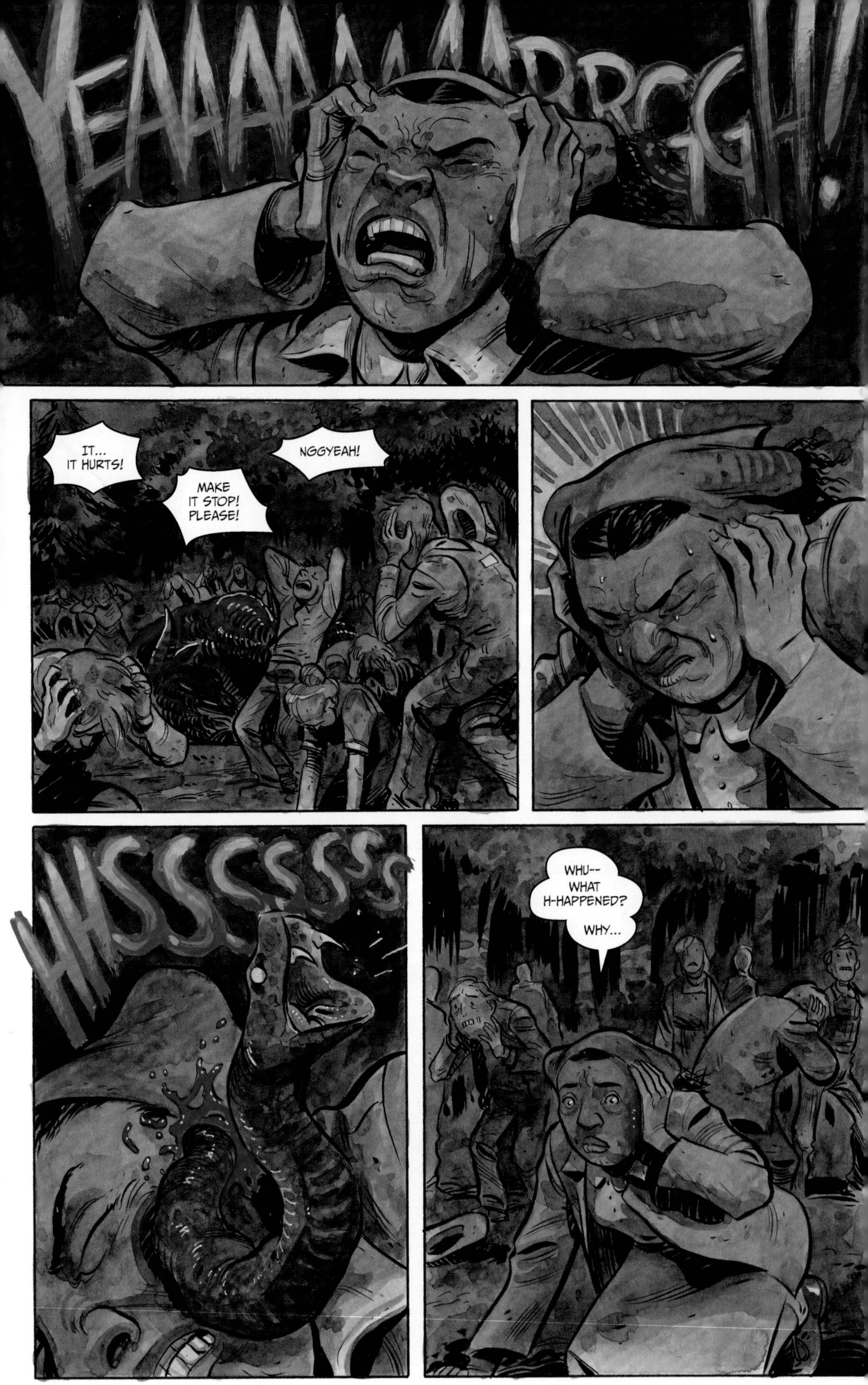
YEAAAAAAARRGGH!!
IT... IT HURTS!
MAKE IT STOP! PLEASE!
NGGYEAH!
HSSSSSSS
WHU-- WHAT H-HAPPENED?
WHY...

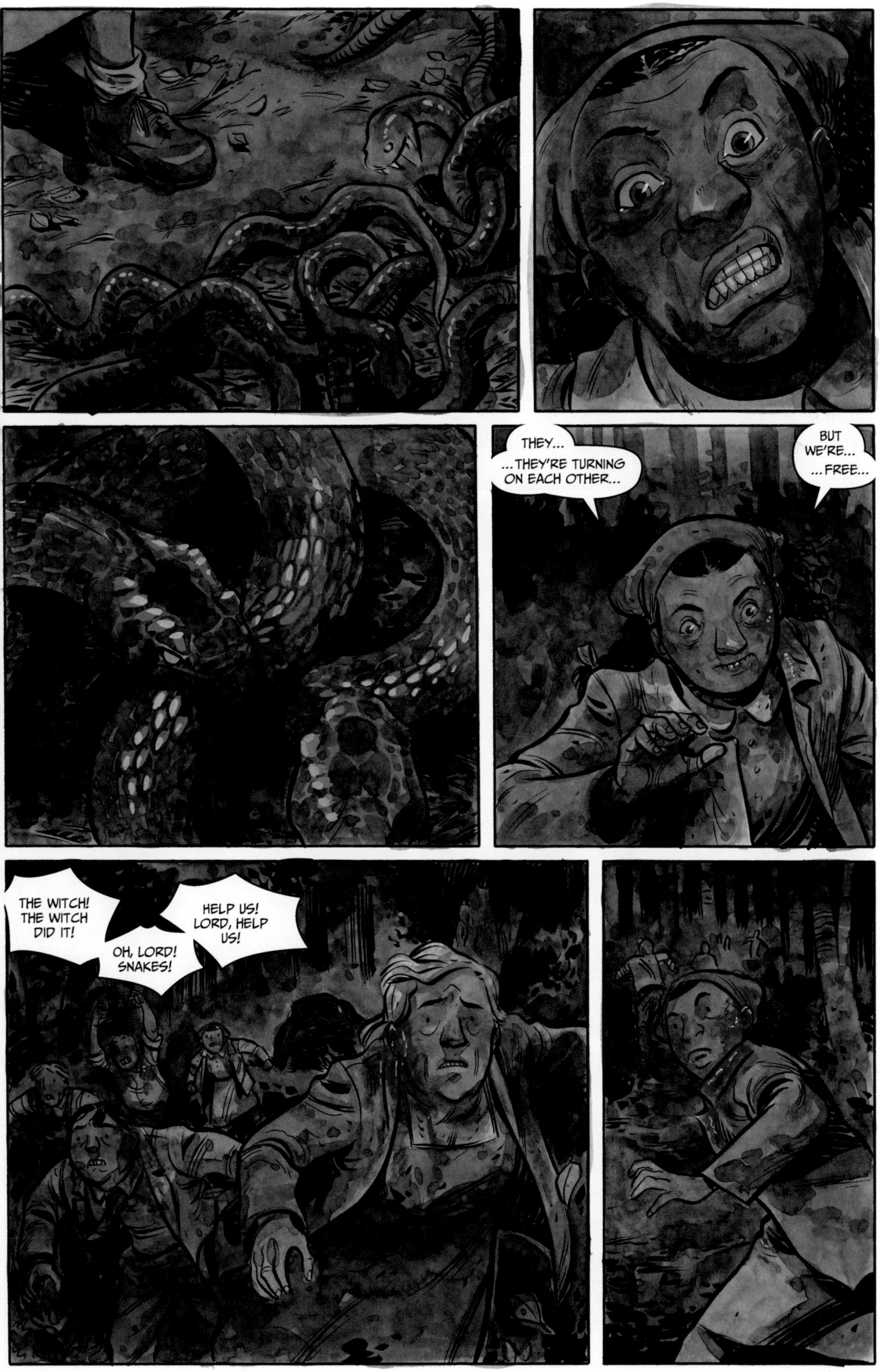
THEY...
...THEY'RE TURNING ON EACH OTHER...
BUT WE'RE...
...FREE...
THE WITCH! THE WITCH DID IT!
OH, LORD! SNAKES!
HELP US! LORD, HELP US!

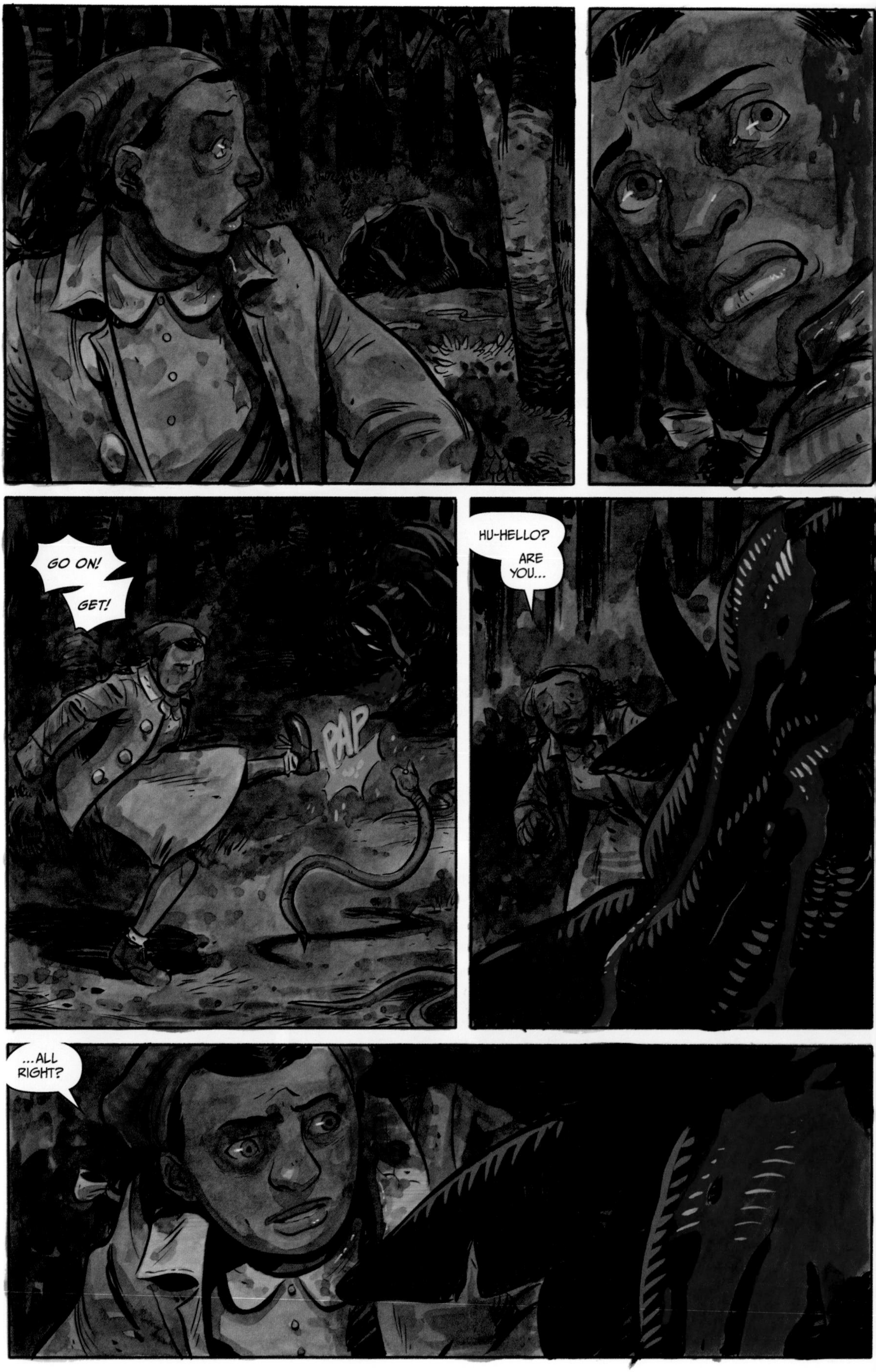
GO ON!
GET!
PAP
HU-HELLO?
ARE YOU...
...ALL RIGHT?

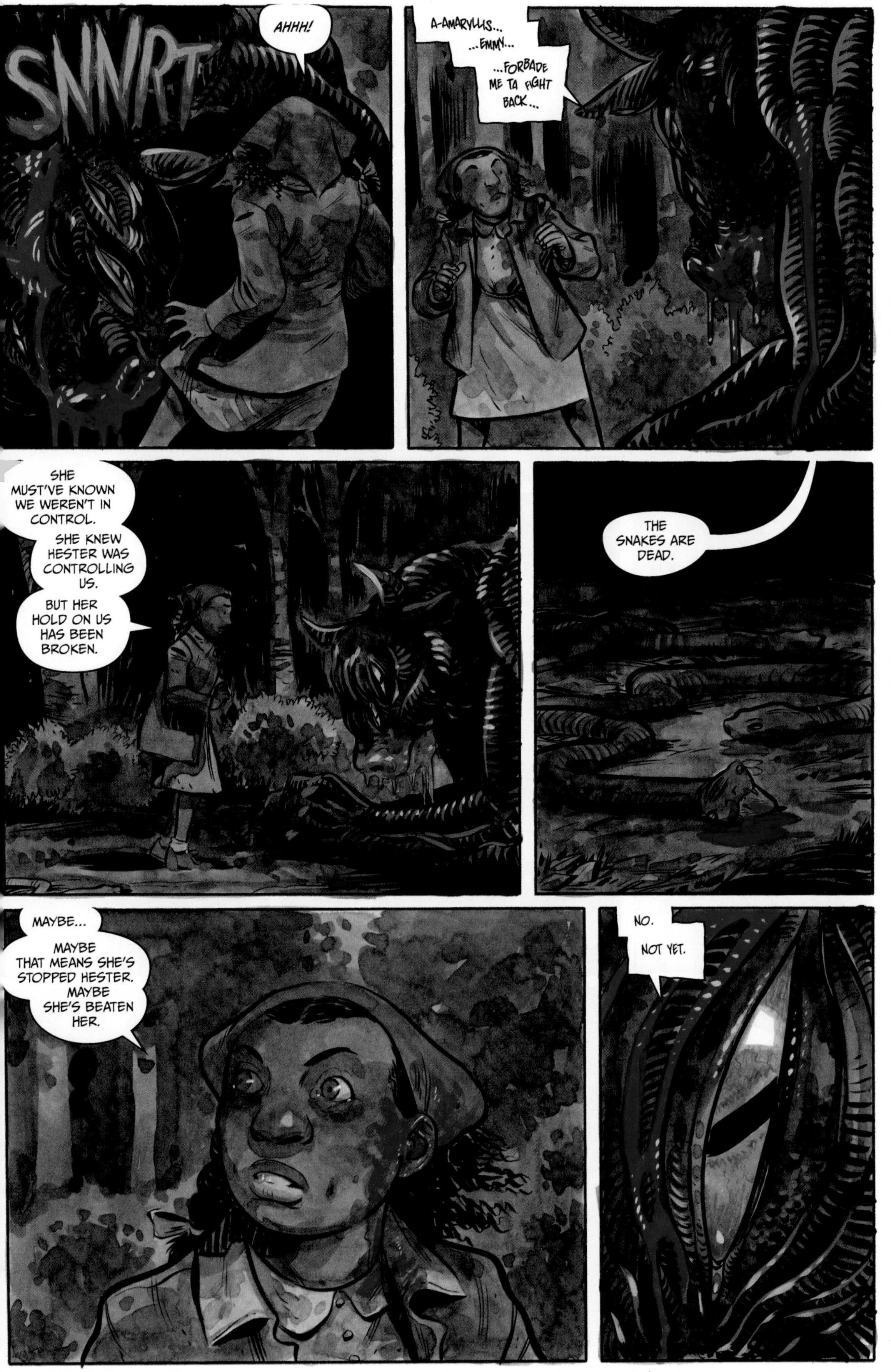
SNNRT
AHHH!
A-AMARYLLIS...
...EMMY...
...FORBADE ME TA FIGHT BACK...
SHE MUST'VE KNOWN WE WEREN'T IN CONTROL.
SHE KNEW HESTER WAS CONTROLLING US.
BUT HER HOLD ON US HAS BEEN BROKEN.
THE SNAKES ARE DEAD.
MAYBE...
MAYBE THAT MEANS SHE'S STOPPED HESTER.
MAYBE SHE'S BEATEN HER.
NO.
NOT YET.

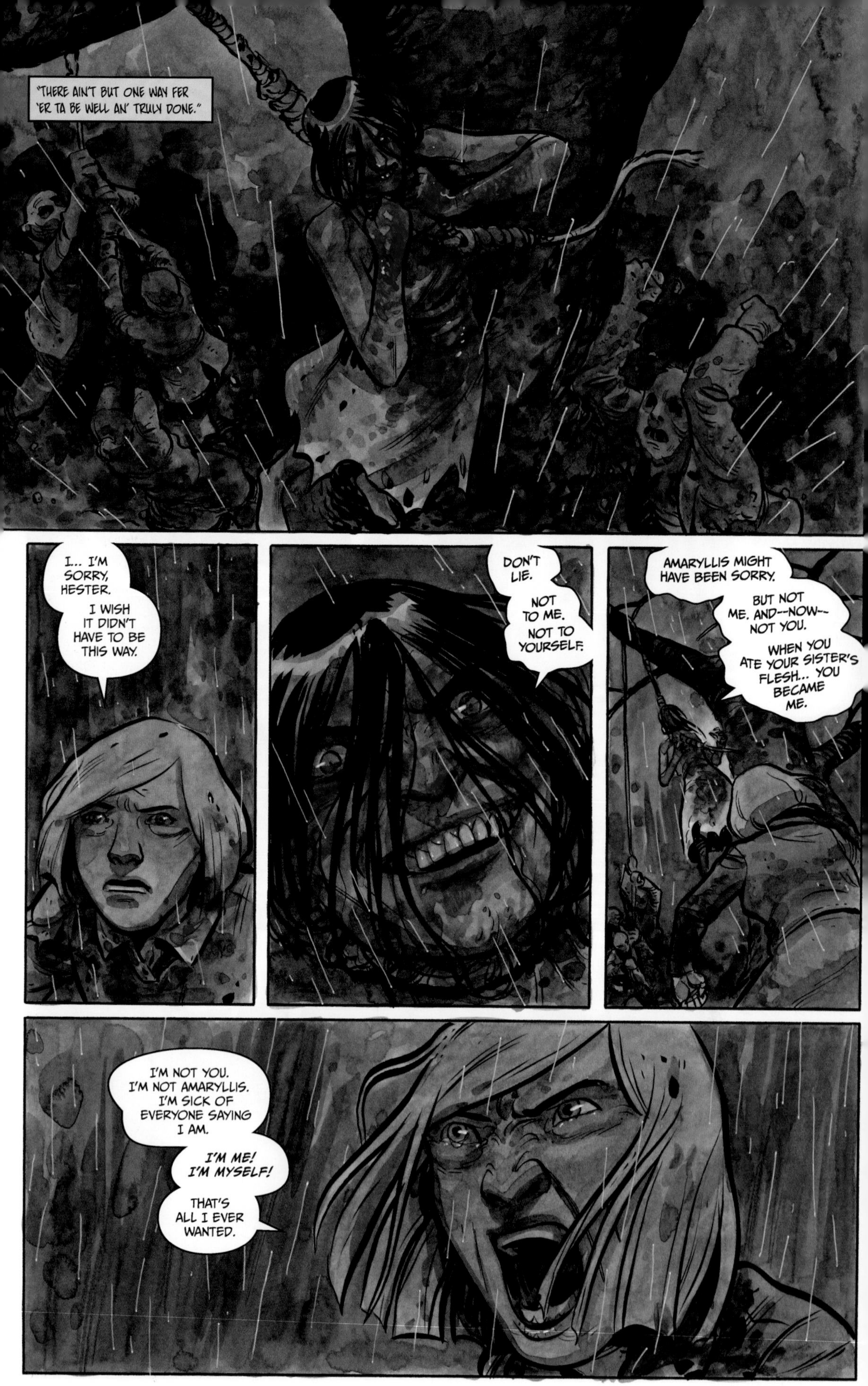
"THERE AIN'T BUT ONE WAY FER 'ER TA BE WELL AN' TRULY DONE."
I... I'M SORRY, HESTER.
I WISH IT DIDN'T HAVE TO BE THIS WAY.
DON'T LIE.
NOT TO ME.
NOT TO YOURSELF.
AMARYLLIS MIGHT HAVE BEEN SORRY.
BUT NOT ME. AND--NOW-- NOT YOU.
WHEN YOU ATE YOUR SISTER'S FLESH... YOU BECAME ME.
I'M NOT YOU. I'M NOT AMARYLLIS. I'M SICK OF EVERYONE SAYING I AM.
I'M ME! I'M MYSELF!
THAT'S ALL I EVER WANTED.

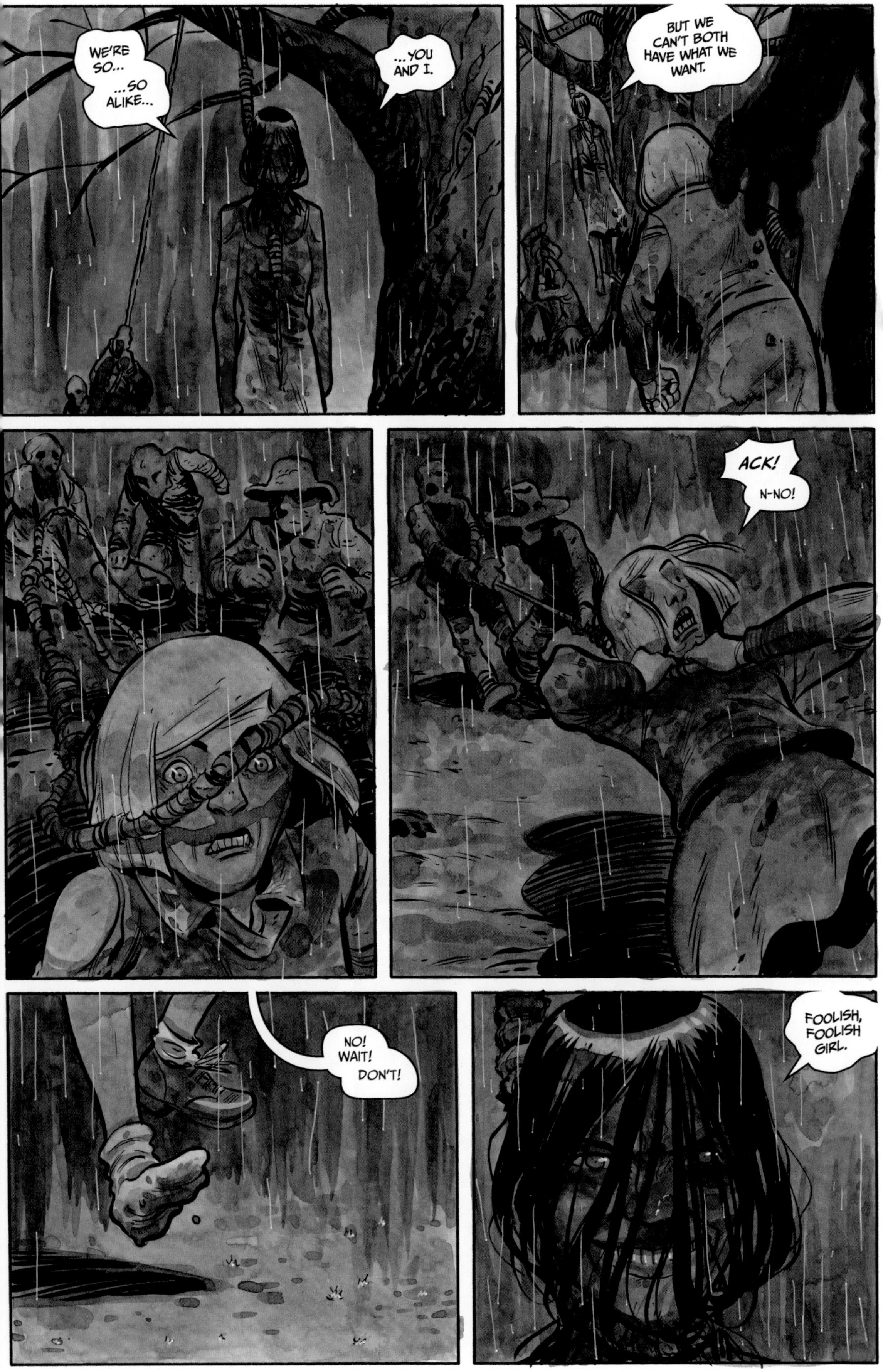
WE'RE SO...
...SO ALIKE...
...YOU AND I.
BUT WE CAN'T BOTH HAVE WHAT WE WANT.
ACK!
N-NO!
NO! WAIT!
DON'T!
FOOLISH, FOOLISH GIRL.

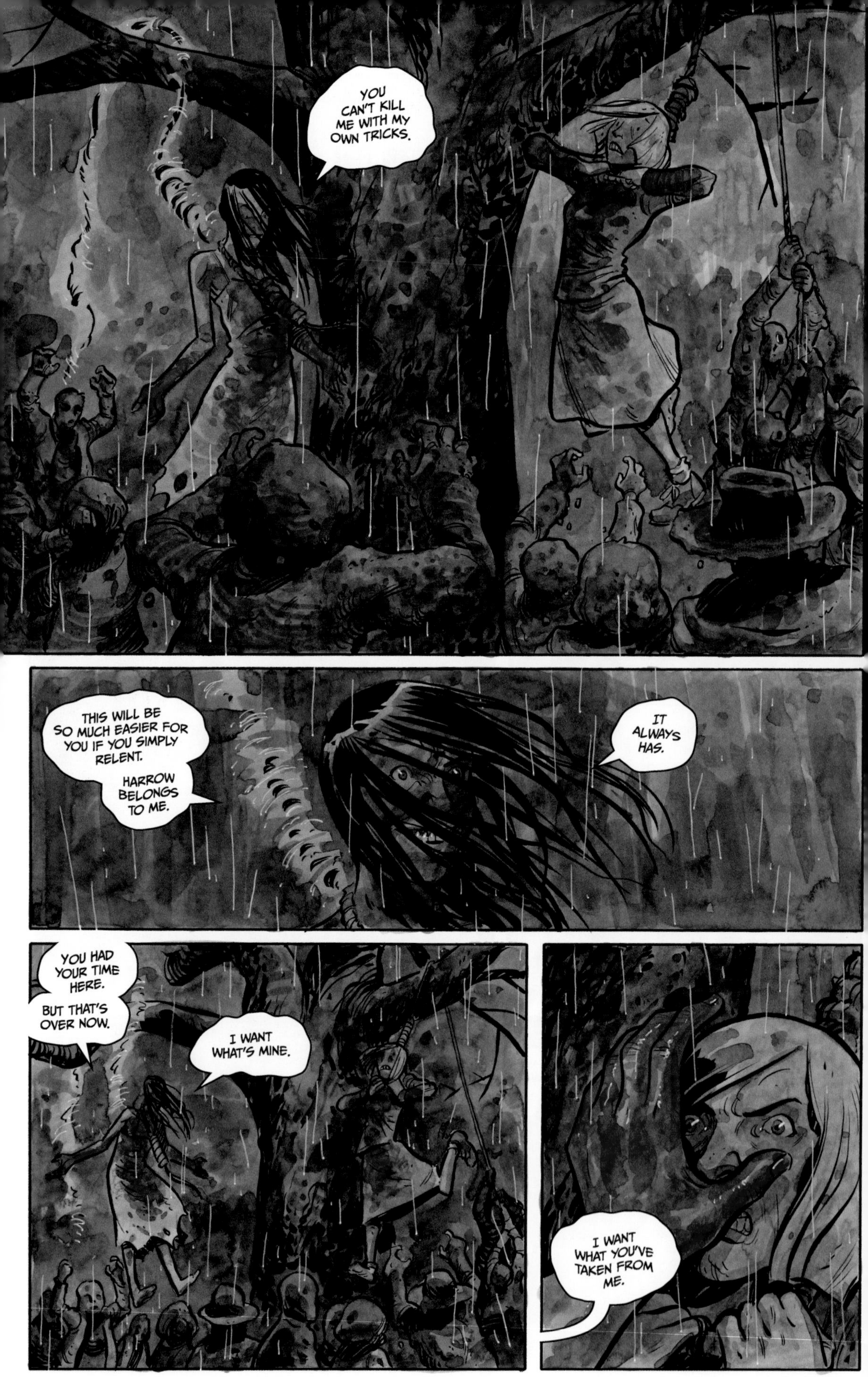
YOU CAN'T KILL ME WITH MY OWN TRICKS.
THIS WILL BE SO MUCH EASIER FOR YOU IF YOU SIMPLY RELENT.
HARROW BELONGS TO ME.
IT ALWAYS HAS.
YOU HAD YOUR TIME HERE.
BUT THAT'S OVER NOW.
I WANT WHAT'S MINE.
I WANT WHAT YOU'VE TAKEN FROM ME.

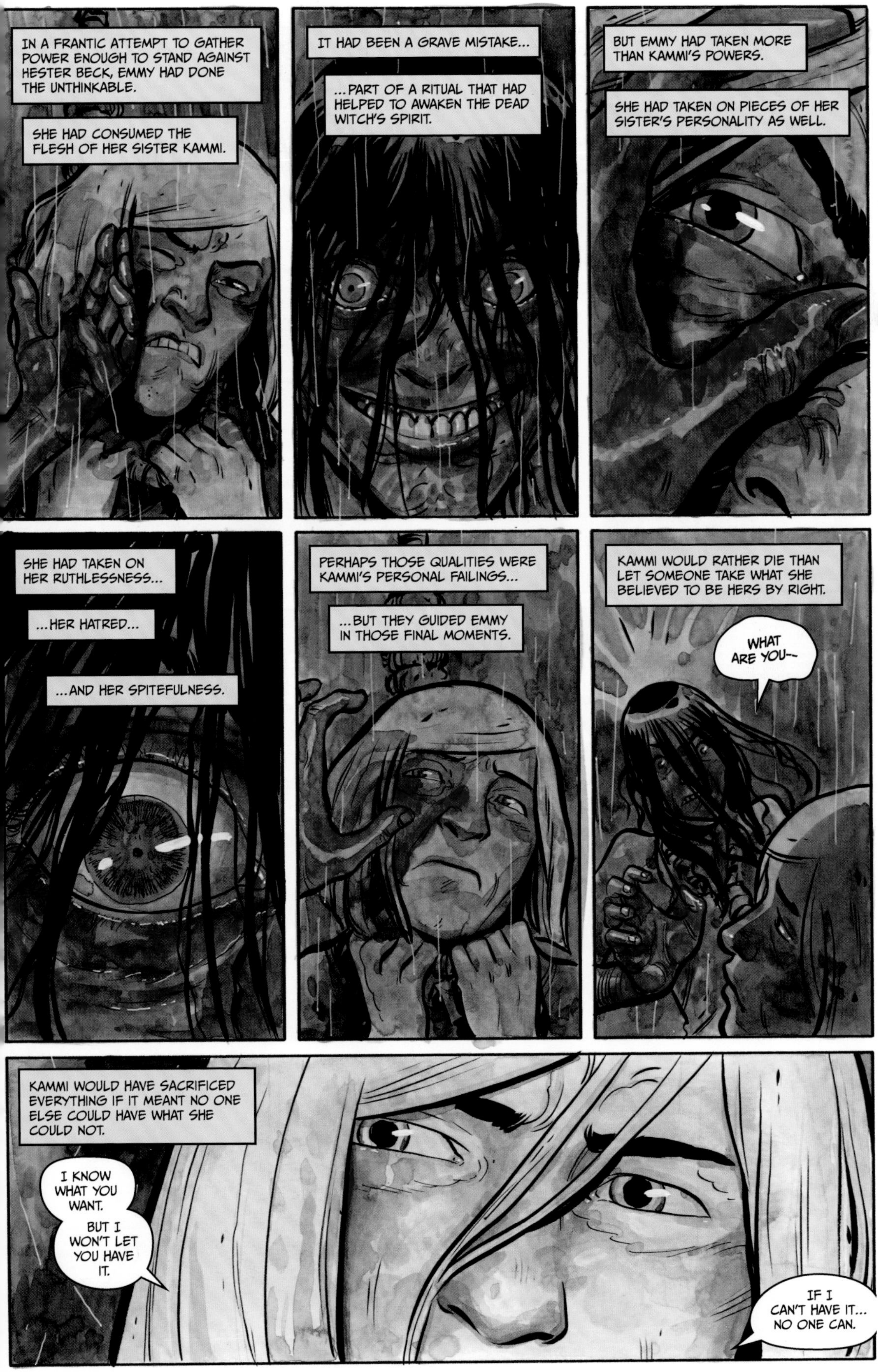
IN A FRANTIC ATTEMPT TO GATHER POWER ENOUGH TO STAND AGAINST HESTER BECK, EMMY HAD DONE THE UNTHINKABLE.
SHE HAD CONSUMED THE FLESH OF HER SISTER KAMMI.
IT HAD BEEN A GRAVE MISTAKE...
...PART OF A RITUAL THAT HAD HELPED TO AWAKEN THE DEAD WITCH'S SPIRIT.
BUT EMMY HAD TAKEN MORE THAN KAMMI'S POWERS.
SHE HAD TAKEN ON PIECES OF HER SISTER'S PERSONALITY AS WELL.
SHE HAD TAKEN ON HER RUTHLESSNESS...
...HER HATRED...
...AND HER SPITEFULNESS.
PERHAPS THOSE QUALITIES WERE KAMMI'S PERSONAL FAILINGS...
...BUT THEY GUIDED EMMY IN THOSE FINAL MOMENTS.
KAMMI WOULD RATHER DIE THAN LET SOMEONE TAKE WHAT SHE BELIEVED TO BE HERS BY RIGHT.
WHAT ARE YOU--
KAMMI WOULD HAVE SACRIFICED EVERYTHING IF IT MEANT NO ONE ELSE COULD HAVE WHAT SHE COULD NOT.
I KNOW WHAT YOU WANT.
BUT I WON'T LET YOU HAVE IT.
IF I CAN'T HAVE IT... NO ONE CAN.

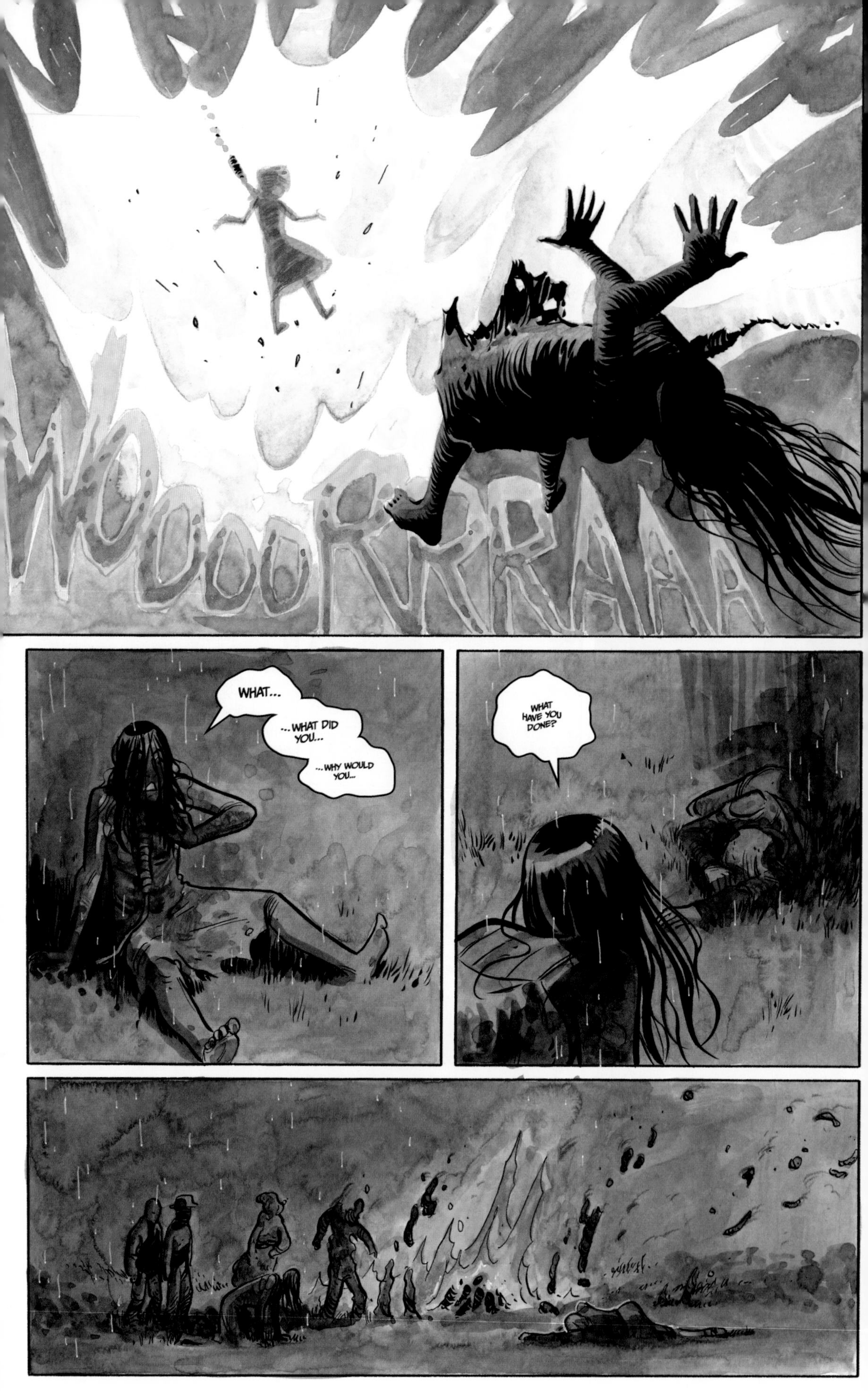
WOOODORRRAAA
WHAT...
...WHAT DID YOU...
...WHY WOULD YOU...
WHAT HAVE YOU DONE?

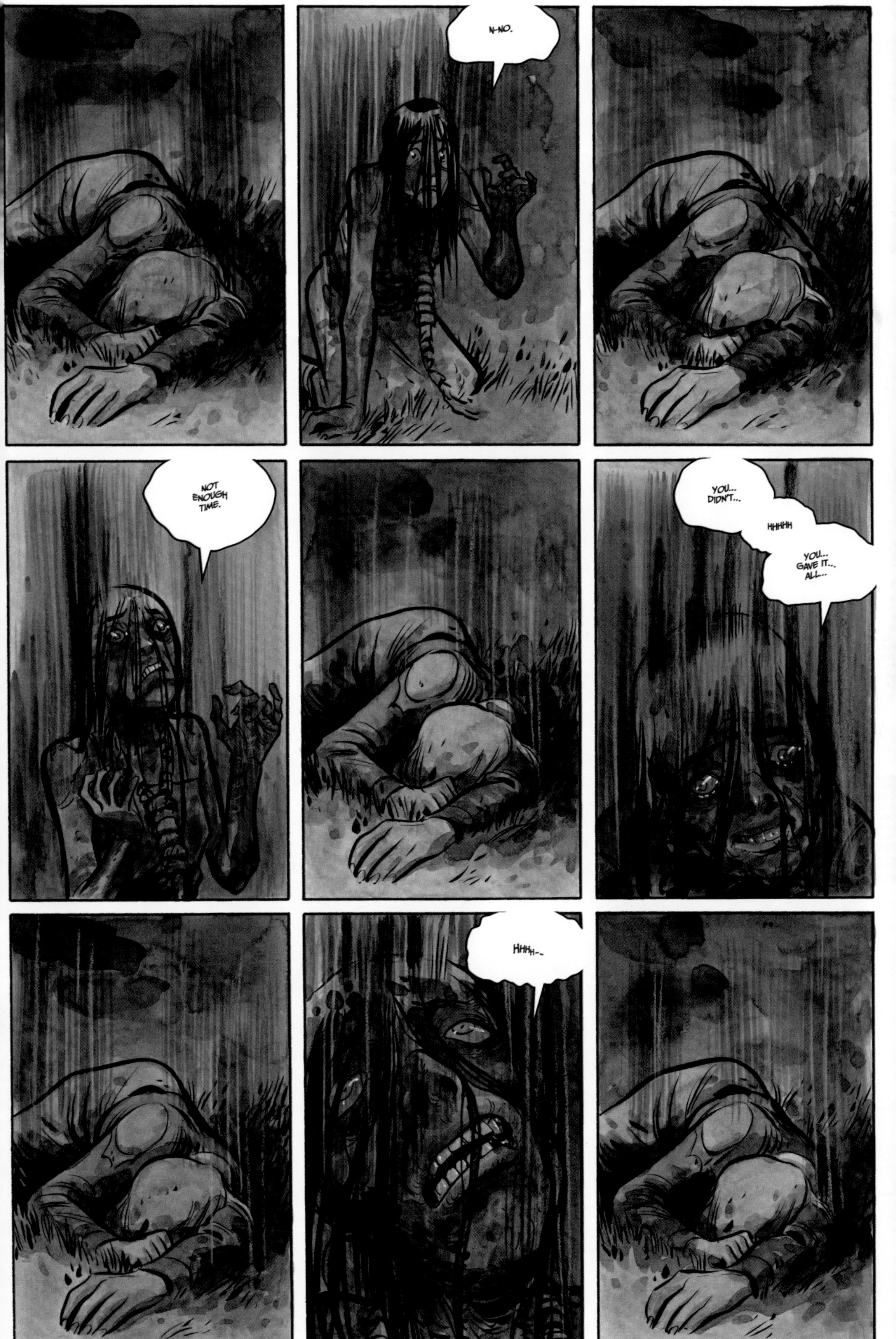
N-NO.
NOT ENOUGH TIME.
YOU... DIDN'T...
HHHHH
YOU... GAVE IT... ALL...
HHHH-.

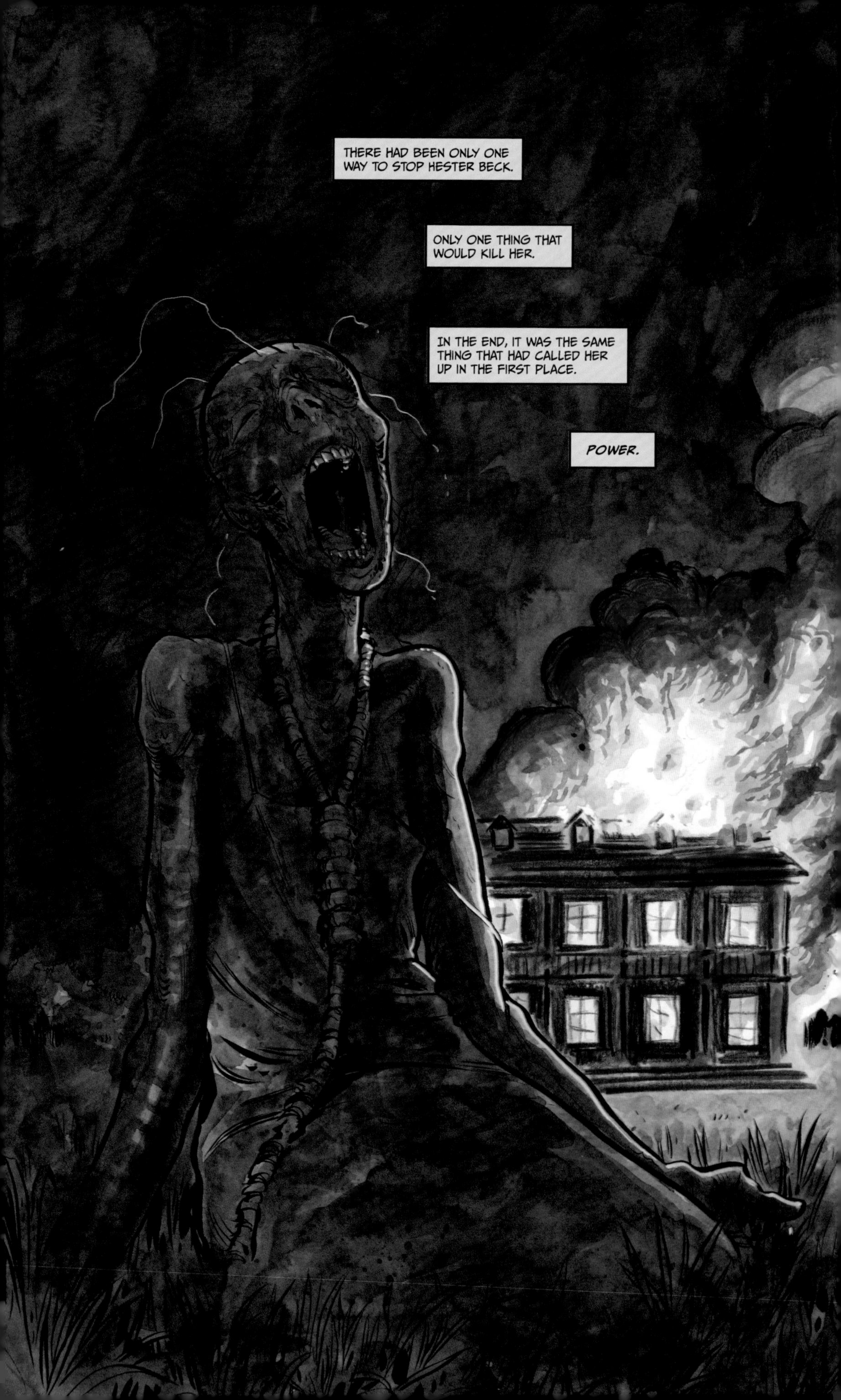
THERE HAD BEEN ONLY ONE WAY TO STOP HESTER BECK.
ONLY ONE THING THAT WOULD KILL HER.
IN THE END, IT WAS THE SAME THING THAT HAD CALLED HER UP IN THE FIRST PLACE.
POWER.

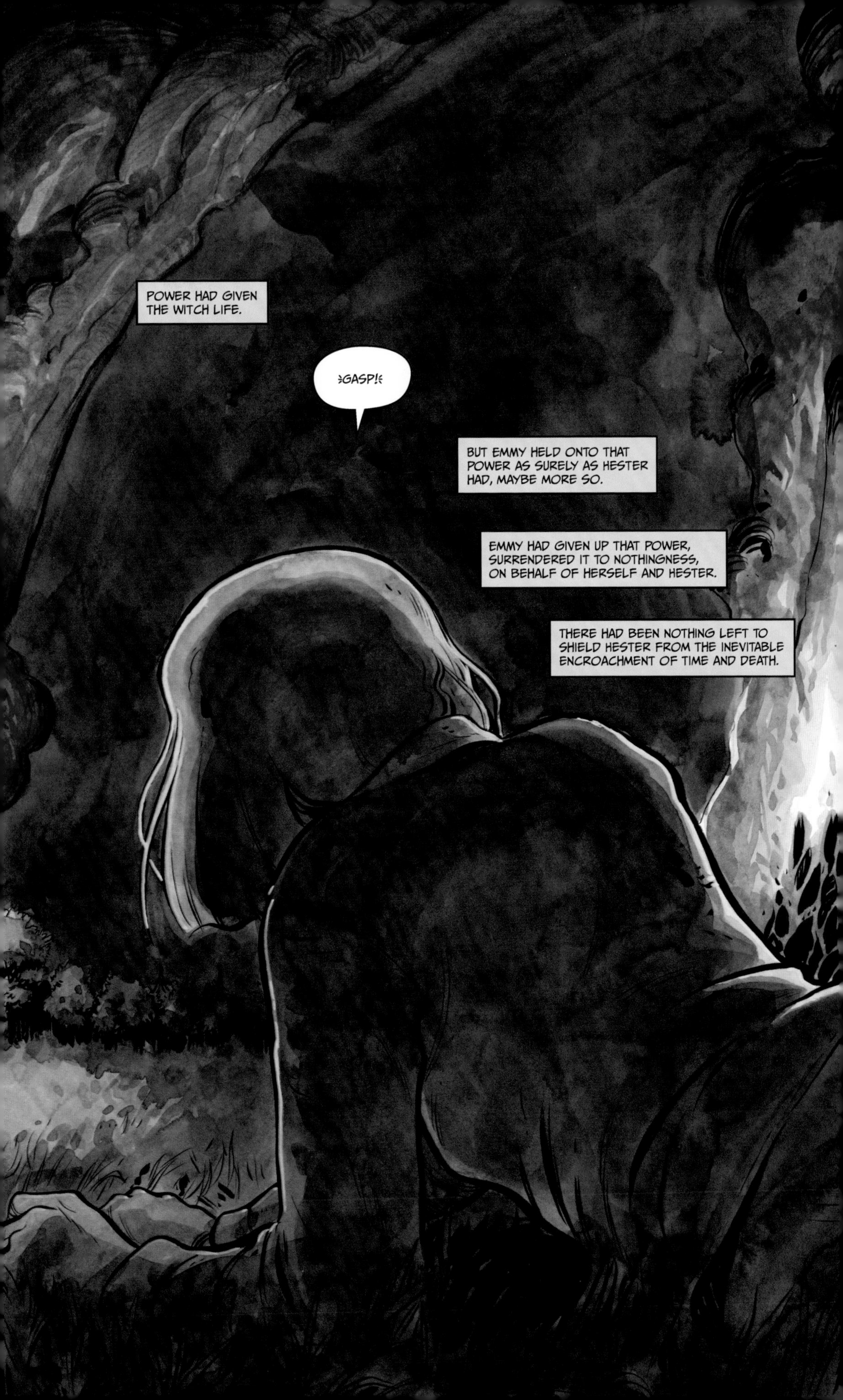
POWER HAD GIVEN THE WITCH LIFE.
GASP!
BUT EMMY HELD ONTO THAT POWER AS SURELY AS HESTER HAD, MAYBE MORE SO.
EMMY HAD GIVEN UP THAT POWER, SURRENDERED IT TO NOTHINGNESS, ON BEHALF OF HERSELF AND HESTER.
THERE HAD BEEN NOTHING LEFT TO SHIELD HESTER FROM THE INEVITABLE ENCROACHMENT OF TIME AND DEATH.

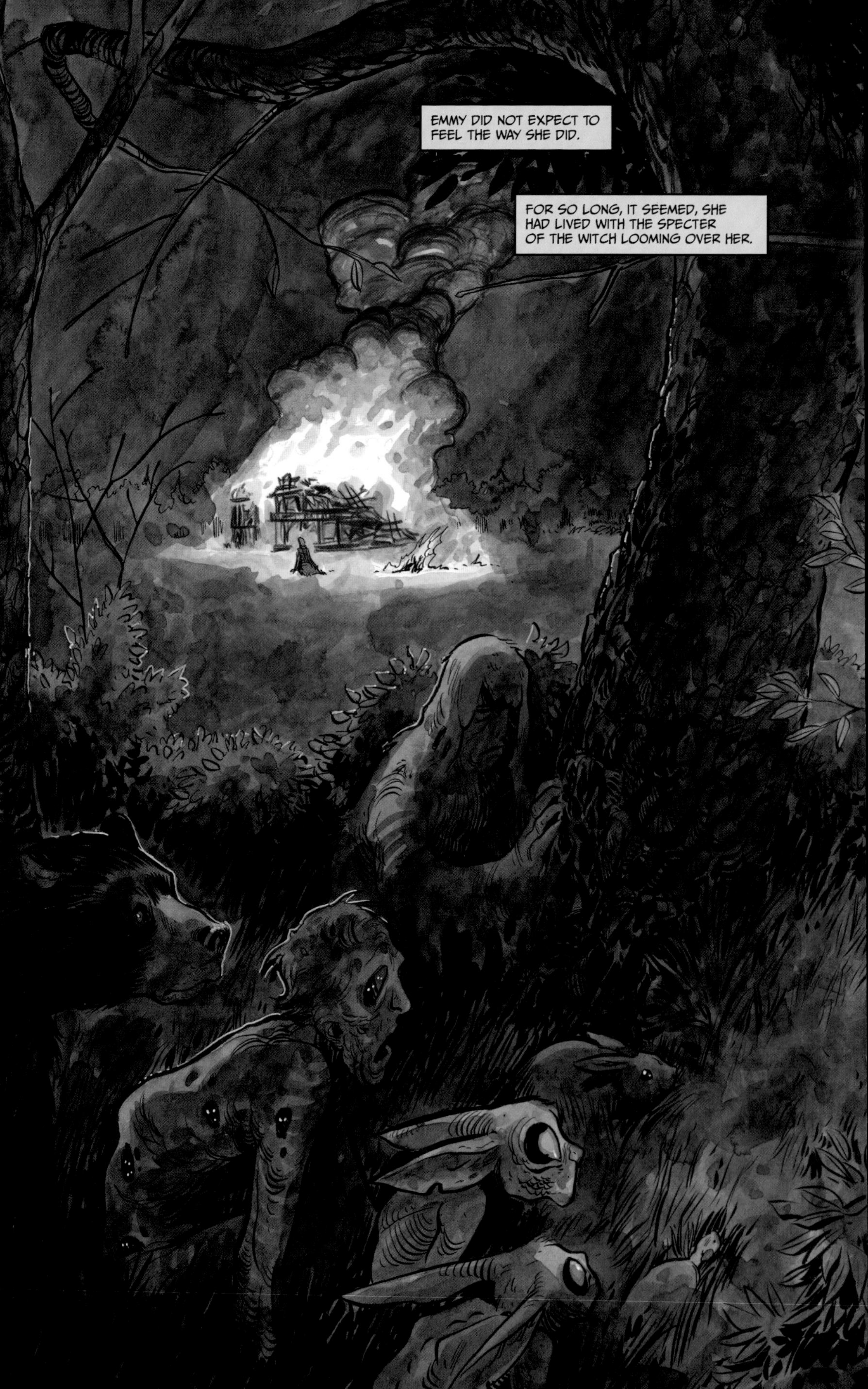
EMMY DID NOT EXPECT TO FEEL THE WAY SHE DID.
FOR SO LONG, IT SEEMED, SHE HAD LIVED WITH THE SPECTER OF THE WITCH LOOMING OVER HER.

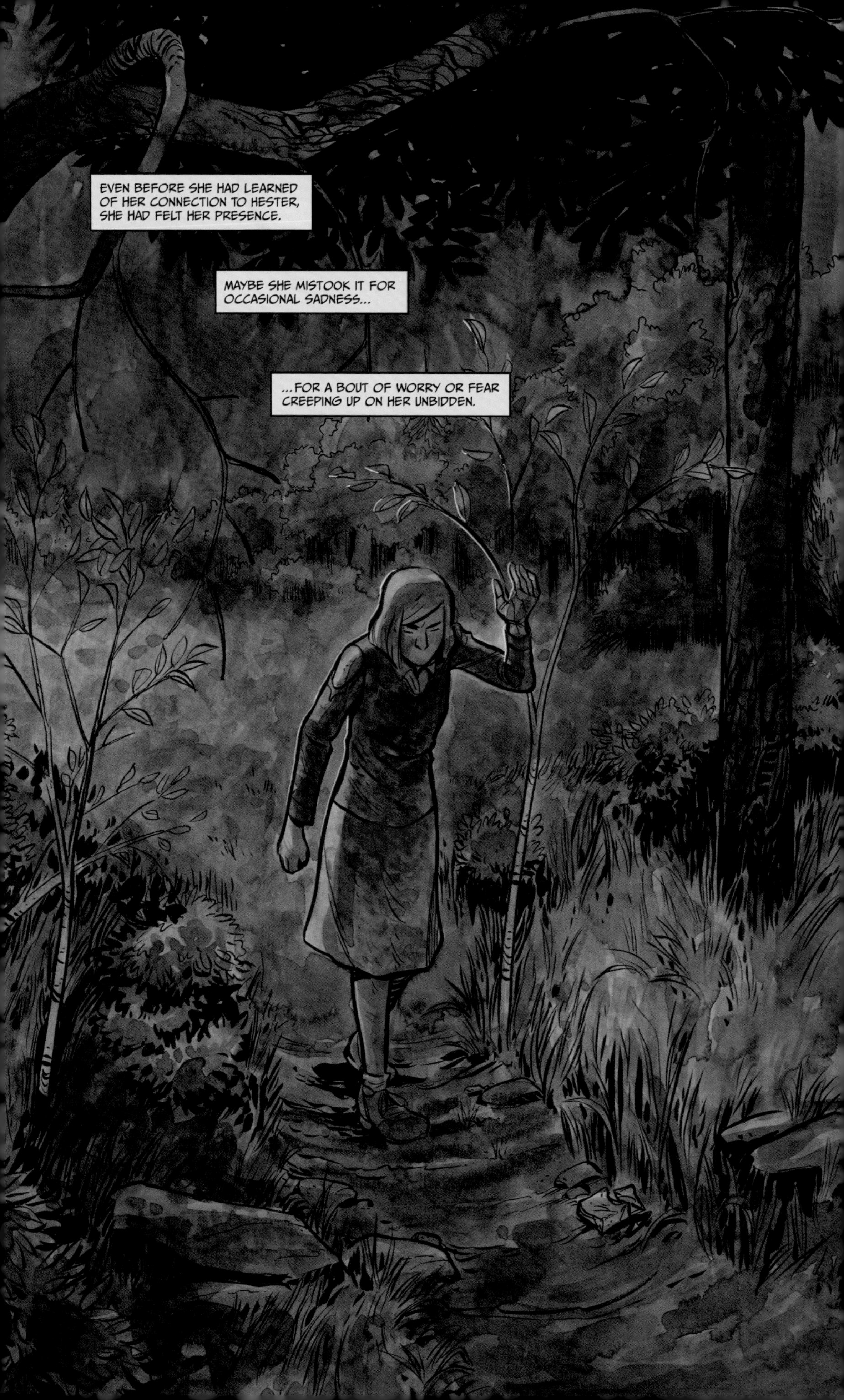
EVEN BEFORE SHE HAD LEARNED OF HER CONNECTION TO HESTER, SHE HAD FELT HER PRESENCE.
MAYBE SHE MISTOOK IT FOR OCCASIONAL SADNESS...
...FOR A BOUT OF WORRY OR FEAR CREEPING UP ON HER UNBIDDEN.

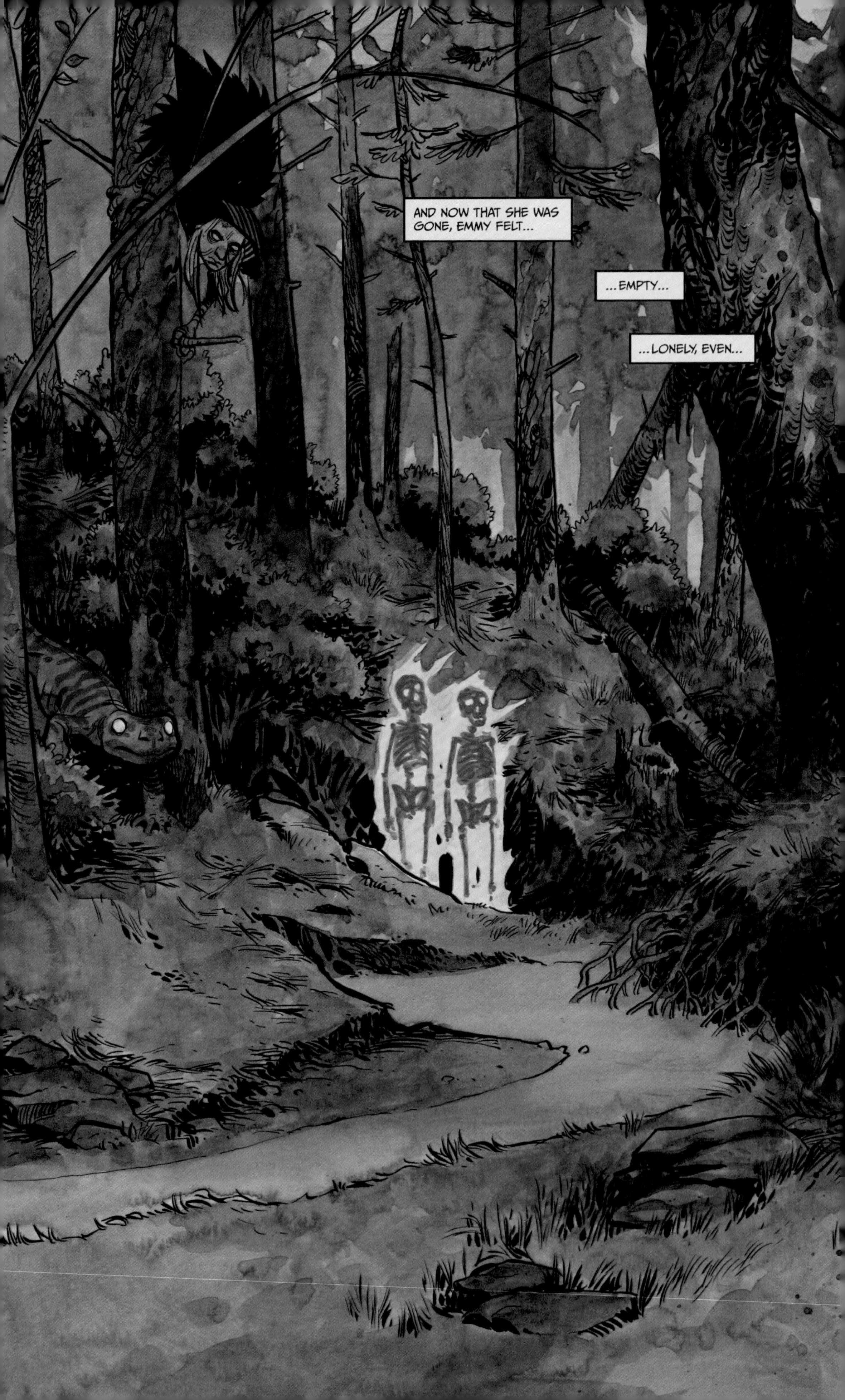
AND NOW THAT SHE WAS GONE, EMMY FELT...
...EMPTY...
...LONELY, EVEN...

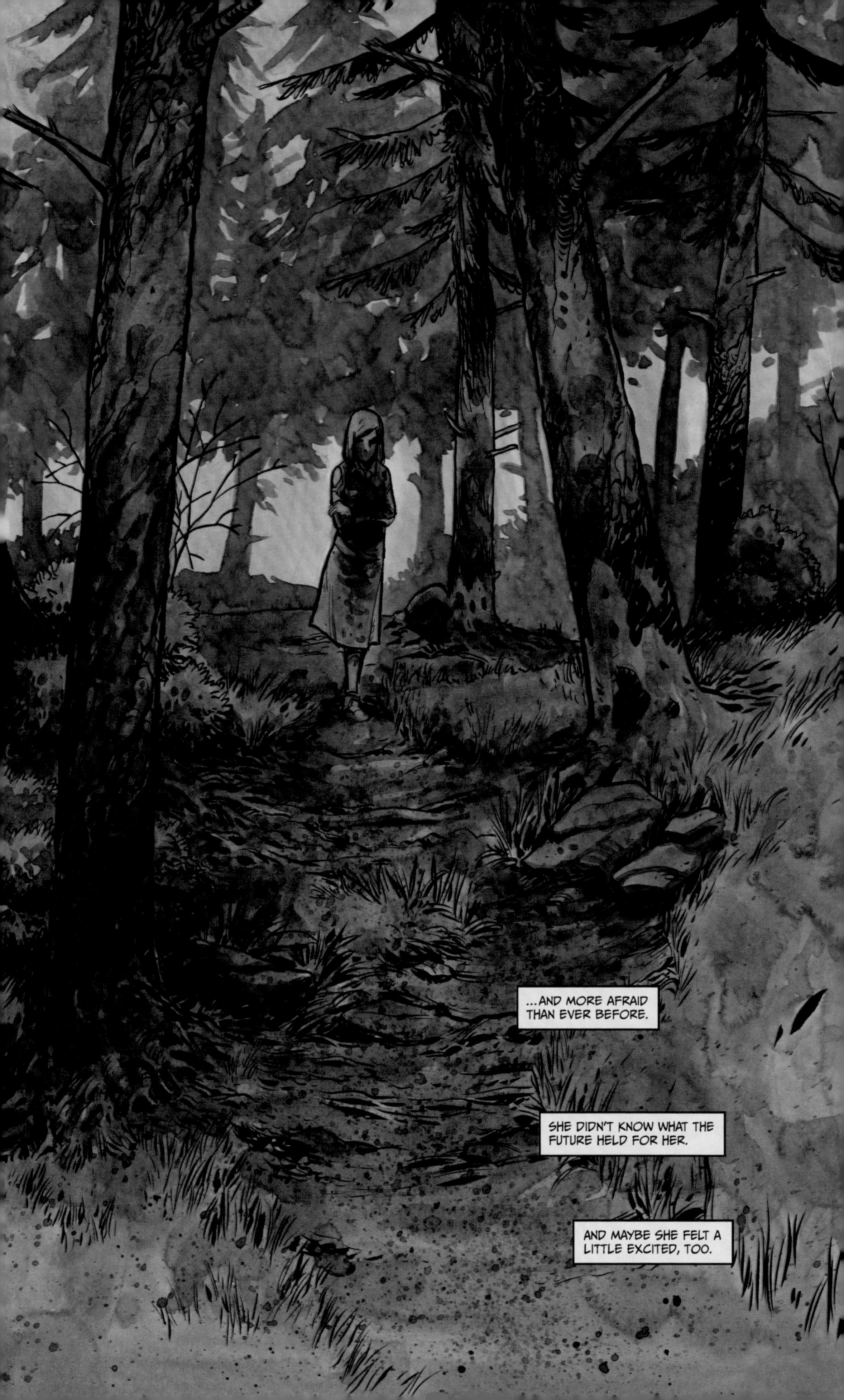
...AND MORE AFRAID THAN EVER BEFORE.
SHE DIDN'T KNOW WHAT THE FUTURE HELD FOR HER.
AND MAYBE SHE FELT A LITTLE EXCITED, TOO.

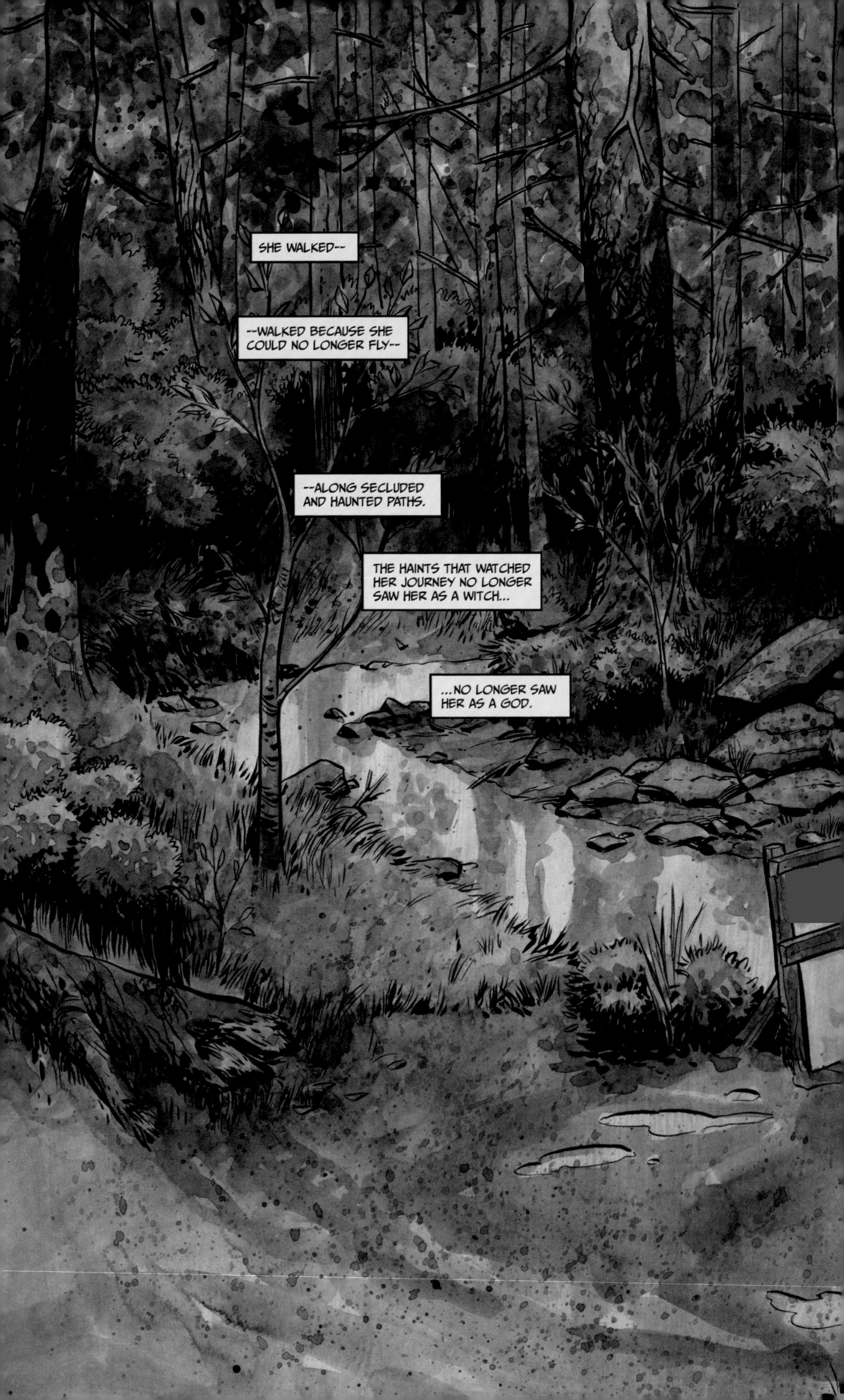
SHE WALKED--
--WALKED BECAUSE SHE COULD NO LONGER FLY--
--ALONG SECLUDED AND HAUNTED PATHS.
THE HAINTS THAT WATCHED HER JOURNEY NO LONGER SAW HER AS A WITCH...
...NO LONGER SAW HER AS A GOD.

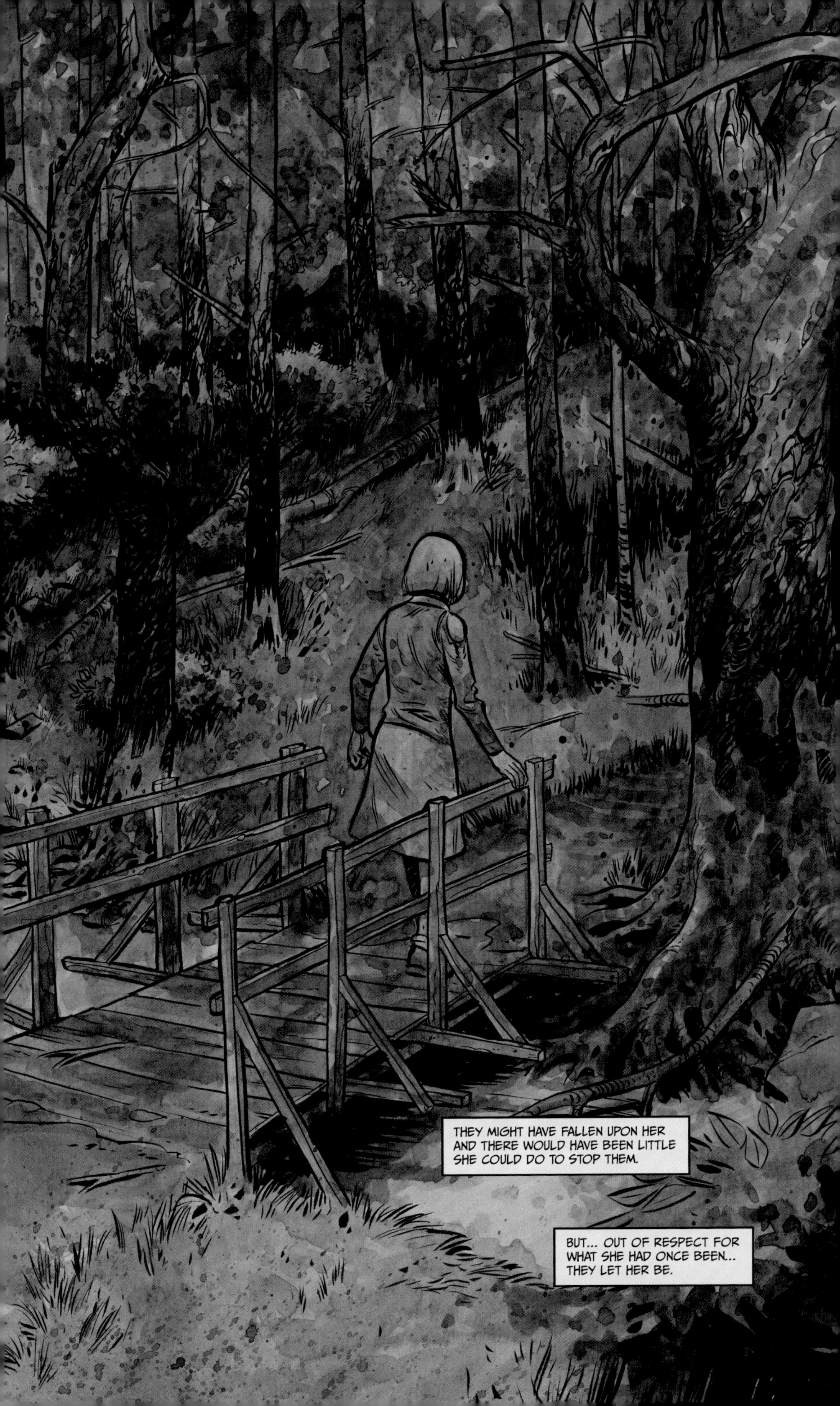
THEY MIGHT HAVE FALLEN UPON HER AND THERE WOULD HAVE BEEN LITTLE SHE COULD DO TO STOP THEM.
BUT... OUT OF RESPECT FOR WHAT SHE HAD ONCE BEEN... THEY LET HER BE.

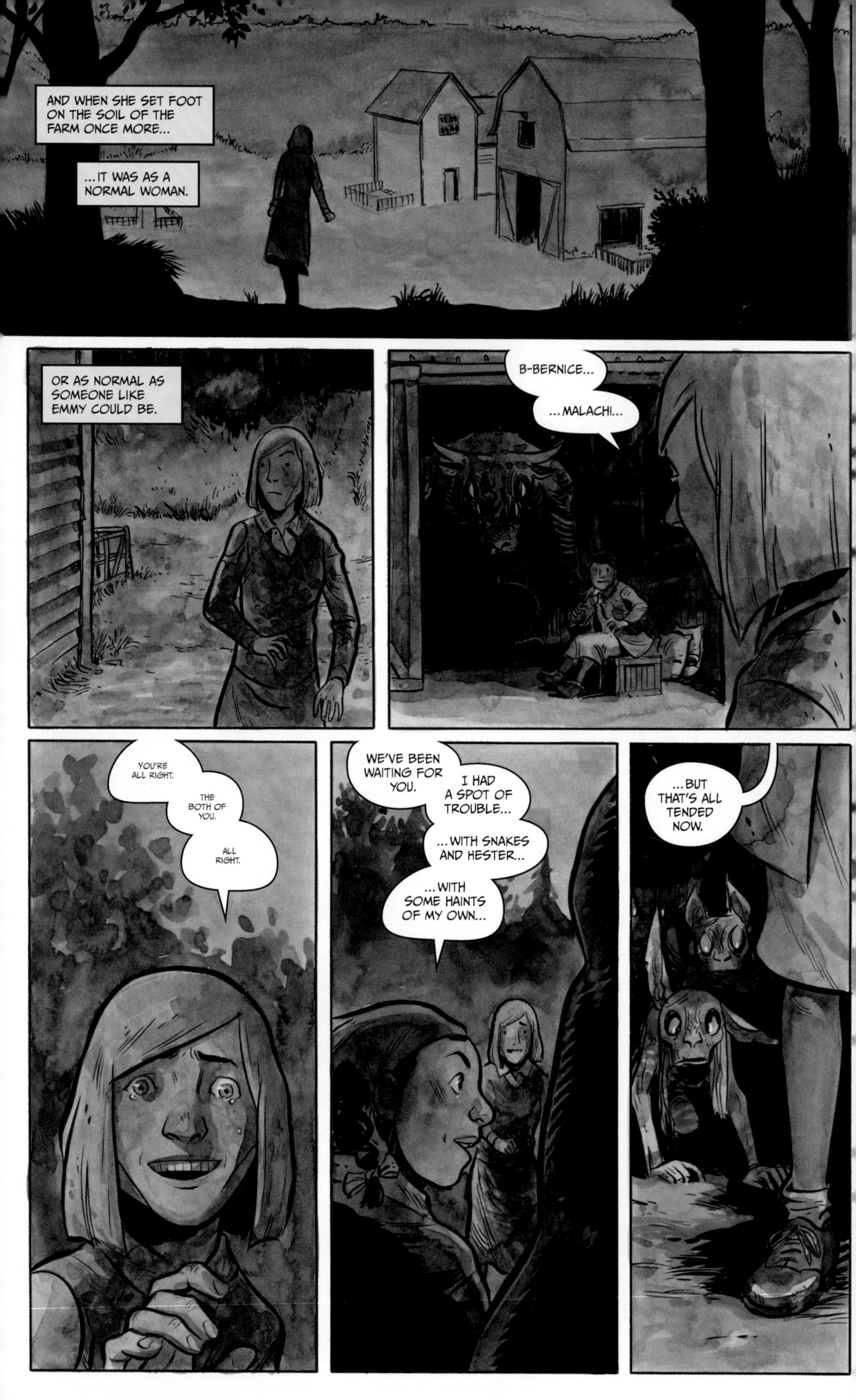

AND WHEN SHE SET FOOT ON THE SOIL OF THE FARM ONCE MORE...
...IT WAS AS A NORMAL WOMAN.
OR AS NORMAL AS SOMEONE LIKE EMMY COULD BE.
B-BERNICE...
...MALACHI...
YOU'RE ALL RIGHT.
THE BOTH OF YOU.
ALL RIGHT.
WE'VE BEEN WAITING FOR YOU.
I HAD A SPOT OF TROUBLE...
...WITH SNAKES AND HESTER...
...WITH SOME HAINTS OF MY OWN...
...BUT THAT'S ALL TENDED NOW.

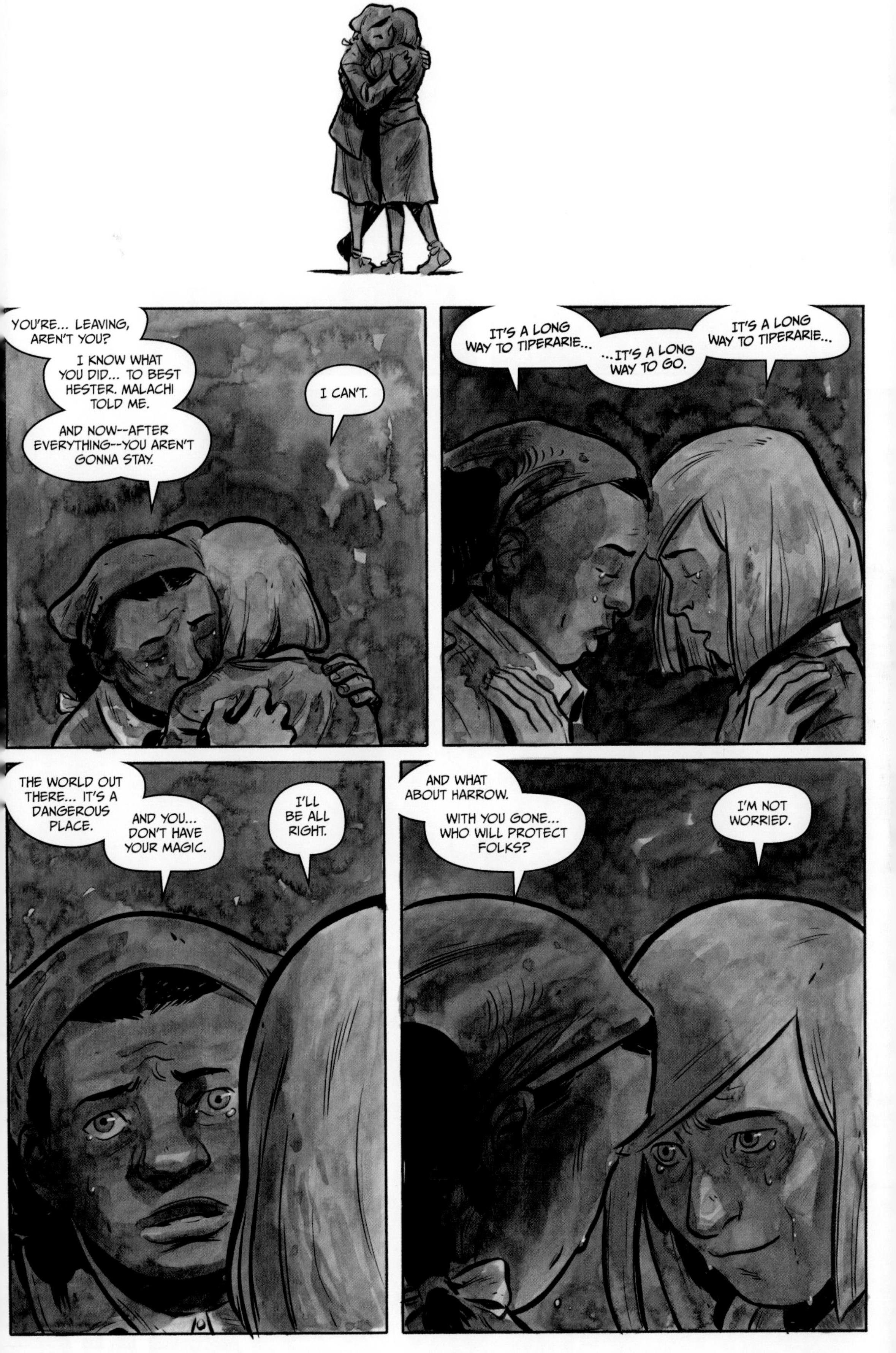
YOU'RE... LEAVING, AREN'T YOU?
I KNOW WHAT YOU DID... TO BEST HESTER. MALACHI TOLD ME.
AND NOW--AFTER EVERYTHING--YOU AREN'T GONNA STAY.
I CAN'T.
IT'S A LONG WAY TO TIPERARIE...
...IT'S A LONG WAY TO GO.
IT'S A LONG WAY TO TIPERARIE...
THE WORLD OUT THERE... IT'S A DANGEROUS PLACE.
AND YOU... DON'T HAVE YOUR MAGIC.
I'LL BE ALL RIGHT.
AND WHAT ABOUT HARROW.
WITH YOU GONE... WHO WILL PROTECT FOLKS?
I'M NOT WORRIED.

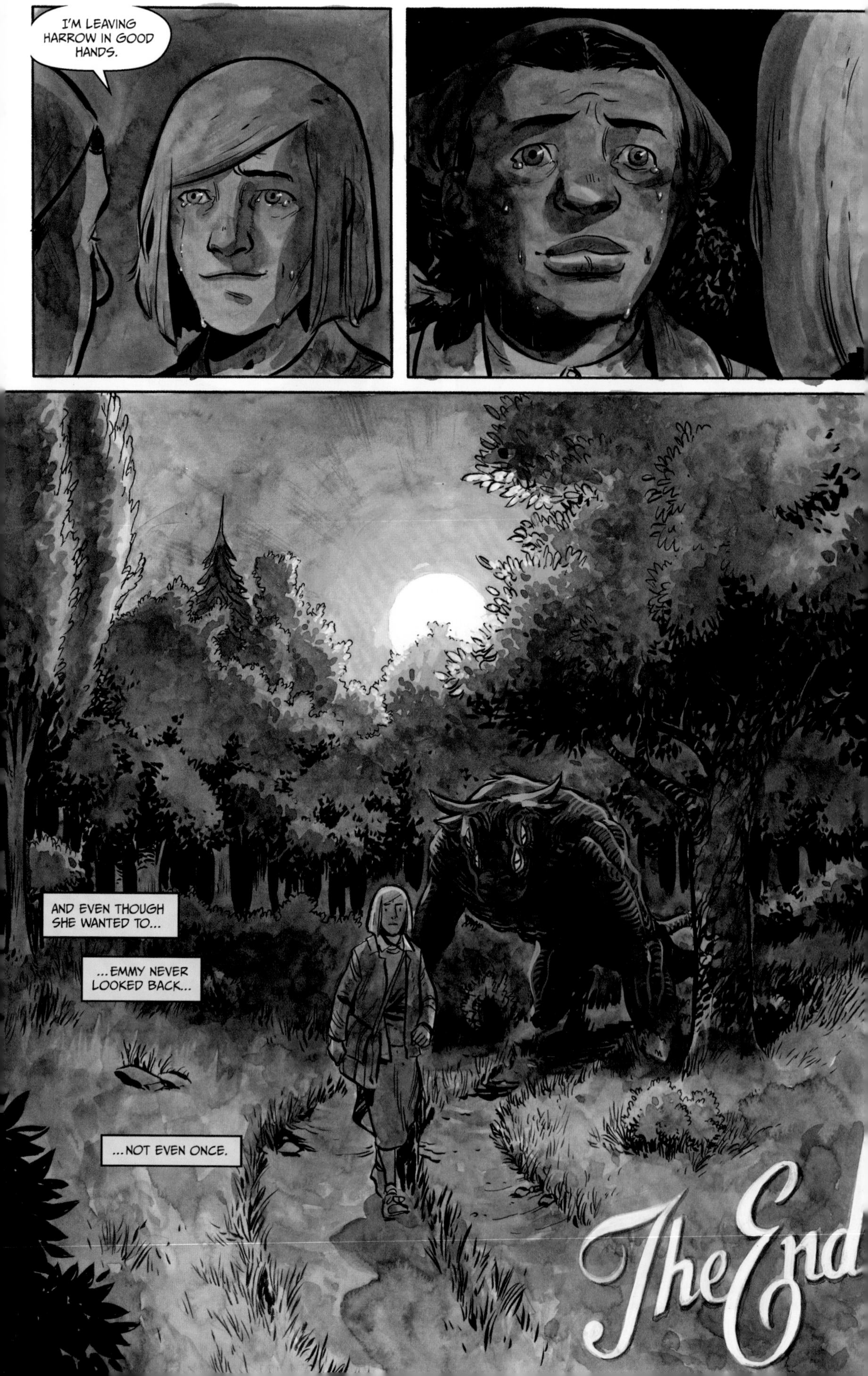
I'M LEAVING HARROW IN GOOD HANDS.
AND EVEN THOUGH SHE WANTED TO...
...EMMY NEVER LOOKED BACK...
...NOT EVEN ONCE.
The End

HARROW COUNTY

◄ AFTERWORD ►

So, a bunch of years back, I started to spin a yarn about a young woman named Madrigal who might have been the reincarnation of a nasty ol' witch. The first line of that story read, "Her earliest memories were of the taste of freshly turned earth and the bleating of goats." The story was set near the fictional town of Ahmen's Landing (called "Ominous Landing" by some of the local riffraff). Madi had strange abilities. Ghosts—or haints, as we call them—were drawn to her. A strange, haunted tree lurked in her dreams. She found a tattered skin in the woods and that skin became a familiar of sorts. I called the story "Countless Haints." I wrote several chapters of the story before I got distracted and started working on something else.

I moved on from Madrigal, but I never forgot about her.

Some time later, Tyler Crook and I started talking about working together on a story. We knew we wanted to do a supernatural tale, but we didn't have anything planned beyond that. We kicked around a bunch of ideas before I asked Tyler if he'd like to read the first few chapters of "Countless Haints." He read it and liked it. We agreed that this was the story we wanted to tell.

We changed little bits and pieces here and there. The story was originally set in the here-and-now, but we felt that the past might be more visually appealing. Ahmen's Landing vanished and was re-placed by Harrow County, for which the comic book series was named. And Madrigal—named after a witch I've written about many times . . . the cruel Maddie Someday—became Emmy.

We kept the haints, though.

Tyler and I took that initial concept and made it into something completely different from what I had originally envisioned. My plans prior to starting on the comic book did not include Bernice or Priscilla or the Family or the Meeting Lodge or even Kammi. As a comic book, *Harrow County* became its own thing, and I fell in love with the setting and the characters and even the monsters in a way I never did while working on the prose story.

And now I'm saying goodbye.

This is a tough one. I hate to let these characters go. I'm going to miss Emmy and Bernice and the Skinless Boy terribly. I'll miss Kammi and Hester Beck (perhaps a cousin of Maddie Someday). I'll miss the Abandoned and the twisted old tree that whispered such cruel things to Emmy. We've told the story we wanted to tell, and we're ending the story where it is supposed to end. We're going out at a good place.

I wanted to take this opportunity to thank you, the reader, for supporting this book and following along with us. Witnessing reader reaction to this story of witches and ghosts has been one of the rewarding, exciting, and humbling experiences of my career. Sincerely, you mean the world to me.

Will there ever be more *Harrow County*?

Who knows? There are certainly other stories to tell, and there are, of course, countless haints. Bernice and Priscilla are likely to get into all sorts of trouble in the days following this story. Maybe there are other members of the Family we haven't met. Emmy's story has come to a close, I think, but who's to say she isn't embarking on a new adventure in the great big world beyond Harrow County?

I can say this: I'm sitting outside as I write this. It's not quite yet summer, but it's getting there. And the first dragonfly—the first snake doctor—of the season just swooped by my head.

An omen?

I bet Emmy would think so.

Cullen Bunn

Cullen Bunn
2018

When we started Harrow County, we weren't sure if it would last beyond four issues. We hoped but we didn't know. You can never really know with a weird, little, creator-owned book like this so it's wild to be sitting here three and a half years later, writing about the experience.

In the time it took us to make thirty-two issues of *Harrow County*, my wife and I moved to Portland then we moved away from Portland, we bought a house, we got a second dog, my wife got cancer and then got an operation so now she doesn't have cancer, the American political landscape went bananas, I went to Poland and France—and that's just the stuff I want to talk about. It's been an intense time and through all of it, if I was awake, I was probably working on Harrow County. I don't even want to think about the amount of coffee I've consumed in that time.

Making *Harrow County* has been hard but it's also been a wonderfully fulfilling experience. I loved going to Harrow County every day and exploring the world and the people there. I love the woods and the monsters. I was enriched by the fans whose reaction to the book always left me delighted and energized. I loved the challenge of making a fully painted book.

I want to thank Keith Wood and the Dark Horse production staff. They made the book look great and made Cullen and I look like we might be professionals.

And I'd also like to thank you for supporting this weird, sweet horror comic and for supporting us in the making of it. I hope the experience was as fun and meaningful for you as it has been for me.

Keep a song in your heart and the snakes out of your ears.

CROOK 18

Tyler Crook
2018